# Elementary Standard ML

Greg Michaelson
*Heriot-Watt University*

UCL
PRESS

First published in 1995 by UCL Press

UCL Press Limited
University College London
Gower Street
London WC1E 6BT

The name of University College London (UCL) is a registered
trade mark used by UCL Press with the consent of the owner.

ISBN: 1-85728-398-8 PB

**British Library Cataloguing-in-Publication Data**
A CIP catalogue record for this book is available from the British Library.

Typeset in Palatino and Univers.
Printed and bound by
Page Bros (Norwich) Ltd, England.

# Contents

# Preface

## Overview

*Between thought and expression there lies a lifetime.* Lou Reed

This book is intended to support a first level course in programming in Standard ML (SML). No previous programming experience is required. No mathematical ability is required beyond competence at senior school year 4 mathematics. It is assumed that you have access to a computer running SML, and know how to prepare and modify a raw text file using an editor.

SML is a member of a family of programming languages known as the functional languages. It has many differences to the imperative programming languages like Basic, C, Pascal and COBOL. If you have already used one of these languages then it is important that you leave any preconceptions behind and approach SML with an open brain.

The material is organized as a continuous argument and each chapter assumes that the previous chapters have been understood. Thus, you should work steadily through the book rather than trying to dip in and out. Programming is ultimately about persuading computers to run programs. As you progress through this book it is well worth using a computer to try out the examples in the text. Each chapter is followed by exercises which are based on the preceding material. While time should be spent on thinking about how to solve the exercises and working out answers on paper, the use of a computer is fundamental.

This book has been developed from courses taught at Heriot-Watt University to 1st year undergraduate BSc Computer Science students (1993 to present) and to MSc Knowledge Based System students (1987 to present).

## Approach

### Where to start?

Learning to program is a confusing and puzzling business. It is necessary to learn simultaneously how to analyze problems, how to design a solution, how to encode a solution in a programming language and how to use a computer system to run and modify programs. To begin with, a great deal of elementary but vital detail must be absorbed which often obscures more general concepts.

This book does not pretend to teach a discipline of problem analysis and design as well as programming. Trying to cover all of these topics in one text leads either to vast books, to inadequate treatment of individual topics or to never progressing beyond trivial problems. Rather, this book is based on the premise that the best way to learn to program is by seeing and attempting lots of simple examples where the problem area is already well analyzed and constrained. From these examples, more general constructs and techniques are drawn out. Thus, you will soon notice that for each new topic a couple of concrete examples are presented and a general case is then elaborated by looking at where the examples are different and abstracting accordingly. The general case is then applied to more concrete examples.

The book explicitly draws on the distinction between programming in the small and in the large, plumping exclusively for the former. I think that it is best to become competent at getting the guts of elementary algorithms right before trying to assemble such algorithms into larger systems. Thus, there are no case studies or large worked problems until very late on. Instead, there are lots and lots of very similar simple examples which are used to present a variety of quite low level but nonetheless fundamental techniques. Furthermore, there is no material here on advanced searching and sorting methods, or on data structures beyond simple lists and unbalanced trees. I think that such subtleties are best left to a second level course concentrating on programming in the large, where they can be tackled in conjunction with abstract data types and modular or object oriented programming.

## Functional programming

Functional programming has its roots in mathematical logic and computability theory from the 1930s. Coming to prominence as a research area in the 1970s, it is now in the mainstream of Computing. Alas, functional programming is still seen by many as a hard, advanced subject, bearing an unwarranted aura of mathematics and theory. This is partly because of the manner in which it is traditionally presented.

Some texts are based on the comparative ease of deriving, proving and transforming functional programs and seek to use these techniques to elaborate rigorous disciplines of programming. Alas, programming tends to be overwhelmed by formal detail which is off-putting for beginners. Such approaches are also unconvincing at first level: beginners can often understand a program intuitively but lack the mathematical sophistication to get to grips with its derivation or proof. Furthermore, the sizes of proofs and derivations explode as programs get larger.

We teach low level imperative programming but we do not expect students to hand translate substantial high level programs into machine code: we have compilers. In the same way, while it is vital for students to understand formal approaches and to apply them by hand to small problems, we need appropriate tool sets to support both the teaching and application of such techniques.

Other texts try to treat functional programming as paradigmatic of all Computing and cover issues in semantics and implementation as well as programming. I do not think that such an all-embracing approach is appropriate for first level teaching. Too many disparate issues are covered and their significance is lost in the absence of a general overview of Computing.

Functional programming is really just another way of constructing computer programs. Because of its theoretical grounding it certainly has many attractive formal properties. At heart though, it is an eminently practical activity. There is no need to have any background in or awareness of matters theoretical to learn functional programming. Indeed, it is a positive advantage for teaching to not treat functional programming as anything out of the ordinary. In this book there is nothing on derivation, proof and transformation. Nor are semantics or implementation issues considered. Instead, as indicated above, the focus is solidly on practical functional programming through examples.

## Why start with a functional language?

There is much anecdotal evidence that, as with natural language, a first programming language colours and clouds the learning of the second, particularly where there are substantial paradigmatic differences. It seems appropriate to teach a simple, abstract language before a more complex, concrete one. Thus, high level imperative languages are usually taught before assembly languages. Functional programming is both simpler and more abstract than high level imperative programming and there are many advantages to learning it first. Topics which are either presented as advanced or ignored completely in first level imperative programming courses are a natural, indeed essential part of a functional programming course.

In functional programming, function composition and parameter passing are fundamental. Recursive data structures are complemented directly by recursive control for repetition. The combination of case structured function definitions, pattern matching and explicit structure denotations leads to small, succinct programs with a close correspondence between data and program structure. Functions as values and higher order functions follow cleanly and easily from a high degree of orthogonality of abstraction mechanisms. Polymorphic typing combines ease of function reuse with strong checks for type compatibility.

In contrast, the transition to a functional language after a year or two of imperative programming is much harder. People who are used to assignment as the primary means of associating names and values often have conceptual problems with sub-program use through parameter passing, even in imperative languages. Similarly, those who are used to iteration as a repetition mechanism find recursion hard. In the same vein, pattern matching seems arcane after explicit element selection from data structures. In short, people who know about assignment miss it: hence the warning in the first section above.

Of course, functional languages are not some universal panacea for all our programming teaching ills. Functional programming brings different misconceptions, confusions and problems. That is why so much time is spent in this book on basic concepts, repeating and abstracting from concrete examples with stepped variations to build up layers of more general techniques slowly and steadily.

### Why Standard ML?

SML was originally developed in the 1970s at the University of Edinburgh as the *meta-language* for the LCF theorem prover. It is now used widely for teaching and research, and increasingly for industrial computing.

SML was one of the first languages to be defined formally, rather than retrofitted with a formal definition. This provides a solid basis both for implementations and for program proof and transformation. Mature, robust, stable, consistent, free implementations are available for a variety of platforms, in particular for IBM-compatible PCs and for UNIX-based systems. SML is actually an imperative language with a pure functional subset. For practical purposes it may be viewed as a functional language, the approach taken here.

Good but incompatible alternatives are Miranda (a trade mark of Research Software Ltd) and Haskell. Both are pure functional languages. Both differ from SML not just in syntax but in the way that function application is defined. To be somewhat arcane, SML is said to be strict because arguments are always evaluated before functions are applied to them. In contrast, Miranda and Haskell are said to be lazy because argument evaluation is delayed until the argument value is actually needed. Purists argue plausibly that this gives Miranda and Haskell an edge over SML in that it is easier to prove some properties of programs and to characterize particular sorts of computations. However, for first level teaching, I do not think that these are good reasons to choose Miranda or Haskell over SML.

### Contents

It is not the intention to cover full SML here. The major topics are:
- basic types and operations – integer, real, boolean string
- functions as values
- global declarations
- pattern matching with booleans, integers and strings
- integer recursion
- conditional expression
- lists, list pattern matching and list recursion
- list higher order functions
- local declarations
- tuples and tuple pattern matching
- concrete datatypes
- let expressions and simultaneous declarations
- exceptions
- input/output

There is minimal mention of:

- imperative constructs
- abstract data types
- modules

in the final chapter. There is no coverage of:

- records
- user defined operators

## Acknowledgements

I would like to thank:

Tore Bratvold and Sandra Foubister, for carefully checking the contents and exercises of the first draft.

The anonymous reviewer, for incisive and instructive comments, suggestions, corrections and improvements.

Peter King, for making Latex more bearable.

Andrew Carrick, for his support and enthusiasm.

I would particularly like to thank my 1st year BSc Computer Science and MSc in Knowledge Based Systems students who acted as constructively critical consumers of much of the material in this book.

I alone am responsible for the mistakes and misrepresentations in the following pages. If you spot any then please let me know.

Greg Michaelson, Edinburgh, 1994–5

greg@cee.hw.ac.uk

# CHAPTER 1
# Introduction

## 1.1 Introduction

The world is a fiendishly complicated place. To make sense of it, we break it up into manageable chunks and construct abstract descriptions or models of them. If those descriptions are detailed and precise enough then they can be turned into programs to be animated by computers.

In this chapter we are going to consider various aspects of model making. This chapter is really a fairy story. Like all fairy stories it contains nuggets of wisdom but it presents them in an idealized and simplified manner making lots of vague assumptions along the way. Still, we have to start somewhere. The rest of the book will firm up and amplify the ideas sketched out here.

## 1.2 Making models

If we want to solve a problem then one approach is to make a model which captures important aspects of the circumstances of the problem. If the model is accurate and detailed enough then working with it should shed further light on the problem.

Usually, a model means a simplified physical replica of something. For example, many childrens' toys are models of far more complex devices. Models may be constructed at differing levels of closeness to the thing being modelled. For example, a basic toy car has four wheels so that it can be pushed across a floor. A more complex model might have steerable wheels. An even more detailed model might have an electric motor so that it does not need to be pushed. Finally, the model might have remote control so that its speed and direction can be changed without direct contact.

Each level of model encapsulates more and more features of the thing being modelled. However, each level also misses out a lot of detail which is deemed to be inessential: the detail should be appropriate for a model's intended use. For example, a two-year-old will wreck a remote controlled car while a twelve-year-old will be bored by a push-along wagon. Similarly, a child's model car probably does not have leather upholstery or an FM radio whereas a manufacturer's model car at a motor show might have both but no engine.

Models can be made increasingly sophisticated so that they encompass more and more detail and hence provide more and more information about what is being modelled. In civil engineering, for example, models of proposed structures are made to very high tolerances so that measurements made on them can be scaled up directly to the ultimate constructions. Nonetheless, in a model road bridge it is probably not important whether the lines in the centre of the road are white or yellow, or, indeed, if the lines are there at all. A fundamental aspect of problem solving and model making is deciding what detail is relevant.

Models for use with computers are much more abstract than physical replicas. Computer models are programs, that is sequences of instructions for manipulating information. The information represents static details of the problem and the instructions describe the dynamic behaviour of those static details. Thus, a program is much more general than a physical model: the instructions describe dynamic behaviour for general cases and the information provides details for a specific case of interest. A physical model is frozen with one set of properties but a computer model can be used in any circumstances which fit the general case. For example, in using a computer program to model a bridge the information might include the dimensions of the girders and the strength of the material they are made from, and the instructions might describe how girders of arbitrary dimension and material bend and fracture when they bear weight. This program could then be used to model the behaviour of bridges made from steel or concrete provided the strengths of steel and concrete beams are known.

An important aspect of abstract model making is identifying general cases. One way to do this is to look at lots of individual cases to try and spot regularities or common patterns in static detail and dynamic behaviour. It is very useful to clarify how the individual cases are similar and how they differ. A general case can then be formed by freezing the points of similarity and leaving open the points of difference. Subsequently, the general case can be applied in a new individual case by filling in the open points with appropriate information and instructions. The tricky thing is knowing what are going to be useful points of comparison, once again separating out relevant from irrelevant detail.

For example, suppose we want to investigate the factors determining car fuel consumption. We know that cars have a number of common features such as wheels and engines and bodies and seats and so on: all the things that constitute "carness". We also know that cars can be of different colours, have varying numbers of doors, have different sized engines, travel at different speeds and have different weights. We could then measure the fuel consumptions of lots of cars and try and relate the consumption to these different factors. It is likely that we would find that the car colour and number of doors were not relevant to fuel consumption whereas engine size, car weight and speed were relevant. Furthermore, we might find that fuel consumption increased in a simple way with engine size and car weight and in a complex way with speed. We could then construct a model which given an arbitrary car's weight, engine size and speed would tell us its fuel consumption. We could check the model with the original information and if we were happy with its accuracy we could then apply it to new cars.

Of course, if we had thought a little bit more about cars we might not have bothered to see if the colour and number of doors were important. That is, we actually already have a model in our brains based on our experience of cars and what we have read or have been told about them. If we are totally ignorant about a problem then we can ask someone else or read about it or see if it is similar to a problem that we already have some information about. We will then incorporate a first model in our brains as a starting point. We never approach a problem blind. Rather, we have presuppositions and we should always make them explicit. If our presuppositions are wrong then our experimentation and model making will show that up.

## 1.3 Things, collections and properties

When we make an abstract model we have to actually write down its description. Above, we introduced a distinction between static information and instructions for manipulating it. To begin with, let us assume that information consists of collections of descriptions of things.

Note that collections are also things so we can have collections of collections. Note also that instructions are things and so are programs, structured collections of instructions. Hence the distinction between information and instructions is not hard and fast in our world of thingfulness, or, as we shall see, in computer programs.

Now, when we make a collection of things we do not do so arbitrarily: we have some criteria for identifying them and grouping them together, some common properties that they all share. That is, we must have some way of determining which things should be in the collection and which should not. For example, when we are collecting cars to investigate fuel consumption we might specify that a car has four wheels, an engine and enclosed seating. Thus, we should exclude bicycles, which have two wheels, no engine and are not enclosed, motorcycles, which have two wheels, an engine and are not enclosed, and stagecoaches, which have four wheels, no engine and are enclosed.

Note that we have become a bit more specific about descriptions of things in collections. We are now including properties as parts of descriptions and we can define a thing itself as a group of properties. We will come back to just what constitutes a property a little later on.

This gives us a first way of representing a collection of things as a table of properties. For example, for vehicles we might have:

| name | wheels | engine | enclosed |
|------|--------|--------|----------|
| car | 4 | yes | yes |
| bicycle | 2 | no | no |
| motorcycle | 2 | yes | no |
| stagecoach | 4 | no | yes |

At the top of the table is a row of properties. Each subsequent row is a sequence of property values for an individual thing.

Note that a thing will often have more properties than those needed to decide if it should be in a particular collection. For example, individual cars have particular colours but having a specific colour is irrelevant for whether or not something is a car. For example, in the collection of cars we might want to compare engine size, weight and speed but once again these are not properties that determine whether or not something is a car.

## 1.4 Properties of properties

In the above discussion of cars we introduced implicitly a number of different ways of describing properties. Now we will tease out just how we form property descriptions.

First of all, we said that a car should have enclosed seating and should have an engine. Enclosed-seatingness and engine-bearingness are two valued or binary properties: either a thing has or does not have enclosed seating; either a thing has or does not have an engine. To put it another way, the questions "Does the thing have enclosed seating?" and "Does the thing have an engine?" can both be answered yes or no. To put it yet another way, the statements "The thing has enclosed seating." and "The thing has an engine." can be either true or false. True and false are called truth values or logical values or boolean values. Boolean values are named after George Boole, the 19th-century mathematician who was one of the first people to formalize the mathematics of truth values. He thought that he had found the answer to the ultimate question and called his book on logic *The laws of thought*.

Next, we said that a car should have four wheels. We know that a wheel is an indivisible sort of an entity and so wheels are counted in whole numbers. Here there is an unstated implication that in determining the number of wheels on a thing we use a whole number, an integer value.

We also said that cars have weights and speeds. We know that these are not whole numbers of kilograms or of metres per second but can vary to an infinitely fine degree. Hence, the implication here is that we use decimal numbers, real values, to describe them.

Finally, we said that cars have colour. Colours have fixed names, for example "red", "green" and "blue". Here, we can use the word or words for the colour name. In principle, any colour name is valid, for example "metallic blue" or "racing green", provided the names can be distinguished. Words are a special case of the more general strings. Where a word is a sequence of alphabetic letters, a string is any sequence of any letters between double quotes, including spaces, digits and punctuation marks. Thus, we can use strings to represent arbitrary sequences of words.

These property descriptions – booleans, integers, reals and strings – are pleasingly general, certainly not specific to car properties. We can use truth values to represent any property involving the presence or absence of something, for example whether or not something has marmalade fur or eats fish. In the same way, we can use integers to represent any property involving a whole number of something, for example how many marmalade hairs something has. Similarly, we can use reals to represent any property involving a variable quantity of something, for example how many kilograms of fish something eats. And we can use strings to represent a property involving a fixed range of describable possibilities, for example whether something is not very, quite, very or extremely furry.

Note that we are being somewhat luxurious in allowing so many different sorts of generalized property descriptions because we can use some of them to represent others. For example, we could use integers to represent truth values, say using "0" for "false" and "1" for "true". We could also use integers to represent strings, for example "0" for "red" and "1" for "orange" and so on. Equally well, we could use strings to represent integers, for example "zero" for "0" and "one" for "1" and so on. Or we could use pairs of integers to represent reals, for example "12" and "34" for "12.34". However, we gain in expressive power by separating out different property classes. By introducing additional general properties we cannot necessarily describe more things but we can make richer descriptions.

## 1.5 Types and methods

For making models, just putting things into collections is rather more involved than it seems at first. We have said that for something to go into a collection it must have certain properties. Thus there must be some way of selecting properties from the description of a thing. That suggests that there must also be some way of constructing descriptions of things out of properties in the first place. In turn, that suggests that there must be some way of constructing properties themselves. Similarly, once we have selected the properties from a thing's description there must be ways of testing them. Furthermore, we may want to make new descriptions out of old descriptions: if those new descriptions are not just simple copies then the properties from the old descriptions must be changed. These ways of constructing, accessing and manipulating properties and descriptions are known as methods. As we shall see, they are the basis for the instructions in model building.

Above we looked at the use of booleans, integers, reals and strings to describe properties. Each of these general property descriptions is more than just collections of values for us to choose from. They also come with their own methods which we use implicitly all the time. A collection of values and associated methods is known as a type. Let us now look at methods for these types in more detail.

First of all, all of these types enable two values to be compared. We can ask "Is '5' the same as '7'?" or "Does 'true' equal 'true'?" or "Is '3.14' different to '3.15'?" or "Is 'tomato' identical with 'tomato'?". Note that all of these questions require a binary answer, either "yes" or "no", or "true" or "false". That is, methods for testing equality return boolean values.

Note that it does not really make sense to compare values from different types. When we compare two values we assume that we are comparing "like with like" and not comparing "apples and oranges" as the old saws have it. If two values are from different types then they are necessarily different, so there is no point in comparing them.

For the boolean type, we can ask whether or not two values are both "true". This method is called conjunction. We can also ask if one or both of two values is "true", known as disjunction. Or, we could ask if one follows from the other. This method is called implication. As we shall see, we can build up involved logical arguments from these methods. Note that these methods return boolean values.

For the integer and real types, we have methods to do arithmetic, that is to add or multiply two values together or subtract one from another or divide one by another. As we shall see later, we can construct complex sums from these methods. Note that these methods return numerical values.

We can also carry out magnitude comparisons on integer and real values to see if one is bigger or smaller than another. We can use these methods to choose amongst things and to put things in order. Such methods return boolean values.

For the string type, we can join two strings together to form a new string, or we can ask how many letters are in a string, to get an integer, or we can select parts of strings to get what are effectively more strings. Once again, we can carry out quite elaborate textual manipulation using these simple methods.

Note that methods are type specific. That is, they must be used with values of particular type and return values of particular type. For example, it does not make sense to add an integer and a string, or to test if a real is bigger than a boolean. As we will see, this is important for ensuring that the methods that make up programs are fitted together correctly.

## 1.6 Choosing types

A fundamental aspect of model making is deciding which types to use to represent properties. Above we suggested using booleans for binary choices, integers for counting, reals for measuring and strings for words. Note, however, that different types may be appropriate for what is apparently the same property in different contexts.

For example, consider working with dates of the form:

*day month year*

First of all, suppose we want to check if two people have the same birthday. We only need compare their dates of birth, so they might be represented as strings, for example:

        `"24th September 1953"`

or

        `"1/3/39"`

Here we have two radically different possible ways of writing down dates but they are both represented as strings. So long as we use consistently just one way of writing down dates as strings then we can compare them letter by letter from left to right. Thus we can see that:

        `"24th July 1961"`

is the same as:

        `"24th July 1961"`

and:

        `"29/4/56"`

is not the same as:

```
"24/12/58"
```

However, if we want to find the date of the day after someone's birthday then the representation as a single string is not very flexible. We need to add 1 to the day, suggesting representing the day as an integer. If the new day is bigger than the number of days in the month then we need to reset it to 1 and somehow get to the next month. This suggests representing the month as an integer between 1 and 12:

```
1  ==  January
2  ==  February
...
12 ==  December
```

which we can add 1 to. If the new month is bigger than 12 then we need to reset it to 1 for January and get to the next year. This again suggests representing the year as an integer.

We can also use this representation as three integers to compare dates but now we have to explicitly compare three different integer properties instead of one string property.

In general, the choice of type to represent a property should be determined by how the property is used, that is what methods are used to manipulate it. It is important to try and find a balance between ease of manipulation and simplicity of representation.

## 1.7 Characterizing things and collections

Let us now begin to firm up the differences between things and collections of things. A thing is described by a fixed number of properties. We decide once and for all which properties are needed to describe something and, thereafter, we cannot add or remove properties. In contrast, a collection of things can have a variable number of things in it. In particular, it can be empty. However, all the things must have common properties. As we will see much later on, requiring things to be a fixed number of properties is not as restricting as it sounds because some of the properties could be other things or variable sized collections of other things.

The reasons for this distinction are to do with various technical aspects of ensuring that models are correctly constructed: we are not yet in a position to go into more details but introduce the distinction to ease presentation. So, from now on we will distinguish fixed sized descriptions of things from variable sized collections of things.

When we want a new value from one of our basic types we just write it down or form an expression to generate it. In the same way, we will need to have some way of writing down a thing as a fixed group of values and of writing down a collection as a potentially variable bundle of things.

Above we saw that we can represent collections of things as tables. For example, suppose we have a collection of vehicles each with its own name, a certain number of wheels, and the presence or absence of an engine. Thus, we might include a Morris 1000 car with four wheels and an engine, an Elswick Ambler bicycle with two wheels and no engine, a Honda 90 motorcycle with two wheels and an engine, a Wells Fargo stagecoach with four wheels and no engine, and a Fiat 127 car with four wheels and an engine. The corresponding table is:

```
Vehicles collection
name                    wheels    engine
"Morris 1000"           4         true
"Elswick Ambler"        2         false
"Honda 90"              2         true
"Wells Fargo"           4         false
"Fiat 127"              4         true
```

Notice that down each column all the values are of the same type: the name is always a string, the number of wheels is always an integer and the presence or absence of an engine is always a boolean. Thus, each row has the same combination of a fixed number of types.

We have introduced tables as a first informal representation of collections of things. However, we are going to delay making a more definite commitment to specific representations for things and collections of things until later chapters. Nonetheless, we can begin to consider in broad terms how we can manipulate collections of things.

Because things and collections are so fundamental to model making, it would be very useful to have general ways of manipulating them, that is general purpose methods. Thus, we want types for things and collections which we can firm up for particular problems. However, just as we are evading questions of thing and collection representation, we will also evade questions to do with the corresponding methods. We have also assumed that we can extract properties from things. In the same way, we will assume that we have ways of putting things into and taking them out of collections. We will also assume that we can make an empty collection and that we can tell if a collection is empty.

## 1.8 New types from old types

We have said that a car description is a collection of properties formed from values of general types. We could now consider a car description to be a value in its own right. Furthermore, we could consider the instructions to find a car's name or the number of wheels or its travel distances as methods for manipulating car values. That is, we can use general types and their methods to start building a new type for cars.

This is the essence of model making and programming. We analyze a problem to identify the types within it. We then use the general types we know about already to make values and methods for new types appropriate to the problem. We then plug the methods for the new types together to solve the problem. Once we have become adept at building new types we can then use them in turn to make yet more types to solve further problems.

## 1.9 The story so far

Let us summarize the above musings. Models are abstract descriptions and are composed of static information and dynamic instructions. Information is based on collections of things. Things are groups of properties. Properties are values of particular types. Types are general purpose aggregates of values and methods. Methods enable the manipulation of values of appropriate types and are the building blocks of programs, that is sequences of instructions.

Thus, knowing what we want to model we have to decide what things are relevant, which properties are important and how they need to be manipulated. We then choose appropriate types for describing those properties and hence the things.

We will now turn to how we use methods to construct instructions for thing manipulation through their properties. In particular, we will look at the use of naming properties of things as a way of specifying general, abstract instructions.

## 1.10 Expressions from methods

Methods seem to be very simple instructions for manipulating properties of things and returning values which might be further properties. We can plug methods together to build up more complex instructions. However, we must make sure that the types match up. That is, if the result of one method is to be used by another method then the result type of the first method must be the same as the required type for the second method. Instructions built from methods are called expressions.

For example, suppose we write * to mean integer multiplication. Then, if we know that a car travels at 110 kilometres per hour for 2 hours, the distance covered is:

```
110 * 2 ==> 220
```

kilometres. Note the use of:

```
==>
```

to mean that the result of the expression on the left is the value on the right.

For example, suppose we write < when we want to see if one integer is less than another. If we know that one car has a top speed of 130 kilometres per hour and another has a top speed of 150 kilometres per hour then the first car has a slower top speed than the second car because:

```
130 < 150 ==> true
```

For example, if we know that one car travels at 150 kilometres per hour for 2 hours and another travels at 90 kilometres per hour for 3 hours then the first car does not travel a lesser distance than the second car because:

```
150 * 2 < 90 * 3 ==> false
```

Let us make the stages in carrying out this expression explicit. First of all, we work out the distance travelled by the first car:

```
150 * 2 ==> 300
```

Next we work out the distance travelled by the second car:

```
90 * 3 ==> 270
```

Finally, we compare the distances travelled:

```
300 < 270 ==> false
```

Recall that `*` multiplies one integer by another integer to return an integer and `<` compares two integers. Thus, it is fine to build an expression from other expressions using `*` to return integers for subsequent comparison by `<`.

Note that there is an implicit order in which the expression is carried out. First we did the expressions involving arithmetic methods. Then we did the expression involving a comparison method. In a complex expression, arithmetic methods are said to have greater precedence than comparison methods. When carrying out an expression, the expressions it is composed of are carried out in order of precedence from highest to lowest.

Notice also that after we had carried out the multiplication expressions we replaced them in the original expression with their results. We will assume that we can always replace something with something else provided they are equivalent.

## 1.11 Generalizing through naming

In the above discussion we were working with specific things with specific properties. Thus, we had a first car with a speed of 110 kilometres per hour and a duration of 2 hours. Then we had two cars with top speeds of 130 and 150 kilometres per hour respectively. Then we had another two cars with speeds of 150 and 90 kilometres per hours and travel durations of 2 and 3 hours respectively. In all the examples, we ignored any other properties of the cars.

All the expressions we constructed and evaluated involved those specific property values being frozen in place. For example, we carried out three similar calculations to find the distance travelled from three cars' speeds and durations. Each time we wrote down a slightly different expression with the same method but different specific values for the speed and duration. This is all very well for finding the distance travelled by 3 cars but would be dull for 30 cars, tedious for 300 cars and mind bogglingly boring for 3000 cars. It would be much better if we could make an expression to find the distance from the speed and duration for an arbitrary car and then reuse that expression for lots of specific cars.

We want to be able to talk about arbitrary values of properties rather than specific values. We can do so by naming the properties and writing expressions that refer to the names rather than the specific values.

For example, suppose we want to know how far a car travels in 2 hours given its speed. We could refer to the speed by the name **speed** and write:

```
speed * 2
```

We could generalize further by referring to an arbitrary duration of travel as **duration**, and then write:

```
speed * duration
```

This technique of generalizing specific values with a name is called abstraction.

As we shall see, abstraction is central to programming. In particular, an abstracted expression is called a function.

The subsequent use of functions is eased if we always make explicit the names that are used for abstraction. For example, we could write something like:

```
replace speed
  in speed * 2
```

to make it clear that **speed** needs to be replaced with a specific value. Similarly, we could write:

```
replace speed
  replace duration
    in speed * duration
```

to stress that first **speed** and then **duration** need to be replaced with values.

## 1.12 Specializing abstractions

In order to use an abstracted expression to carry out a calculation we need to replace the names with specific values. This is called specializing an abstraction. For each name, we need to state the values that will replace it. For example, to find the distance travelled by a car going at an average speed of 100 kilometres per hour for 2 hours using the first function above, we might write:

```
replace speed
  in speed * 2
with 100
```

This tells us to replace **speed** with **100** giving:

```
100 * 2 ==> 200
```

Similarly, using the second function above to find the distance travelled by a car at 120 kilometres per hour for 4 hours, we might write:

```
replace speed
  replace duration
    in speed * duration
with 120
with 4
```

First of all, we replace **speed** with **120** giving:

```
replace duration
  in 120 * duration
with 4
```

Next we replace **duration** with **4** giving:

```
120 * 4 ==> 480
```

Specializing an expression abstraction by replacing names with values is known as calling or applying a function.

## 1.13 Abstraction by comparison

We could have used the approach of case comparison for generalization suggested above to guide us in the abstraction. The three original calculations were:

```
110 * 2
150 * 2
90 * 3
```

If we compare the first two they have the duration **2** in common but different values for the speed. This suggests that we might abstract for speed:

```
replace speed
  in speed * 2
```

to form a function. We could abstract in the third example in the same way:

```
replace speed
  in speed * 3
```

to form another function. If we now compare these two functions they have **speed** in common but different values for the duration. This suggests that we might abstract for duration:

```
replace speed
  replace duration
    in speed * duration
```

to form a third function.

This way of comparing things and abstracting at the points where they are different is incredibly useful for model making and programming. Indeed, this is often a good way to start solving a problem when we know roughly what things we are interested in and how we want to manipulate them but are not clear how to proceed. We can write down lots of individual examples, compare them, spot the common features and introduce names at the points of difference.

## 1.14 Naming functions

We have just seen how we can use names to generalize values in expressions. We can also associate names with functions so that in future when we refer to the name we know to use the associated function.

For example, we might write:

```
distance is replace speed
            replace duration
              in speed * duration
```

to give the name **distance** to the function to find distance travelled from speed and travel duration. Suppose we want to find the distance travelled by a car doing 20 kilometres per hour for 10 hours, we could write:

```
distance
with 20
 with 10
```

First we replace **distance** with the associated function:

```
replace speed
 replace duration
  in speed * duration
with 20
 with 10
```

and then we replace **speed** and **duration** as before:

```
20 * 10 ==> 200
```

## 1.15 Deciding what to do next

Above, we fitted methods together to form expressions. An expression is a one off activity but often we need to choose amongst a group of possible actions depending on the properties of the things that we are investigating. We will now introduce a simple way of describing such decisions.

For example, suppose that any car that has a top speed of over 150 kilometres per hour is said to be fast and all other cars are said to be slow. Consider deciding whether a car that has a top speed of 160 kilometres per hour is fast or slow. We would like to get back the string "fast" or the string "slow" as the result of the decision. Suppose we use the method called > to decide if one integer is bigger than another. We might write:

```
if 160 > 150
then "fast"
else "slow"
```

The intention here is that if the expression after the **if** has the value **true** then the result is whatever follows the **then**. Otherwise the expression after the **if** must have the value **false** and so the result is whatever follows the **else**. Thus, in the above example:

```
160 > 150 ==> true
```

so for:

```
if true
then "fast"
else "slow"
```

the result is **"fast"**.

Note that first we worked out the value of the expression after the **if** which should return a boolean value. We then replaced the expression with its value before proceeding.

For example, for a car with a top speed of 110 kilometres per hour, the fastness check is:

```
if 110 > 150
then "fast"
else "slow"
```

Here, the expression after the **if** gives:

```
110 > 150 ==> false
```

so for

```
if false
then "fast"
else "slow"
```

the result is **"slow"**.

This way of making a decision is called a conditional expression.

Incidentally, comparing these two conditional expressions, they are the same apart from the speed so we could abstract over the speed to form a function:

```
replace speed
  in if speed > 150
     then "fast"
     else "slow"
```

We could then name this function:

```
speedname is replace speed
               in if speed > 150
                  then "fast"
                  else "slow"
```

and call it with, for example, a speed of 120 kilometres per hour:

```
speedname
with 120 ==>
replace speed
 in if speed > 150
    then "fast"
    else "slow"
with 120 ==>
if 120 > 150
then "fast"
else "slow" ==>
if false
then "fast"
else "slow" ==> "slow"
```

As another example, suppose that one car travels for 2 hours and another travels for 3 hours and we want to know which duration is longer. We could write:

```
if 2 > 3
then 2
else 3
```

that is, if the first car's duration, 2, is bigger than the second car's duration, 3, then the result is the first car's duration, 2. Otherwise the result is the second car's duration, 3. In fact:

```
2 > 3 ==> false
```

so:

```
if 2 > 3
then 2
else 3 ==>
if false
then 2
else 3 ==> 3
```

so the second car's duration is the longer.

Perhaps the first car has a longer duration than one which travels for 1 hour:

```
if 2 > 1
then 2
else 1 ==> 2
```

Indeed it has.

Comparing these two conditional expressions they differ in the second duration, so we could abstract to form a function to compare the duration 2 with an arbitrary second duration called duration2:

```
replace duration2
 in if 2 > duration2
    then 2
    else duration2
```

Now we are returning the arbitrary value **duration2** if it is not smaller than **2**. For example, suppose the second car travels for 3 hours:

```
replace duration2
  in if 2 > duration2
     then 2
     else duration2
with 3
```

Replacing the name **duration2** with the value **3**, we get:

```
if 2 > 3
then 2
else 3 ==>
if false
then 2
else 3 ==> 3
```

so the second duration was longer.

We could now abstract for the first car's duration:

```
replace duration1
  replace duration2
    in if duration1 > duration2
       then duration1
       else duration2
```

to make a general purpose function to compare two durations. We could name the function:

```
longer is replace duration1
              replace duration2
                in if duration1 > duration2
                   then duration1
                   else duration2
```

and call it, for example to find the longer of an 11 hour and a 7 hour journey:

```
longer
  with 11
  with 7 ==>
replace duration1
  replace duration2
    in if duration1 > duration2
       then duration1
       else duration2
with 11
  with 7 ==>
replace duration2
  in if 11 > duration2
     then 11
     else duration2
with 7 ==>
if 11 > 7
then 11
else 7 ==>
if true
then 11
else 7 ==> 11
```

## 1.16 Names are arbitrary

This new function will actually find the bigger of any two integers: it is not specific to travel durations even though we used the names `duration1` and `duration2`. Similarly, our distance function:

```
distance is replace speed
            replace duration
            in speed * duration
```

will multiply any two integers together, not just speeds and distances.

Nonetheless, when we make abstractions we should certainly choose names that have meanings for us. Otherwise our functions can become incomprehensible. For example,

```
thingumywhatsit is replace yibble
                replace yabble
                in yibble * yabble
```

is just as good as:

```
distance is replace speed
            replace duration
            in speed * duration
```

as a way of generalizing multiplication but the names `thingumywhatsit`, `yibble` and `yabble` tell us nothing about their intended use for our particular problem.

Part of the art of model making is, on the one hand, choosing names that reflect the values they generalize but, on the other hand, recognizing that the resulting functions may have applications beyond the immediate problem. For example, because the duration comparison function works with any two integers, we might use more general names, say:

```
bigger is replace first
          replace second
          in if first > second
             then first
             else second
```

Here the names tell us that we are working with two values and that we supply the values in a particular order.

Names' meanings are significant to us because they remind us of what they are generalizing in the model that we are building. However, it is important to remember that the names themselves are only significant in functions as indicators as to where replacements are to take place.

## 1.17 New collections from old collections

We have talked about solving a problem by starting with an initial collection of things for subsequent manipulation. For a problem to be solved, we will need to construct a final collection of things satisfying various criteria by selecting, inspecting and possibly changing things from the initial collection. The final collection may consist of the same sorts of thing as the initial collection or it may be full of different things. The final collection may be empty or may just have one thing in it. Indeed the initial collection may be empty or have just one thing in it. Of course, for elaborate problems we may well start with several initial collections and finish with several final collections, but we shall keep things simple for the moment.

Consider the following outline of solving a common simple sort of problem by creating a final collection of things from an initial collection of things:

> If the initial collection is empty then the final collection is empty. Otherwise, manipulate the next thing from the initial collection to decide whether or not to add something to the final collection that results from dealing with the rest of the initial collection.

That is, we go through the initial collection taking out things until there are none left. Next we make an empty final collection. Then we look at each of the things that we took out of the initial collection and decide whether or not to put something into the final collection.

We will now consider some concrete examples of this general approach, using four variants of it. The examples are based on a collection of cat descriptions. Each description consists of the cat's name, a string, its fur colour, a string, and its weight in kilogrammes, a real number. We might represent the cat descriptions using the following table:

```
Initial collection
name          colour     weight
"Wallace"     "tabby"    4.0
"Mog"         "black"    4.5
"Spider"      "tabby"    2.8
```

Note again that we are not making any firm commitment to representations for things or collections: rather we note that a table is one possible representation for a collection of things.

## 1.18 Mapping

Suppose each cat eats 200 grammes of delicious dolphin flavoured soya cat food and we want to know how much each one now weighs.

If the initial collection is empty then we make an empty final collection. Otherwise we take out the first cat and add 0.2 to its weight. We then add it to the final collection from finding new weights for all the cats in the rest of the initial collection.

Let us try this out. We start with the whole initial collection:

```
Initial collection
name          colour     weight
"Wallace"     "tabby"    4.0
"Mog"         "black"    4.5
"Spider"      "tabby"    2.8
```

The collection is not empty. After eating, the next cat:

```
Old next cat
"Wallace"     "tabby"    4.0
```

gains weight:

```
New next cat
"Wallace"     "tabby"    4.2
```

and we add it to the result of dealing with the rest of the collection:

```
Initial collection
name            colour        weight
"Mog"           "black"       4.5
"Spider"        "tabby"       2.8
```

The collection is not empty. After eating, the next cat:

```
Old next cat
"Mog"           "black"       4.5
```

is also plumper:

```
New next cat
"Mog"           "black"       4.7
```

and we add it to the result of dealing with the rest of the collection:

```
Initial collection
name            colour        weight
"Spider"        "tabby"       2.8
```

The collection is not empty. After eating, the next cat:

```
Old next cat
"Spider"        "tabby"       2.8
```

is somewhat stouter:

```
New next cat
"Spider"        "tabby"       3.0
```

and we add it to the result of dealing with the rest of the collection:

```
Initial collection
name            colour        weight
```

The collection is empty so the final collection is empty to begin with:

```
Final collection
name            colour        weight
```

The new next cat is added:

```
Final collection
name            colour        weight
"Spider"        "tabby"       3.0
```

The new next cat is added:

```
Final collection
name            colour        weight
"Mog"           "black"       4.7
"Spider"        "tabby"       3.0
```

The new next cat is added:

```
Final collection
name            colour        weight
"Wallace"       "tabby"       4.2
"Mog"           "black"       4.7
"Spider"        "tabby"       3.0
```

Note that we unwound our way through the collection until it was empty, doing something to each thing. We then made a new empty collection and wound our way back up, picking up the new things and adding them to the new collection.

This activity is called mapping because it involves doing something to everything in a collection to form a new collection. The final collection has as many things in it as the initial collection and each thing in the final collection results from doing something to a corresponding thing in the initial collection.

It is important to note that each stage has its own distinct initial and final collections. We are not working with one initial collection and one final collection which are common to all stages. Rather, we are using the rest of the initial collection at each stage as the initial collection for the next stage. Similarly, we used the expanded final collection from each stage as the basis of the final collection for the previous stage. In the same way, each stage had its own old and new next cats. When we moved from stage to stage we remembered the collections and next cats for the previous stages. When we returned to a stage we picked up the appropriate collections and cats.

## 1.19 Filtering

Suppose we want to find all the tabby cats from the collection we used above:

```
Initial collection
name          colour        weight
"Wallace"     "tabby"       4.0
"Mog"         "black"       4.5
"Spider"      "tabby"       2.8
```

If the initial collection is empty then we make an empty final collection. Otherwise, we take out the first cat. If it is tabby then we add it to the final collection from finding all the tabby cats in the rest of the initial collection. If the first cat is not tabby then we just make a final collection from all the tabby cats in the initial collection.

Once again we start with the initial collection. The collection is not empty. The next cat:

```
Old next cat
"Wallace"     "tabby"       4.0
```

is tabby so we add it:

```
New next cat
"Wallace"     "tabby"       4.0
```

to the result of dealing with the rest of the collection:

```
Initial collection
name          colour        weight
"Mog"         "black"       4.5
"Spider"      "tabby"       2.8
```

The collection is not empty. The next cat:

```
Old next cat
"Mog"         "black"       4.5
```

is not tabby, so we ignore it and just deal with the rest of the collection:

```
Initial collection
name          colour        weight
"Spider"      "tabby"       2.8
```

The collection is not empty. The next cat:

```
            Old next cat
            "Spider"      "tabby"      2.8
```

is tabby so we add it:

```
            New next cat
            "Spider"      "tabby"      2.8
```

to the result of dealing with the rest of the collection:

```
            Initial collection
            name          colour      weight
```

The collection is empty so the final collection is empty to begin with:

```
            Final collection
            name          colour      weight
```

First we add the next cat:

```
            Final collection
            name          colour      weight
            "Spider"      "tabby"      2.8
```

Then we do not add the next cat:

```
            Final collection
            name          colour      weight
            "Spider"      "tabby"      2.8
```

Finally we add the next cat:

```
            Final collection
            name          colour      weight
            "Wallace"     "tabby"      4.0
            "Spider"      "tabby"      2.8
```

Once again, we wound our way down through the collection but this time we decided whether or not to keep each thing. When the collection was empty we started a new empty collection and wound our way back up again, picking up things that we had kept.

This activity is known as filtering because it involves selecting things which satisfy some criterion. The final collection does not necessarily contain as many things as the initial collection as some of the things in the initial collection do not meet that criterion.

## 1.20 Folding

Suppose we want to find the total weight of all the cats:

```
      Initial collection
      name          colour      weight
      "Wallace"     "tabby"      4.0
      "Mog"         "black"      4.5
      "Spider"      "tabby"      2.8
```

This is slightly different to mapping and filtering as we want a single final thing, a value, rather than a collection of things.

If the collection is empty then we start with a final total weight of 0.0. Otherwise, we add the weight for the first cat in the initial collection to the total weight for all the other cats in the initial collection.

As before, we start with the whole collection. The collection is not empty so we add on the next cat's weight:

```
Next cat
"Wallace"    "tabby"    4.0
```

to the result of dealing with the rest of the collection:

```
Initial collection
name          colour      weight
"Mog"         "black"     4.5
"Spider"      "tabby"     2.8
```

The collection is not empty so again we add on the next cat's weight:

```
Next cat
"Mog"         "black"     4.5
```

to the result of dealing with the rest of the collection:

```
Initial collection
name          colour      weight
"Spider"      "tabby"     2.8
```

The collection is not empty so add on the next cat's weight:

```
Next cat
"Spider"      "tabby"     2.8
```

to the result of dealing with the rest of the collection:

```
Initial collection
name          colour      weight
```

The collection is empty. Here though, we are not forming a final collection but an overall weight. We start the overall weight at 0.0:

```
Final weight
0.0
```

First we add in the next cat's weight:

```
Final weight
2.8
```

Then we add in the next cat's weight:

```
Final weight
7.3
```

Finally, we add in the next cat's weight:

```
Final weight
11.3
```

As before, we wound through the collection, picking up the cats. At the end we started an overall weight and wound back up again adding in the cats' weights.

This activity is called folding or reducing because it involves combining together properties of all the things in a collection to form a final value.

## 1.21 Checking

Suppose we want to check if every cat weighs more than 2.0 kilograms. We want either "true" or "false" as the result. If the final collection is empty then we must have successfully checked every cat so the final check is "true". Otherwise, if the next cat weighs more than 2.0 kilograms then we check the rest of the collection. Otherwise, we have found a cat which does not weigh more than 2.0 kilograms: there is no point in checking any other cats so we stop with the final check as "false".

Once again we start with the initial collection. The collection is not empty. The next cat:

```
Old next cat
"Wallace"    "tabby"    4.0
```

weighs more than 2.0 kilograms so we check the rest of the collection:

```
Initial collection
name            colour        weight
"Mog"           "black"       4.5
"Spider"        "tabby"       2.8
```

The collection is not empty. The next cat:

```
Old next cat
"Mog"           "black"       4.5
```

weighs more than 2.0 kilograms so we deal with the rest of the collection:

```
Initial collection
name            colour        weight
"Spider"        "tabby"       2.8
```

The collection is not empty. The next cat:

```
Old next cat
"Spider"        "tabby"       2.8
```

weighs more than 2.0 kilograms so we deal with the rest of the collection:

```
Initial collection
name            colour        weight
```

The collection is empty so the final check is "true" to begin with:

```
Final check
true
```

So the final check is "true":

```
Final check
true
```

So the final check is "true":

```
Final check
true
```

So the final check is "true":

```
Final check
true
```

Once again, we wound our way down through the collection but this time we passed a boolean value back up.

## 1.22 Higher order functions

Let us summarize the mapping activity to find the weights of the fed cats:

```
     replace initial collection
      in if the initial collection is empty
         then the result is an empty final collection
         else the result is found by
               adding a new description
***            from adding 200 grammes to the weight ***
                with the next in the initial collection
               to the final collection
               from dealing with the rest of the initial
               collection
```

Note that we have abstracted for the initial collection so that we could apply this function to an arbitrary collection of cats.

Suppose we had wanted the names of all the cats. We might try:

```
     replace initial collection
      in if the initial collection is empty
         then the result is an empty final collection
         else the result is found by
               adding a new description
***            from taking the name ***
                with the next in the initial collection
               to the final collection
               from dealing with the rest of the initial
               collection
```

For example, starting with:

```
Initial collection
name          colour       weight
"Wallace"     "tabby"      4.0
"Mog"         "black"      4.5
"Spider"      "tabby"      2.8
```

The collection is not empty. The next cat's:

```
Old next cat
"Wallace"     "tabby"      4.0
```

name is:

```
New name
"Wallace"
```

and we add it to the result of dealing with the rest of the collection:

```
Initial collection
name          colour       weight
"Mog"         "black"      4.5
"Spider"      "tabby"      2.8
```

The collection is not empty. The next cat's:

```
Old next cat
"Mog"         "black"      4.5
```

name is:

```
New name
"Mog"
```

and we add it to the result of dealing with the rest of the collection:

```
Initial collection
name          colour       weight
"Spider"      "tabby"      2.8
```

The collection is not empty. The next cat's:

```
Old next cat
"Spider"      "tabby"      2.8
```

name is:

```
New name
"Spider"
```

and we add it to the result of dealing with the rest of the collection:

```
Initial collection
name          colour      weight
```

The collection is empty so the final collection is empty to begin with:

```
Final collection
name
```

The new name is added:

```
Final collection
name
"Spider"
```

The new name is added:

```
Final collection
name
"Mog"
"Spider"
```

The new name is added:

```
Final collection
name
"Wallace"
"Mog"
"Spider"
```

Now compare these two mapping functions:

```
replace initial collection
  in if the initial collection is empty
     then the result is an empty final collection
     else the result is found by
          adding a new description
***          from adding 200 grammes to the weight ***
             with the next in the initial collection
          to the final collection
          from dealing with the rest of the initial
          collection

replace initial collection
  in if the initial collection is empty
     then the result is an empty final collection
     else the result is found by
          adding a new description
***          from taking the name ***
             with the next in the initial collection
          to the final collection
          from dealing with the rest of the initial
          collection
```

They are pretty much the same apart from what is done to the next thing in the collection. For heavy cats, the action is:

```
adding 200 grammes to the weight
```

and for cat names the action is:

```
taking the name
```

We could abstract over this action:

```
replace action
  replace initial collection
   in if the initial collection is empty
      then the result is an empty final collection
      else the result is found by
            adding a new description
***          from applying action ***
               with the next in the initial collection
            to the final collection
            from dealing with the rest of the initial
            collection
```

When we made functions before, we abstracted by introducing names for values. Now we have abstracted by introducing a name for a function. We have constructed a general mapping function which has no connection whatsoever with cats or weights or colours or cat names. We can replace the names **action** and **initial collection** with any function and collection, provided the function can be applied to things from the collection. In other words, the function must apply to things of the same type as the things in the collection.

For example, if we wanted to use this function to find the weights of pampered cats we would call it with a function to make a new cat description from an old cat description by adding on the weight of food. Similarly, to find the names of cats we would call it with a function to extract the name from a cat description.

This function is said to be higher order because it can be applied to other functions. As we shall see, higher order functions are extremely useful for model making and programming because they enable us to reuse the same general problem solving instructions in specific circumstances.

As we shall see, filtering and folding can also be cast as higher order functions.

## 1.23 Naming and recursion

In the above description of weighing fed cats, it says that the result from an initial collection which is not empty includes:

```
... the final collection
    from dealing with the rest of the initial collection
```

The intention is that in "dealing with the rest of the collection" we should in some sense "do the same again" to the rest of the initial collection. Let us now try and make "doing the same again" a little clearer. What we want to do again is the function itself. Suppose we associated the function with the name **fed weight**:

```
fed weight is
 replace initial collection
 in if the initial collection is empty
    then the result is an empty final collection
    else the result is found by
          adding a new description
           from adding 200 grammes to the weight
            with the next in the initial collection
          to the final collection
           from dealing with the rest of the initial
           collection
```

We can then indicate "doing the same again" by referring to the function through its associated name:

```
fed weight is
 replace initial collection
 in if the initial collection is empty
    then the result is an empty final collection
    else the result is found by
          adding a new description
           from adding 200 grammes to the weight
            with the next in the initial collection
          to the final collection
***        from fed weight ***
            with the rest of the initial collection
```

Whenever we get to **fed weight** on the second last line, we can replace it with all the instructions, which will result in them being carried out all over again. Each time, the rest of the initial collection from the previous stage becomes the initial collection for the next stage.

We can use the same approach to firm up the general mapping function. Let us call it **mapping** and put a reference to **mapping** in the instructions:

```
mapping is
 replace action
  replace initial collection
   in if the initial collection is empty
      then the result is an empty final collection
      else the result is found by
            adding a new description
             from applying action
              with the next in the initial collection
            to the final collection
***          from mapping ***
              with action
               with the rest of the initial
               collection
```

Once again, when the name **mapping** is reached it should be replaced by all the instructions associated with it, causing them to be done all over again.

Note that **mapping** has two abstraction points so it needs to be called with two values. The first abstraction point is for the generalized action **action** so it must be passed to the call along with the rest of the initial collection.

This technique where a function can invoke itself by referring to a name that is associated with its own instructions is called recursion. As we shall see, recursion is a fundamental technique for repeatedly carrying out a sequence of instructions.

Note that we said "a name that is associated with its instructions" not "its name". There is no necessary connection between a particular name and a particular sequence of instructions: the same name may be associated with different instruction sequences in different places; different names may be associated with the same instruction sequences in different places. This holds for associations between names and things in general. While it is often convenient to treat a name and a thing as if they are intimately connected they are really quite separate. A name simply identifies a place where it may be replaced by a thing.

## 1.24 Summary
And they all lived happily ever after? Well, we are at the end of this particular fairy story and it has given us an overview of problem solving and model making. Let us sum up what we have discussed in this chapter.

We have a bundle of tools for making models. Our basic general types – booleans, integers, reals and strings – can be used to describe things as groups of fixed numbers of property values. These types have methods which can be plugged together to form expressions to manipulate property values. Expressions can be generalized as functions by abstracting over values. We can regard thing descriptions and functions as the values and methods of new types. Decisions can be made by using the values of boolean expressions to choose between possible actions. Collections of things can be empty or have arbitrary numbers of the same type of thing. New collections can be constructed from old collections by repeatedly inspecting and changing things from the old collection to make things for the new collection. Functions can be generalized as higher order by abstracting over functions called within them. Recursion enables repetition by naming a function and then referring to the names associated with a function in that function.

However, despite introducing some *ad hoc* notation we have barely begun to write programs. Our models are just about detailed enough for human use but still far too vague for a computer to animate.

A programming language may be regarded as a model making notation which computers understand. Most programming languages provide a number of basic types like the ones we have been using, and ways of making collections of type values. Similarly, they provide methods, often called operations, for manipulating type values and collections. Furthermore, they provide abstraction mechanisms, that is ways of generalizing through naming and specializing by binding names to values and collections and instruction sequences. Finally, they provide control mechanisms for making decisions and repeating instruction sequences. One way to tell different programming languages apart and to classify them is to find out how specifically these different aspects are supported.

The rest of this book is concerned with programming in the language Standard ML (SML), that is using SML to make precise models for computer animation. We will not say much more about problem solving. Instead, we will look mostly at writing programs where the problem is well defined already. Furthermore, there are no hard details here about how computers work: we will assume that a computer is organized to accept a program and either run it or reject it because it contains errors, without caring about how it is able to do this.

This book is based on the premise that the best way to learn how to write programs is to write lots of programs. Thus, there are lots and lots of exercises at the ends of chapters and you are urged to try them out. Most exercises are based directly on ideas that have been covered in the text or can be solved by extrapolating from something in the text.

## 1.25  Book structure

The rest of the book is organized as follows.

In Chapter 2 we will meet the basic SML types for booleans, integers, reals and strings, and their associated methods or operations. Next we will look at how the methods can be plugged together to form expressions. We will also introduce briefly the representation of things as tuples.

In Chapter 3 we will look at abstraction over expressions to form functions. We will then consider how to call functions to specialize expression abstractions.

In Chapter 4 we will consider the use of pattern matching to enable the functional representation of a limited form of collection of things. We will also look at recursion with integer values.

In Chapter 5 we will meet the list type for representing collections. We will then consider a wide variety of functions for general purpose list manipulation. Here, the focus will be on lists of basic values.

In Chapter 6 we will take a further look at list processing, in particular at a number of list higher order functions.

In Chapter 7 we will move on to the manipulation of collections of things as lists of tuples. Here we will extend many of the simple list processing approaches from Chapters 5 and 6.

In Chapter 8 we will look at techniques for manipulating texts represented as lists of strings.

In Chapter 9 we will consider a more general representation for collections called concrete datatypes which enable collections of mixed type. We will use concrete datatypes in building lexical analyzers to recognize symbol sequences represented as strings.

In Chapter 10 we will look at the use of concrete datatypes to represent collections as tree structures. After discussing general tree manipulation, we will build simple syntax analyzers to check that symbol sequences correspond to grammatical rules and to represent the sequences' structures as trees. We will then consider briefly how to manipulate such symbol sequences by traversing the equivalent trees.

In Chapter 11, we will consider simple techniques for input and output to let SML programs communicate with the outside world.

Finally, in Chapter 12 we will look briefly at further aspects of SML not covered in the previous chapter.

Appendix A contains details of how to use a Standard ML system.

Appendix C contains details of SML's standard functions and operators.

## 1.26 Syntax notation

In introducing SML we will need to be clear about the general form of information and instructions. To be more formal, we will need to specify the syntax of SML constructs, that is those combinations of SML words that are valid parts of or whole programs. In particular, we will need to refer to arbitrary instances of constructs. To do so, we will write down the names of constructs in italics.

For example:

*name*

will mean an arbitrary name,

*integer*

will mean an arbitrary integer,

*expression*

will mean an arbitrary expression and so on.

There is a full grammar in Appendix B for the parts of SML which we will study here.

## 1.27 Typefaces

Different typefaces are used to distinguish different contexts.

English text is in Palatino.

`SML programs and program fragments are in Courier.`

Computer responses are in Univers.

*As noted above, the names of SML program constructs are in italics.*

## 1.28 Exercises

1) For each of the following descriptions of problems, identify the relevant initial collections, things and their properties. Specify the type of each property
   a) find the capital of a specified country
   b) find the time of the next showing of a specified play at a specified theatre
   c) find the names of all the cacti in a plant shop
   d) count how many varieties of tree in a plant shop are evergreen
   e) find the names of all the 6th form students over 1.5 metres tall in a school
   f) count how many items on a fast food restaurant menu cost more than $5
   g) find the names of all the people in the 5th form of a school with the same birthday as someone in the 4th form of the same school
   h) check if someone in a specific university department was born before 1977
   i) find the names of all the people in a cinema who wear glasses

    j)  find the names of all the varieties of fruit from Namibia in a super-market

2) Given the following table of city details:

| city | area | country |
|------|------|---------|
| Dundee | Tayside | Scotland |
| Brisbane | Queensland | Australia |
| Glasgow | Strathclyde | Scotland |
| Newcastle | New South Wales | Australia |
| Victoria | British Columbia | Canada |
| Newcastle | Northumbria | England |

describe how to solve the following problems in terms of doing something to the first entry having done something to the rest of the entries, or doing something with no entries:

a) find all the cities
b) find all the areas and corresponding countries
c) find all the cities in Scotland
d) find all the cities and areas in Australia
e) find all the countries with a city called Newcastle
f) count all the entries
g) count all the Australian entries

In each case, check your description by working through it by hand.

3) Given the following table of people:

| name | sex | age | swims |
|------|-----|-----|-------|
| Chris | female | 22 | yes |
| Pat | male | 17 | no |
| Jo | female | 21 | yes |
| Chris | male | 20 | yes |
| Pat | female | 19 | no |
| Jo | male | 18 | yes |

describe how to solve the following problems in terms of doing something to the first entry having done something to the rest of the entries, or doing something with no entries:

a) count how many female people swim
b) find the ages of all the male people who don't swim
c) find the names and sexes of all the people whose ages are at least 20
d) find the total age of all the people
e) find the total age of all the people called Jo
f) find the total age of all the female people who swim
g) count how many people are called Pat and are less than 20
h) count how many people are called Pat or called Jo
i) check if everyone swims
j) check if everyone swims or is called Jo
k) check if everyone who is male also swims
l) check if everyone who is female is also over 19

In each case, check your description by working through it by hand.

# CHAPTER 2

# Basic types

## 2.1 Introduction
In this chapter we are going to look at the SML boolean, integer, real and string types. We will use them to represent property values. We will also briefly consider tuples as a way of making things as groups of fixed numbers of property values.

## 2.2 Expressions and types
SML programs consist of function definitions and expressions that use the defined functions. We will see how expressions are formed as the book progresses. At its simplest, an expression may be a value from a basic type.

Types and typing are central to SML, as we shall see. They enable thorough checks on whether operations and functions are put together correctly.

Types are described by what are called type expressions. We will also see how type expressions are formed as the book progresses. To begin with, we will note that a type expression may be the name of a basic type, also known as a type constructor.

## 2.3 Basic system use
When an SML system is started up it displays a:

    -

to prompt for input and waits for an expression to be entered followed by a **;** :

    -   *expression* **;**

After you enter an SML expression into the system, it carries it out and tells you its value and type, and prompts for another expression:

    -   *expression*  **;**
    >   *value : type*
    -

We will use this convention throughout this book to present examples.

There are more details of system use in Appendix A. Please read it now.

## 2.4 Boolean type

The boolean type has the type constructor **bool** and has the values **true** and **false**. For example:

```
-   true;
>   true : bool
```

Here, the system tells us that the expression **true** consisting of a single boolean value has the value **true** and is a **bool** value.

We use the boolean type to represent the presence or absence of some property.

## 2.5 Case sensitivity

It is important to note that SML views upper and lower case letters as distinct. If, for example, you try to use **TRUE** or **True** instead of **true** then the SML system will reject them as unknown names.

In the next chapters we will see how we can introduce our own new names to generalize values. Once we have chosen a name we must spell it consistently. Changing just one letter in a name from lower to upper case will result in the SML system seeing it as a different name.

In general, SML's special words like **bool**, **true** and **false** are all lower case.

## 2.6 Integer type

The integer type has type constructor **int** and consists of positive and negative whole numbers and zero. A positive integer is a sequence of the digits:

```
1 2 3 4 5 6 7 8 9 0
```

There is a convention in Computing that non-zero integers should not start with **0**. For example:

```
-   42;
>   42 : int
```

Here the system tells us that the expression **42** consisting of a single integer value has value **42** and is an **int** value.

Negative integers start with ~. For example:

```
-   ~42;
>   ~42 : int
```

We use the integer type to represent properties which involve a discrete quantity.

## 2.7 Real type

The real type has type constructor **real** and consists of negative, zero and positive real numbers, written as a decimal number:

*integer* **.** *integer*

for example:

```
-   4.2;
>   4.2 : real
```

Real numbers may also be written as floating point numbers in the form:

    *integer1* **E** *integer2*

The idea here is that *integer1* is multiplied by **10** to the power of *integer2*. For example:

```
-  3E3;
>  3000.0 : real
```

because:

```
3E3 ==> 3*10*10*10 ==> 3000.0
```

*integer2* is called the exponent.

    An exponent may also be a negative integer. Then, *integer1* is divided by **10** to the power of *integer2*. For example:

```
-   3E~3;
>   0.003 : real
```

because:

```
3E~3 ==> 3/(10*10*10) ==> 0.003
```

Finally, real numbers may be written as floating point decimal numbers:

    *integer1* **.** *integer2* **E** *integer3*

Here, the decimal fraction *integer1*.*integer2* is multiplied by **10** to the power of *integer3*. For example:

```
-   4.2E3;
>   4200.0 : real
```

because:

```
4.2E3 ==> 4.2*10*10*10 ==> 4200.0
```

Once again, the exponent may be a negative integer.

    Negative real numbers also start with ~:

```
-   ~4.2E1;
>   ~42.0 : real
```

We use the real type to represent properties involving an effectively continuously varying amount.


## 2.8 Numeric precision

It is usual to think that integer and real numbers may be arbitrarily large or small. In practice, computers can only represent numbers to a fixed number of places. Furthermore, different sorts of computer represent numbers to different degrees of precision.

    You may hear of a computer performing 32- or 64-bit integer arithmetic. The word "bit" refers to the binary representation of integers as sequences of 1s and 0s. The number of bits is an indication of the range of values that can be represented; in general, the more bits the wider the range of values. Very crudely, if a computer performs $N$-bit arithmetic then the biggest integer cannot be larger than $2^{N-1}-1$, and the smallest integer cannot be less than $-2^{N-1}$.

    Computers can represent substantially bigger and smaller real numbers than integers but nothing like as accurately. Very roughly, while integers are precise, the computer represents real numbers as decimal multiples of powers of two. This enables a much wider range of values to be covered but there are lots of gaps in the range even with fixed precision. One real number representation effectively covers several real values both immediately larger and smaller.

It is hard to explain this in more detail without a major digression on binary representation, which we will avoid here. You might consult a textbook on computer organization for more details. The point to bear in brain is that if you get an error message referring to numeric overflow or underflow then you have tried to use a number which is larger or smaller than those permitted.

## 2.9  String type

The string type has type constructor **string** and consists of zero or more characters between double quotes:

```
"
```

For example:

```
-   "banana";
>   "banana" : string
```

Strings may be entered over several lines, with a back slash:

```
\
```

at the end of each line and at the start of the next line. However, the string will be treated as if it were all on one line. For example:

```
-   "This\
\string\
\is on four\
\lines?";
>   "Thisstringis on fourlines?" : string
```

Note that the beginning of each line abuts the end of the previous line: we should have put spaces at the ends of the lines:

```
-   "This \
\string \
\is on four \
\lines?";
>   "This string is on four lines?" : string
```

A double quote can be included in a string by preceding it with a back slash:

```
-   "double \" quote!";
>   "double " quote!" : string
```

A back slash can also be included in a string by preceding it with a back slash:

```
-   "back \\ slash?";
>   "back \ slash?" : string
```

Finally, for an explicit end of line character:

```
\n
```

is used. We will see the significance of this much later on when we consider input and output.

The empty string, that is a string with no letters, is:

```
""
```

We use the string type to represent properties described by words.

## 2.10 Tuple type

Tuples are fixed length sequences of mixed type and may be used to represent things as groups of property values. A tuple is written as a sequence of values separated by , s within ( and ).

For example, a car description might be:

```
("Morris 1000",4,true)
```

for a Morris 1000 with four wheels and an engine. This tuple consists of a string, an integer and a boolean value.

Similarly, a cat description might be:

```
("Mog","black",4.0)
```

for a black cat called Mog which weighs 4.0 kilogrammes. This tuple consists of a string, a string and a real value.

A given and a family name might be represented as a tuple consisting of two strings:

```
("Donald","Duck")
```

A department and phone number might be represented as a tuple of a string and an integer:

```
("Emergency",999)
```

A volume description, consisting of a volume name, height, depth and length might be represented by a tuple of a string and three integers:

```
("box",3,5,8)
```

Tuples may contain tuples. For example, someone's full name and age might be represented as a tuple consisting of a tuple, consisting of two strings, and an integer:

```
(("Minnie","Minx"),9)
```

Tuples may be nested to arbitrary depth. For example:

```
("Scotland",
  ("Glasgow",("Caledonia","Glasgow","Paisley","Strathclyde")))
```

is a tuple of a string and a tuple of a string and a tuple of four strings.

The components of tuples are known as elements.

The type of a tuple is given by the types of its elements separated by * s. For a tuple:

( *expression1* , *expression2* , ... *expressionN* )

if the types of the expressions are:

*expression1* : *type1*
*expression2* : *type2*
...
*expressionN* : *typeN*

then the tuple's type is:

*type1* * *type2* * ... * *typeN*

For example:

```
-   ("Morris 1000",4,true);
>   ("Morris 1000",4,true) : string * int * bool
```

```
-    ("Mog","black",4.0);
>    ("Mog","black",4.0) : string * string * real

-    ("Donald","Duck");
>    ("Donald","Duck") : string * string

-    ("Emergency",999);
>    ("Emergency",999) : string * int

-    ("box",3,5,8);
>    ("box",3,5,8) : string * int * int * int

-    ("Minnie","Minx",9);
>    ("Minnie","Minx",9) : string * string * int
```

For tuples with tuples as elements, the element tuple types are bracketed in the overall type expression. Compare the last example with:

```
-    (("Minnie","Minx"),9);
>    (("Minnie","Minx"),9) : (string * string) * int
```

Here, the whole of the first element is a tuple so its type is in brackets. For example:

```
-    ("Scotland",("Edinburgh",
                   ("Edinburgh","Heriot-Watt","Napier")));
>    ("Scotland",("Edinburgh",
                   ("Edinburgh","Heriot-Watt","Napier"))) :
     string * (string * (string * string * string))
```

Note that we refer to a tuple as a value even though it is made up of other values.

Tuples are known as product types. A

*type1 * type2*

tuple may consist of any value of *type1* followed by any value of *type2*. If there are, say, $M$ possible *type1* values and, say, $N$ possible *type2* values then there are $M \times N$ possible *type1 * type2* tuple values. Hence the name "product" type.

## 2.11 Function type overview

As we shall see, functions are central to programming in SML.

Alas, SML systems cannot display the instructions for functions as they are converted into a special representation for use by the computer hardware. For a function, only the type is displayed:

```
-    function ;
>    function type
```

We saw in Chapter 1 that a function has a number of named abstraction points. These are called formal parameters or bound variables. A function is defined from a domain, determined by the types of the formal parameters, to a range, determined by the types of the final result. Thus, a function type is displayed as:

*domain type -> range type*

When a function is applied to values corresponding to *domain type* the result is a *range type*.

The values a function is applied to are called its actual parameters or arguments. A function application has the general form:

*expression1 expression2*

where *expression1* returns a function value and *expression2* returns a value of the same type as the function value's domain.

A function application is itself an expression.

Most SML functions are prefix, that is they are written before their arguments. However, SML provides special syntax for type methods that are applied to two values and are usually written as infix operators between their arguments, such as arithmetic and comparison operators. In SML, almost all such operators are disguised functions. The arguments of infix operators are called operands.

A function application with an infix operator has the form:

*expression1 operator expression2*

and is also an expression.


## 2.12 Boolean operators

The function **not** negates a boolean value, that is it converts **true** to **false** and **false** to **true**. For example:

```
-    not true;
>    false : bool
```

In this function call, the name **not** is the function expression and the value **true** is the argument expression.

For example:

```
-    not false;
>    true : bool
```

**not** is a function from a boolean argument to a boolean result. We can enter **not** into the system to find its type:

```
-    not;
>    fn : bool -> bool
```

This says that **not** has a boolean domain and a boolean range. That is, **not** takes a boolean argument and returns a boolean result.

SML has a special built-in operator for testing if two boolean values are **true**. This is known as conjunction. The infix operator for conjunction is **andalso**. We can explain how **andalso** behaves with the following truth table. Here **x** and **y** stand for arbitrary truth values. The table shows all possible combinations of values of **x** and **y**, and the final values of **x andalso y**:

```
X       Y       X andalso Y
false   false   false
false   true    false
true    false   false
true    true    true
```

Note that the result is **true** only when both **x** and **y** are true. Otherwise, the result is **false**.

For example:

```
-   true andalso false;
>   false : bool
```

In this function application with an infix operator, the operands are **true** and **false**.

SML also provides a special built-in infix operator **orelse** for testing if either or both of two values are **true**. This is known as disjunction. **orelse** has the following truth table:

```
X       Y       X orelse Y
false   false   false
false   true    true
true    false   true
true    true    true
```

Note that the result is **true** unless both values are **false**. For example:

```
-   true orelse false;
>   true : bool
```

SML systems will not display the types of **andalso** and **orelse**.

## 2.13 Precedence and boolean expressions

Complex boolean expressions may be built up by using expressions as arguments or operands in further expressions. The order in which expressions are carried out or evaluated is determined by what is called the precedence of their operators. In boolean expressions, function applications have higher precedence than expressions with **andalso**, and expressions with **andalso** have higher precedence than those with **orelse**. Thus, the order of evaluation is function applications, then **andalso** and finally **orelse**.

For example, in:

```
-   not true andalso false;
>   false : bool
```

first of all:

```
not true ==> false
```

is evaluated and then:

```
false andalso false ==> false
```

Also in:

```
-   true orelse not true andalso false;
>   true : bool
```

first of all:

```
not true ==> false
```

giving:

```
true orelse not true andalso false ==>
true orelse false andalso false
```

Next:

```
false andalso false ==> false
```

giving:

```
true orelse false andalso false ==> true orelse false
```

Finally:

```
true orelse false ==> true
```

Note that each time, a function is applied to the value immediately to its right and an operator is applied to the values immediately on either side.

If we need to override the precedence of functions and operators then we can use the brackets ( and ) to group parts of expressions together. Bracketed expressions have higher precedence than function calls, so they are evaluated right at the beginning. For example consider a bracketed variant of the previous example:

```
-   (true orelse not true) andalso false;
>   false : bool
```

First of all:

```
true orelse not true
```

is evaluated because it is bracketed. Here, first of all:

```
not true ==> false
```

so:

```
true orelse not true ==> true orelse false
```

Next:

```
true orelse false ==> true
```

so for the original expression:

```
(true orelse not true) andalso false ==> true andalso false
```

Finally:

```
true andalso false ==> false
```

Putting in those brackets made **(true orelse not true)** be evaluated as the left operand for **andalso** rather than **not true**.

Note that brackets are always needed if the result of an operator expression is to be the argument for an infix operator or function. For example, in:

```
-   not true andalso false;
>   false : bool
```

**not true** is identified as a function call and evaluated first. If **not** is to be applied to the result of **true andalso false** then the argument expression must be bracketed:

```
-   not (true andalso false);
>   true : bool
```

This is because function calls have higher precedence than operators in expressions.

## 2.14 Integer operators

SML provides a variety of infix integer operators. The addition operator is:

```
+
```

for example:

```
-   22+20;
>   42 : int
```

The subtraction operator is:

```
-
```

for example:

```
-   55-13;
>   42 : int
```

The multiplication operator is:

```
*
```

for example:

```
-   3*14;
>   42 : int
```

The division operator is:

```
div
```

for example:

```
-   126 div 3;
>   42 : int
```

Finally:

```
mod
```

which is short for "modulo" finds the remainder after division. For example:

```
-   171 mod 43;
>   42 : int
```

The prefix integer negation function is ~. These operators may again be used with the brackets ( and ) to build up complex expressions.

The precedence of brackets and operators in decreasing order is:

```
(...)
function call
~
* div mod
+ -
```

so bracketed expressions are evaluated before function calls which are evaluated before negation which is evaluated before multiplication, division and remainder which are evaluated before addition and subtraction.

For example, in:

```
-   3+4*5;
>   23 : int
```

first of all:

```
4*5 ==> 20
```

so:

```
3+4*5 ==> 3+20 ==> 23
```

However in:

```
-   (3+4)*5;
>   35 : int
```

because first:

```
3+4 ==> 7
```

so:

```
(3+4)*5 ==> 7*5 ==> 35
```

Again, in:

```
-   16-9 mod 5;
>   12 : int
```

first of all:

```
9 mod 5 ==> 4
```

so:

```
16-9 mod 5 ==> 16-4 ==> 12
```

However in:

```
-   (16-9) mod 5;
>   2 : int
```

first of all:

```
16-9 ==> 7
```

so:

```
(16-9) mod 5 ==> 7 mod 5 ==> 2
```

When operators of the same precedence are used they are evaluated from left to right. For example:

```
-   6 div 3*2;
>   4 : int
```

because:

```
6 div 3 ==> 2
```

so:

```
6 div 3*2 ==> 2*2 ==> 4
```

This left to right order of evaluation is important because a different order can give a different result. For example, we could get the effect of evaluating the previous expression from right to left with some judicious brackets:

```
-   6 div (3*2);
>   1 : int
```

The same operator may be repeated in an expression without bracketing. As with operators of the same precedence, expressions involving a repeated operator are evaluated from left to right. For example:

```
-   1+2+3;
>   6 : int
```

This is significant for -, div and mod. For example for left to right:

```
-   6-4-2;
>   0 : int
```

but for right to left:

```
-   6-(4-2);
>   4 : int
```

For reasons which will become apparent later, SML cannot display the types of ~, +, - and *. We will see how to display the types of div and mod below.

## 2.15 Tuple type operators

**div** and **mod** are really special SML notation for operators which apply to tuples of two integers. The function **op** is used to convert such special operators into functions on tuples. For example:

```
-   (op div) (126,3);
>   42 : int
```

is the same as:

```
-   126 div 3;
>   42 : int
```

Similarly:

```
-   (op mod) (97,55);
>   42 : int
```

is the same as:

```
-   97 mod 55;
>   42 : int
```

Thus, we can use **op** to convert such operators into functions and thence display their types. For example:

```
-   op div;
>   fn : int * int -> int
```

and:

```
-   op mod;
>   fn : int * int -> int
```

shows that **op div** and **op mod** are functions from **int * int** domains to **int** ranges.

## 2.16 Real operators

SML provides a variety of infix real operators. The real addition operator is:

```
+
```

for example:

```
-   3.3+38.7;
>   42.0 : real
```

The real subtraction operator is:

```
-
```

for example:

```
-   81.7-39.7;
>   42.0 : real
```

The real multiplication operator is:

```
*
```

for example:

```
-   8.0* 5.25;
>   42.0 : real
```

The real division operator is:

/

for example:

```
-   189.0/4.5;
>   42.0 : real
```

As for integers, the prefix real negation operator is ~.

These operators may be used with the brackets ( and ) to build up complex expressions.

The precedence of operators and brackets in decreasing order is:

```
(...)
function call
~
* /
+ -
```

For example:

```
-   3.2*11.0+6.8;
>   42.0 : real
```

because:

```
3.2*11.0 ==> 35.2
```

so:

```
3.2*11.0+6.8 ==> 35.2+6.8 ==> 42.0
```

However:

```
-   3.2*(11.0+6.8);
>   56.96 : real
```

because:

```
11.0+6.8 ==> 17.8
```

so:

```
3.2*(11.0+6.8) ==> 3.2*17.8 ==> 56.96
```

For reasons that we will consider next, SML cannot display the types of +, -, and *. However using **op**:

```
-   op /;
>   fn : real * real -> real
```

shows that **op** / is a function from a tuple of two reals to a real:

```
-   (op /) (126.0,3.0);
>   42.0 : real
```

## 2.17 Overloaded operators

Operators which apply to different types are said to be overloaded. Thus +, - and * are called overloaded operators because they apply to two integers or to two reals. Similarly, ~ is overloaded because it applies to an integer or a real. SML cannot display the types of overloaded operators as it cannot tell which version is required. Some languages provide different operators to distinguish integer and real operations. Instead, SML uses the same operator for both cases.

## 2.18 Mixed type arithmetic

In SML, mixed type expressions are not allowed. The overloaded operators +, – and * must always be applied to either two integers or two reals. **div** and **mod** can only be used with integers. **/** can only be used with reals.

To enable mixed type arithmetic SML provides conversion functions.

The function **real** converts an integer to a real. For example:

```
-   real 42;
>   42.0 : real
```

**real** is a function with type:

```
-   real;
>   fn : int –> real
```

The function **floor** returns the largest integer not greater than a real argument. For example:

```
-   floor (84.6/2.0);
>   42 : int
```

**floor** is a function with type:

```
-   floor;
>   fn : real –> int
```

**real** and **floor** must be used to carry out mixed mode arithmetic to ensure type consistency.

For example, to multiply an integer by a real to get an integer:

```
-   3*(floor 14.1);
>   42 : int
```

Again, to multiply a real by an integer to get a real:

```
-   3.0*(real 14);
>   42.0 : real
```

## 2.19 String operators

There are fewer operators for strings than for the other basic types. The function **size** returns the number of characters in a string as an integer. For example:

```
-   size "banana";
>   6 : int
```

Thus, **size**'s type is:

```
-   size;
>   fn : string –> int
```

The infix operator ^ joins two strings end to end. For example:

```
-   "fish"^"finger";
>   "fishfinger" : string
```

Thus, **op** ^'s type is:

```
-   op ^;
>   fn : string * string –> string
```

^s may be repeated in expressions. For example:

```
-    "fish"^" "^"finger";
>    "fish finger" : string
```

## 2.20 Comparison operators

SML provides overloaded infix operators for comparing values of the same type. The operator:

=

checks if two values are the same and:

<>

checks if two values are different. These return boolean values and are defined for most types of values. Note that = and <> are not defined for functions.

For example:

```
-    2=2;
>    true : bool
-    "chalk"="cheese";
>    false : bool
```

For tuples, corresponding elements are compared. The tuples are the same if the corresponding elements are the same. For example:

```
-    (42,42.0)=(42,42.0);
>    true : bool
-    ("forty","two")=("forty","three");
>    false : bool
```

Tuples must be of the same types to be compared.

These operators may have expressions as well as values as operands. Both operands must be of the same type. The comparison operators have lower precedence than boolean, arithmetic, real and string expressions so they are carried out after such operands. For example:

```
-    2=1+1;
>    true : bool
```

because:

```
2=1+1 ==> 2=2 ==> true
```

Again:

```
-    size "fish"=3;
>    false : bool
```

because:

```
size "fish"=3 ==> 4=3 ==> false
```

Also:

```
-    floor 42.23=42;
>    true : bool
```

because:

```
floor 42.23=42 ==> 42=42 ==> true
```

Finally:

```
-    real (size "haddock")=6.0;
>    false : bool
```

because:

```
real (size "haddock")=6.0 ==> real 7=6.0 ==> 7.0=6.0 ==>
false
```

There are also overloaded infix comparison operators for testing orderings on values of the same type. They are:

```
<
```

to see if one value is less than another:

```
<=
```

to see if one value is less than or equal to another:

```
>=
```

to see if one value is greater than or equal to another and:

```
>
```

to see if one value is greater than another.

These return boolean values and are defined for integers and reals. For example:

```
-   42 <= 41;
>   false
```

Many SML systems also allow order comparisons on strings which test for alphabetic order. For example:

```
-   "haggis"<"oatcake";
>   true : bool
```

As with = and <>, these operators may have expressions as operands provided they return values of the same type. These operators also have lower precedence than integer, real and string expressions so they are evaluated last. For example:

```
-   real 42>41.5;
>   true : bool
```

because:

```
real 42>41.5 ==> 42.0>41.5 ==> true
```

Also:

```
-   "t"^"his"<"t"^"hat";
>   false : bool
```

because:

```
"t"^"his"<"t"^"hat" ==> "this"<"t"^"hat" ==> this"<"that" ==>
false
```

Note that these comparison operators return boolean values so they can be used to make expression operands for **andalso** and **orelse**. For example:

```
-   "a"<"b" andalso "b"<"c";
>   true : bool
```

because:

```
"a"<"b" andalso "b"<"c" ==> true andalso "b"<"c" ==>
true andalso true ==> true
```

## 2.21 Boolean comparison

Note that a boolean expression returns a boolean value so there is never any point in comparing the result of a boolean expression with a boolean value. Consider:

*boolean expression* = **true**

where *boolean expression* is any expression returning a boolean value.

When *boolean expression* is **true** then:

*boolean expression* = **true**

is **true**. When *boolean expression* is **false** then:

*boolean expression* = **true**

is **false**. Either way, the result of the comparison is the same as the result of *boolean expression* alone so the comparison with **true** is not needed. Thus:

*boolean expression* = **true**

is the same as:

*boolean expression*

Similarly:

*boolean expression* = **false**

is **true** when *boolean expression* is **false** and **false** when *boolean expression* is **true**. Thus:

*boolean expression* = **false**

is the same as:

**not** ( *boolean expression* )

## 2.22 Real comparison

Real numbers may be stored in a computer to more places than they are represented. This can lead to problems when trying to compare real values.

Consider calculating:

```
20.0/6.0
```

by hand:

```
20.0/6.0 ==> 3.3333333333333333333333...
```

The **3** repeats endlessly. However, the computer can only hold a fixed number of decimal places and there are rounding errors for real arithmetic. Furthermore, the computer may display real numbers to less places than are actually held.

For example, with:

```
-   20.0/6.0;
>   3.33333333333333 : real
```

the result is displayed to 14 decimal places.

Now consider:

```
-   20.0/6.0=3.33333333333333;
>   false : bool
```

Here, the comparison of **20.0/6.0** with its assumed value accurate to 14 decimal places fails because the result of the calculation is actually held internally to more places than are displayed.

In general comparisons of real expressions and real values should be avoided. Instead, such a comparison should be recast as a subtraction and the result should be tested to see if it is within an acceptable margin of a real value. If reals are displayed to $N$ places then the acceptable margin is half the $N$+1th place. Thus, here the margin is **0.000000000000005**. For example, the above comparison could be recast as:

```
-   20.0/6.0-3.33333333333333<0.000000000000005 orelse
    3.33333333333333-20.0/6.0<0.000000000000005 ;
>   true : bool
```

We do not know whether **20.0/6.0** is going to be slightly bigger or slightly smaller than **3.33333333333333** so we test for both possibilities.

We could avoid doing the main calculation twice by abstracting at those points.

## 2.23 Division and remainder with a negative operand

The behaviours of **div** and **mod** with one negative operand are somewhat counter-intuitive. First of all, for division, the result is rounded down to the nearest integer. For example:

```
-   7 div 3;
>   2 : int
```

but in:

```
-   7 div ~3;
>   ~3 : int
```

and:

```
-   ~7 div 3;
>   ~3 : int
```

the result is **~3** rather than **~2**.

Secondly, for integer $i$ and divisor $d$, SML requires that **div** and **mod** satisfy:

$i$ **div** $d = q$ (quotient) $i$ **mod** $d = r$ (remainder)
$d * q + r = i$
so: $r = i - d * q$

where:

$0 <= r < d$ or $d < r <= 0$

so the remainder with **mod** always has the same sign as the divisor.

Hence, for **mod**, because the quotient is rounded down, the remainder with one negative operand may be bigger or smaller than with two positive or two negative operands. For example:

```
-   7 mod 3;
>   1 : int
```

but:

```
-   7 mod ~3;
>   ~2 : int
```

because:

```
7 div ~3 ==> ~3
```

so:

```
7 - ~3 * ~3 ==> 7 - 9 ==> ~2
```

Similarly:

```
-    ~7 mod 3;
>    2 : int
```

because:

```
~7 div 3 ==> ~3
```

so:

```
~7 - 3 * ~3 ==> ~7 - ~9 ==> 2
```

Thus, you should be careful when using **mod** or **div** with one negative operand as the result may not be what you expect.

## 2.24 Tuples with expressions

Tuples can be constructed from operator expressions as well as values. Each expression is evaluated and the final value placed in the tuple.

For example:

```
-    (real 2,floor 2.8);
>    (2.0,2) : real * int

-    ("cat"^"food",3.0*0.2,"Mog"<"Spider");
>    ("catfood",0.6,true) : string * real * bool
```

## 2.25 Function composition

Function calls may be nested together by making the result of one call the argument in another call. This is called function composition. For example, to find the real value equivalent to the integer length of a string:

```
-    real (size "brolga");
>    6.0 : real
```

Here, **size** is applied to a string and returns an integer for **real** which returns a real:

```
real (size "brolga") ==> real 6 ==> 6.0
```

Functions may be composed to arbitrary depth.

In SML, the infix operator **o** may be used to compose functions. In general:

*( function1* **o** *function2 ) expression*

is the same as:

*function1 ( function2 expression )*

Thus, we could have written:

```
-    (real o size) "bunyip";
>    6.0 : real
```

## 2.26 Introducing exceptions

Sometimes things can go badly wrong in a computer program and the system has to stop running it. The normal sequence of evaluation is halted, the system displays an error message and returns to a state where the user can correct the fault and reinitiate evaluation.

Consider the **div** operator for dividing one integer by another. In arithmetic, dividing by 0 is a special case and is often said to return infinity. However, many programming languages cannot process infinity as a value. Instead, the system halts the program after an attempt to divide by 0.

In SML, a change in the normal flow of evaluation may be initiated through what is called raising an exception. The system will then catch the exception and handle it. If the system does not know how to handle the exception then it will halt evaluation and return to the system prompt after displaying a message. For example, if an attempt is made to divide by 0, the SML system will automatically raise an exception and stop evaluation. On the SML system I use, the effect is:

```
-  11 div 0;
uncaught exception Div
-
```

We will see later on that we can define our own exceptions as a way of dealing with awkward situations.

## 2.27 Summary

In this chapter we met the SML basic types for booleans, integers, reals and strings and introduced the use of tuples to represent things as groups of property values. Then we looked at various operators for these basic types and their use in forming expressions. We saw that we could build up more involved expressions by using expressions as operands of other expressions. Operators have precedence which determines the order in which parts of expressions are evaluated and brackets are used to change the evaluation order. Some operators are overloaded and can be used with different types but mixed type expressions require explicit type conversion. Next, we discussed comparison operators and noted problems with real comparison. We considered building tuples from expressions. We also looked at function composition for nested function calls. Finally, we met exceptions as a way of halting evaluation in dubious circumstances.

It is very important that you now tackle the exercises at the end of this chapter and run your solutions on a Standard ML system: the best way to learn to program is by doing it! Appendix A contains suggestions for Standard ML system use.

## 2.28 Exercises

1) Identify the types of the following values:
   a) **5**
   b) **5.0**
   c) **"five"**

d) `true`
e) `5.0E0`
f) `5E5`
g) `~5`
h) `5E~5`
i) `(5,5,5)`
j) `(5,5.0)`
k) `("five",5.0,5)`
l) `(true,5,"true",5.0)`
m) `(1,(1,1))`
n) `((2,2),2)`
o) `(1.0,(2.0,3.0),4.0)`
p) `("one",(1,1.0))`
q) `(("one",1),("two",2))`
r) `((1.0,("one",1)),(2.0,("two",2)))`
s) `((1,true),("one",false),(1.0,true))`
t) `((1,1,1),(2,4,8),(3,6,9))`
u) `((1,1),(1.1,1.1),("one","one"))`

2) Find the values and types of the following expressions:
   a) `true orelse false`
   b) `true andalso false`
   c) `not true andalso false`
   d) `not (true andalso false)`
   e) `not true orelse false`
   f) `not (true orelse false)`
   g) `false andalso false orelse true`
   h) `false andalso (false orelse true)`
   i) `true orelse false andalso false`
   j) `(true orelse false) andalso false`

3) Find the values and types of the following expressions:
   a) `6*3+4`
   b) `6*(3+4)`
   c) `6.0*3.0+4.0`
   d) `6 mod 7*8`
   e) `6 mod (7*8)`
   f) `floor 4.2E5`
   g) `floor 4.2E~5`
   h) `real 77`
   i) `real 42*real 42`
   j) `floor (real 42)`
   k) `real (floor 42.42)`

4) Find the values and types of the following expressions:
   a) `size "barnacle"`
   b) `size ""`
   c) `"blistering"^"barnacles"`
   d) `"thundering"^" "^"typhoons"`
   e) `size ("Red"^"Rackham")`
   f) `real (size "Unicorn")`
   g) `floor (real (size ("Marlin"^"spike")))`

5) Find the values and types of the following expressions:
   a) `"alphabetic"<="order"`

b) `"alphabetic"<>"order"`

c) `"alpha">"alphabet"`

d) `"1"<"2"`

e) `100000000.0=1.0E8`

f) `1<>1 orelse 1=1`

g) `1<2 andalso "one"<"two"`

h) `"1"<"2" andalso "3"<"4"`

i) `not ((size "wingnut")<3)`

j) `(1,"one")<>(1,"won")`

k) `(true,"true")=(false,"false") orelse`
   `(true,"true")=(true,"true")`

6) Find the values and types of the following expressions:

a) `("a","a"^"b","a"^"b"^"c")`

b) `("eleven",size "eleven",real (size "eleven"))`

c) `(1+1,"one"^"one",1.0+1.0,true andalso true)`

d) `(("one",size "one"),("two",size "two"))`

e) `(not,size,real,floor)`

7) Write expressions to:

a) check if **"mulga"** has more than 5 letters

b) check if the integer part of 6.54 is smaller than 7

c) check if 99 as a real is bigger than 89.9

d) join **"fish"** and **"finger"** with a space in between them

e) check if **";"** comes either before **"a"** or after **"z"** in alphabetic order

f) find the cost of 55 snow gum trees at $100.55 each, as a real

g) find the cost of 77 wattle trees at $120.23 each, as an integer

h) find the cost of 93 heath banksia bushes at $98.75 each with an additional sales tax at 15%, as a real

i) find the cost of 37 jacaranda trees at $246.64 each with an additional sales tax at 17.5%, as an integer

j) find the cost of 29 myrtle trees at $23.79 each, with a discount of 20%, as a real

k) find the cost of 74 paper bark trees at $147.90 each, with a discount of 12% and an additional sales tax at 12%, as an integer

8) Explain why the following expressions are incorrectly formed:

a) `real "three"`

b) `real 3.0`

c) `floor 7`

d) `size 33E33`

e) `false andalso "true"`

f) `6.0+size "grapefruit"`

g) `72.4 div 4`

h) `48 mod 7.0`

i) `126/3`

j) `size "Red"^"Rackham"`

k) `not 3<4`

l) `real 4+5`

m) `floor 6.2+7.3`

n) `1 (not =) 2`

o) `op +`

# CHAPTER 3

# Global declarations and functions

## 3.1 Introduction

In Chapter 1 we saw that abstraction is based on generalization through the introduction of names. Specializing an abstraction then involves replacing the names with particular values. Abstraction mechanisms are central to programming languages and provide a way of classifying and distinguishing between different classes of languages.

In this chapter we are going to start to look at how we can introduce names and associate them with values in SML. SML provides a variety of ways of associating names with values and we will discuss four in this book. Global declarations, which we will meet shortly, are a simple way of associating names and values for the duration of an SML session. Functions, which we will consider in some detail for most of this chapter, are expression abstractions where a formal parameter, a name, identifies the abstraction point. A function call then associates the formal parameter, the abstraction name, with the actual parameter, the argument value, for the duration of that call. Local declarations and let expressions, which we will discuss in later chapters, are useful for structuring programs.

To begin with we will use rather long winded notations for function descriptions and use. In the next chapter we will see more succinct notations which are short hand for the long winded notations. However, we will start with the longer notations to help to clarify the underlying concepts of function use.

## 3.2 Names

In SML, at its simplest, a name may be a sequence of alphabetic, numeric and underbar characters, starting with an alphabetic character. For example:

```
x banana legs_11 M90 Highway_61
```

As we shall see later, names starting with ' are used to abstract over types, that is to name type variables.

Recall from Chapter 1 that a name serves both to identify an abstraction and to remind us of the intention behind the abstraction. The use of meaningful names is very important for clear programming. However, there is a need for a judicious balance between the meaningfulness and length of names. Very long names clutter up programs.

It is sometimes tempting to introduce *ad hoc* name shortening conventions which are perfectly understood by the person that introduces them but incomprehensible to other people. For example, compare:

```
initial_value init_val initval ival iv
```

The first is on the edge of being too long. The second and third are broadly comprehensible. In the last two the significance of **i** is not apparent. The last name could mean "four" in Roman or "intravenous" for drips or "image vector" for picture processing and so on.

The use of such conventions is appropriate in programming if it is made clear what the conventions are and the conventions are applied consistently. Thus, we will adopt some conventions here to simplify presentation. We will sometimes use:

```
i i1 i2 i3 ...
```

or a name preceded or followed by an **i** for names associated with integers,

```
r r1 r2 r3 ...
```

or a name preceded or followed by an **r** for names associated with reals and

```
s s1 s2 s3 ...
```

or a name preceded or followed by an **s** for names associated with strings. We will also use:

```
v v1 v2 v3 ...
```

for names associated with arbitrary values and

```
l l1 l2 l3 ...
```

for names associated with arbitrary lists.

Names are also known as identifiers.

## 3.3 Reserved words

There are a number of names which are of special significance in SML. These are known as reserved words. They are:

```
abstype and andalso as case do datatype else end eqtype
exception fn fun functor handle if in include infix infixr
let local nonfix of op open orelse raise rec sharing sig
signature struct structure then type val with withtype while
```

Reserved words should not be used as names in programs as the system will always assume that they have the special SML significance.

## 3.4 Global declarations

A global declaration associates a name and a value for the duration of an SML session and takes the form:

**val** *name* = *expression*

The system evaluates the *expression* to get a value *value* of type *type*, associates *name* with that value and responds:

> val *name* = *value* : *type*

For example, to associate the name **pay** and the integer **12000**:

```
-   val pay = 12000;
>   val pay = 12000 : int
```

Or, to associate the tuple:

```
("Dennis","Menace")
```

and the name **name**

```
-   val name = ("Dennis","Menace");
>   val name = ("Dennis","Menace") : string * string
```

The name is then said to be globally declared.

Any subsequent mention of a globally declared name returns the associated value. For example:

```
-   pay;
>   12000 : int
```

```
-   name;
>   ("Dennis","Menace") : string * string
```

Names from global declarations may be used in expressions in place of constants and are effectively replaced by the associated values.

For example, to subtract a tax allowance of **4000** from the value in **pay**:

```
-   pay-4000;
>   8000 : int
```

To calculate tax at 25% on the value in **pay** and associate the resulting value with the name **tax**:

```
-   val tax = pay * 25 div 100;
>   val tax = 3000 : int
```

To associate **payslip** with a tuple of the values from **name**, **pay**, **tax** and the net pay after tax of **tax** on **pay**:

```
-   val payslip = (name,pay,tax,pay-tax);
>   val payslip =
    (("Dennis","Menace"),12000,3000,9000) :
    (string * string) * int * int * int
```

A typical SML program consists of a sequence of global declarations, followed by expressions that use them.


## 3.5 Functions

Functions are used to abstract over expressions. The formal parameters make explicit the names that are used for generalization. They are then used in the function body. When a function is called with actual parameters, the body is evaluated with the formal parameters replaced with the actual parameter values. Thus, defining a function abstracts over an expression and calling a function specializes an abstracted expression.

A function value has the form:

**fn** *name* => *expression*

This says:

replace *name* in *expression*.

The *name* is the formal parameter, also known as the bound variable. The *expression* is known as the body.

If the *name* can be associated with values of type *type1* and the *expression* returns a value of type *type2* then the function's type is:

   *type1* -> *type2*

In other words, the function is a mapping from a domain of type *type1* to a range of type *type2*.

If the final result of an expression is a function then its type is displayed as:

   –   *function* ;
   >   fn : *type*

An important aspect of SML is that the system can often deduce the type of the bound variable from the way it is used in the body.

Let us look at functions in more detail through some examples. Consider finding income tax on 10 000 at 25%;

   –   `10000*25 div 100;`
   >   2500 : int

Now consider finding income tax on 12 000 at 25%:

   –   `12000*25 div 100;`
   >   3000 : int

These two expressions are the same except for the sum of money. We can abstract over the sum of money by introducing a name **sum** to stand for an arbitrary sum of money:

   `sum*25 div 100`

We then specify that **sum** is the bound variable, the abstraction point, for this expression:

   `fn sum => sum*25 div 100`

If we give this function value to the SML system:

   –   `fn sum => sum*25 div 100;`
   >   fn : int – > int

the system tells us that we have entered a function and deduces that the domain is an integer and the range is an integer. Remember that * must have two integer or two real operands. **25** is an integer so in **sum*25** the name **sum** must stand for an integer as well. Hence the domain is an integer. Furthermore, if **sum** is an integer then:

   `sum*25 div 100`

is an integer value as * returns an integer and div takes two integers and returns an integer. Hence the range is an integer.

A function is called (or "applied") with an expression of the following form:

   *function_expression argument_expression*

First the *function_expression* is evaluated to return a function value, say:

   **fn** *name* => *expression*

of type:

   *type1* => *type2*

Next the *argument_expression* is evaluated to return a value, say

*value*

which must be of type:

*type1*

the same as the function's domain type.

Finally, all occurrences of the bound variable *name* in the body *expression* are replaced by the argument value *value* and the body is then evaluated to return a result value of type:

*type2*

This is known as applicative order or strict or eager evaluation or call by value.

If the function expression is a function value or call then it must be in brackets.

If the argument expression is a function call, operator expression or function then it must be in brackets.

For example, to find tax at 25% on 10 000:

```
-   (fn sum => sum*25 div 100) 10000;
>   2500 : int
```

`sum` is replaced by `10000` in the body:

```
10000*25 div 100
```

which is then evaluated.

Similarly, to find tax at 25% on 12 000:

```
-   (fn sum => sum*25 div 100) 12000;
>   3000 : int
```

`sum` is replaced by `12000` in the body:

```
12000*25 div 100
```

which is then evaluated.

As another example, consider making the word **"banana"** plural by putting an **"s"** on the end:

```
-   "banana"^"s";
>   "bananas" : string
```

Or consider making the word **"fishcake"** plural by putting an **"s"** on the end:

```
-   "fishcake"^"s";
>   "fishcakes" : string
```

These expressions are the same except for the word. We can abstract by using the name **word** to stand for an arbitrary word:

```
word^"s"
```

We then make it explicit that **word** is the abstraction point:

```
fn word => word^"s"
```

The type of this function is:

```
-   fn word => word^"s";
>   fn : string -> string
```

The operator ^ applies to two strings so **word** must be a string. Hence the domain is a string. The operator ^ returns a string so the range must be a string. We can now apply this function to make a plural for **"banana"**:

```
-   (fn word => word^"s") "banana";
>   "bananas" : string
```

The bound variable **word** is replaced by the argument in the body:

```
"banana"^"s"
```

which is then evaluated.

Once again, to make a plural for **"fishcake"**:

```
-   (fn word => word^"s") "fishcake";
>   "fishcakes" : string
```

The bound variable **word** is replaced by the argument in the body:

```
"fishcake"^"s"
```

which is then evaluated.

As a further example, the age for voting in the UK is 18 years. Consider checking whether or not someone of age 17 can vote in the UK:

```
-   17 >= 18;
>   false : bool
```

Or consider checking whether or not someone of age 19 can vote in the UK:

```
-   19 >= 18;
>   true : bool
```

These expressions are the same apart from the age being checked. We abstract over the age using the name **age**:

```
age >= 18
```

We then make the abstraction point explicit:

```
fn age => age >= 18
```

The type of this function is:

```
-   fn age => age >= 18;
>   fn : int -> bool
```

The operator **>=** must have two arguments of the same type. **18** is an integer so **age** must be an integer. Thus the domain is an integer. Similarly, **>=** returns a boolean so the range must be a boolean.

So to check if someone age 17 can vote:

```
-   (fn age => age >= 18) 17;
>   false : bool
```

Here, **age** is replaced by **17**:

```
17 >= 18
```

which is then evaluated.

## 3.6 Naming functions

Global declarations may be used to associate names with functions. For the global declaration:

```
-   val name = function
```

where *function* is a function, the system will respond:

```
>   val name = fn : type
```

to show that *name* is associated with a function of the given type. So, to name the tax at 25% function:

```
-   val tax = fn sum => sum*25 div 100;
>   val tax = fn : int -> int
```

To name the plural function:

```
-   val plural = fn word => word^"s";
>   val plural = fn : string -> string
```

To name the voter check function:

```
-   val voter = fn age => age >= 18;
>   val voter = fn : int -> bool
```

A name associated with a function value may then be used as the function expression in a function call. Whenever a globally declared name appears in an expression, it is replaced by the associated value. For example, to use the tax function:

```
-   tax 20000;
>   5000 : int
```

Here, **tax** is replaced by **fn sum => sum*25 div 100** giving:

```
(fn sum => sum*25 div 100) 20000
```

Next, **sum** is replaced by **20000** giving:

```
20000*25 div 100 ==> 5000
```

Similarly, the plural function:

```
-   plural "bat";
>   "bats" : string
```

and the voter function:

```
-   voter 21;
>   true : bool
```

can be called by mentioning the associated names.

In SML, something must be declared before it can be referred to. Thus, if one function calls another function by referring to its associated name then the declaration for the called function must appear before the declaration for the calling function. Sometimes several functions need to call each other: we will see how to deal with this in Chapter 9.

## 3.7 Comments

SML allows textual comments to appear in programs. These may be used to clarify what is going on. A comment consists of text within the comment brackets (* and *). Comments may appear anywhere and are ignored by the SML system. Comments may extend over several lines.

It is good practice to precede function declarations with comments to say briefly what the functions do. For example:

```
-   (* find 25% of an integer *)
    val tax = fn sum => sum*25 div 100;
>   val tax = fn : int -> int
```

```
-    (* add "s" after a string *)
     val plural = fn word => word^"s";
>    val plural = fn : string -> string

-    (* check if an integer is more than 18 *)
     val voter = fn age => age >= 18;
>    val voter = fn : int -> bool
```

In these examples, the comments seem unnecessary because the functions are so simple and we have associated the functions with meaningful names. Nonetheless, it is worth commenting functions as you develop them both to help other people understand what they do and to remind yourself.

It can also be helpful to place comments on the right hand side of each line of longer functions to clarify what each step does.

It is a very common mistake to forget the closing comment bracket *)!

## 3.8 Making the bound variable type explicit

Suppose we try to define a function to find the square of an integer:

```
fn x => x*x;
```

The system cannot type this function because * is overloaded. That is * can be used with either two reals or two integers and the system has no way of telling which **x** is. We have to specify the type of **x** explicitly.

In general, a function's bound variable type may be specified by:

```
fn ( name : type ) => expression
```

This says that in *expression* it is assumed that *name* will only be associated with a value of type *type*

For example, for the above function we need to make it explicit that **x** is an integer:

```
-    (* square an integer *)
     val sq = fn (x:int) => x*x;
>    val sq = fn : int -> int
```

Here, because **x** is nominated as **int** then the integer version of * must be intended.

If the system cannot deduce the type of a formal parameter from its use then its type must be stated explicitly.

In fact, in SML any expression can be typed anywhere by bracketing it with a type. However, it is considered good style to type bound variables when they are first introduced as abstraction points. That way, the reader knows their types immediately.

It is arguable as to whether it is sensible to always type all bound variables even where the system can deduce their types. On the one hand, that certainly provides lots of information to someone who might want to reuse a function somewhere else and is unsure as to what types of values the function may be used with. On the other hand, as with long names, explicit type information can clutter up function declarations. Here, we will tend to only specify a type explicitly if it is needed.

## 3.9 Abstraction over functions

So far, we have abstracted over an expression to form a function. Now we will look at abstracting over a function to form a function that returns a function as result.

Consider the function to find tax at 25%:

```
-    fn sum => sum*25 div 100;
>    fn : int -> int
```

Consider the function to find tax at 30%:

```
-    (* find 30% of an integer *)
     fn sum => sum*30 div 100;
>    fn : int -> int
```

These are the same apart from the rate of tax. We can abstract for tax with a new bound variable **tax**:

```
fn sum => sum*tax div 100
```

and then make the abstraction point explicit:

```
fn tax => fn sum => sum*tax div 100
```

Now we have a function whose body is a function. The type of

```
fn sum => sum*25 div 100
```

is:

```
int -> int
```

so:

```
fn tax => fn sum => sum*tax div 100
```

must be:

```
int -> int -> int
```

This is a function from an integer to a function from an integer to an integer:

```
-    (* find tax% of an integer *)
     val taxdue = fn tax => fn sum => sum*tax div 100;
>    val taxdue = fn : int -> int -> int
```

This function will find the tax at any rate **tax** on any sum **sum** by calling it first with a value for **tax** to get a new function which is then called with a value for **sum**.

For example, to find tax at 40% on 20 000:

```
-    (taxdue 40) 20000;
>    8000 : int
```

First of all, the function expression:

```
taxdue 40
```

is evaluated. **taxdue** is replaced by the associated function giving:

```
(fn tax => fn sum => sum * tax div 100) 40
```

This is evaluated so **tax** is associated with **40** giving:

```
fn sum => sum * 40 div 100
```

The original application is now:

```
(fn sum => sum*40 div 100) 20000
```

so **sum** is associated with **20000** and:

```
    20000*40 div 100
```

is evaluated giving **8000**.

Again, to find tax at 50% on 30 000:

```
-   (taxdue 50) 30000;
>   15000 : int
```

First of all the function expression:

```
taxdue 50
```

is evaluated. **taxdue** is replaced giving:

```
(fn tax => fn sum => sum * tax div 100) 50
```

This is evaluated so **tax** is associated with **50** giving:

```
fn sum => sum*50 div 100
```

The original application is now:

```
(fn sum => sum*50 div 100) 30000
```

**sum** is associated with **30000** and:

```
30000*50 div 100
```

is evaluated giving **15000**.

We can use **taxdue** to define functions to find the tax at specific rates. For example, to find tax at 20% we want a function like **taxdue** but with **tax** set to 20:

```
-   (* find 20% of an integer *)
    val tax20 = taxdue 20;
>   val tax20 = fn : int -> int
```

Note that **taxdue** is:

```
int -> int -> int
```

and **20** is **int** so:

```
taxdue 20
```

is:

```
int -> int
```

because **tax** has been frozen to the **int** value **20**.

Thus, **tax20** is like **taxdue** but with **tax** set to **20**. For example, in:

```
-   tax20 10000;
>   2000 : int
```

**tax20** is effectively replaced with its associated value:

```
(fn tax => fn sum => sum*tax div 100) 20
```

so, in effect, the expression:

```
((fn tax => fn sum => sum*tax div 100) 20) 10000
```

is evaluated as above.

To find tax at 60% we want a function like **taxdue** but with **tax** set to 60:

```
-   (* find 60% of an integer *)
    val tax60 = taxdue 60;
>   val tax60 = fn : int -> int
-   tax60 10000;
>   6000 : int
```

Now, **tax60** is like **taxdue** with **tax** set to **60**.

Let us now look at another example. Consider the function to add an **"s"** on the end of a word:

```
-   fn word => word^"s";
>   fn : string -> string
```

Consider the function to add **"ed"** on the end of a word:

```
-    fn word => word^"ed";
>   fn : string -> string
```

These functions are the same apart from the ending. We can abstract over the ending by introducing a new bound variable to stand for it:

```
fn ending => fn word => word^ending
```

Once again we have a function whose body is a function. The type of:

```
fn word => word^"s"
```

is:

```
string -> string
```

so the type of:

```
fn ending => fn word => word^ending
```

is:

```
string -> string -> string
```

This is a function from a string to a function from a string to a string:

```
-   (* put string ending after string word *)
    val endword = fn ending => fn word => word^ending;
>   val endword = fn : string -> string -> string
```

For example, to add **"ing"** to **"walk"**:

```
-   (endword "ing") "walk";
>   "walking" : string
```

First of all the function expression:

```
endword "ing"
```

is evaluated. **endword** is replaced giving:

```
(fn ending => fn word => word^ending) "ing"
```

This is evaluated so **ending** is associated with **"ing"** giving:

```
fn word => word^"ing"
```

Next:

```
(fn word => word^"ing") "walk"
```

is evaluated. **word** is associated with **"walk"** giving:

```
"walk"^"ing" ==> "walking"
```

Again, to add **"ed"** to **"fish"**:

```
-   (endword "ed") "fish";
>   "fished" : string
```

First of all the function expression:

```
endword "ed"
```

is evaluated. **endword** is replaced giving:

```
(fn ending => fn word => word^ending) "ed"
```

**ending** is associated with **"ed"** giving:

```
fn word => word^"ed"
```

The function application is now:

```
(fn word => word^"ed") "fish"
```

which is evaluated. **word** is associated with **"fish"** giving:

```
"fish"^"ed" ==> "fished"
```

We can use **endword** to define functions to add specific endings to words. For example, to add **"ed"**:

```
-    (* put "ed" after a string *)
     val ended = endword "ed";
>    val ended = fn : string -> string
```

**ended** is like **endword** but with **ending** set to **"ed"**:

```
-    ended "talk";
>    "talked" : string
```

Or, to add "s":

```
-    (* put "s" after a string *)
     val ends = endword "s";
>    val ends = fn : string -> string
```

**ends** is like **endword** but with **ending** set to **"s"**:

```
-    ends "swim";
>    "swims" : string
```

## 3.10 Introducing higher order functions

The last two functions were formed by abstracting for constants in the bodies of functions. Higher order functions can be formed by abstracting for an operation in the bodies of functions. The abstraction point must then be specialized with a function value.

Let us look at another example. Suppose we have the squaring function:

```
-    val sq = fn (x:int) => x*x;
>    val sq = fn : int -> int
-    sq 3;
>    9 : int
```

and the cubing function:

```
-    (* cube an integer *)
     val cube = fn (x:int) => x*x*x;
>    val cube = fn : int -> int
-    cube 3;
>    27 : int
```

Consider finding double the square of an integer:

```
-    (* double the square of an integer *)
     val doublesq = fn n => 2*sq n;
>    val doublesq = fn : int -> int
-    doublesq 3;
>    18 : int
```

Consider finding double the cube of an integer:

```
-   (* double the cube of an integer *)
    val doublecube = fn n => 2*cube n;
>   val doublecube = fn : int -> int
-   doublecube 3;
>   54 : int
```

These functions are the same apart from the function applied to the argument. We can abstract over this function:

```
fn func => fn (n:int) => 2*func n
```

func's type is:

```
int -> int
```

because n is an integer and * with 2 must have another integer argument. Thus, the new function is:

```
-   (* double the result of applying function to integer *)
    val doublefunc = fn func => fn (n:int) => 2*func n;
>   val doublefunc = fn : (int -> int) -> int -> int
```

As we shall see later, we do not actually need to specify explicitly that n is of type int but it eases the presentation.

This is a function from a function from an integer to an integer, to a function from an integer to an integer. That is, it expects its argument to be an integer to integer function.

We can use doublefunc to find two times the square of 4:

```
-   (doublefunc sq) 4;
>   32 : int
```

First of all the function expression:

```
doublefunc sq
```

is evaluated. doublefunc is replaced giving:

```
(fn func => fn (n:int) => 2*func n) sq
```

func is associated with the argument giving:

```
fn (n:int) => 2*sq n
```

The original function application is now:

```
(fn (n:int) => 2*sq n) 4
```

n is associated with 4 giving:

```
2*sq 4 ==> 32
```

Note that to simplify presentation we have left sq in place in fn (n:int) => 2*sq n instead of replacing it with fn (x:int) => x*x.

We can use doublefunc to find two times the cube of 4:

```
-   (doublefunc cube) 4;
>   128 : int
```

First of all the function expression:

```
doublefunc cube
```

is evaluated. doublefunc is replaced giving:

```
(fn func => fn (n:int) => 2*func n) cube
```

func is associated with the argument giving:

```
fn (n:int) => 2*cube n
```

The original function application is now:

```
(fn (n:int) => 2*cube n) 4
```

**n** is associated with **4** giving:

```
2*cube 4 ==> 128
```

We can use **doublefunc** to define **doublesq**:

```
-    val doublesq = doublefunc sq;
>    val doublesq = fn : int -> int
```

**doublesq** is like **doublefunc** but with **func** set to **sq**.
For example, in:

```
-    doublesq 3;
>    18 : int
```

**doublesq** is replaced with the associated value effectively giving:

```
((fn func => fn (x:int) => 2*func x) sq) 3 ==>
(fn (x:int) => 2*sq x) 3 ==> 2*sq 3 ==> 18
```

Similarly, we can use **doublefunc** to define **doublecube**:

```
-    val doublecube = doublefunc cube;
>    val doublecube = fn : int -> int
```

**doublecube** is like **doublefunc** but with **func** set to **cube**:

```
-    doublecube 3;
>    54 : int
```

We will now look at another simple higher order function. Consider applying **sq** twice to a value to raise it to a fourth power:

```
-    (* find the fourth power of an integer *)
     val fourth = fn n => sq (sq n);
>    val fourth = fn : int -> int
```

**sq** is of type **int** -> **int** and is applied to **n** so **n** must be of type **int** and the result must also be of type **int**.

Note the brackets round the argument **(sq n)**.
For example:

```
-    fourth 2;
>    16 : int
```

because:

```
fourth 2
```

is the same as:

```
sq (sq 2) ==> sq 4 ==> 16
```

Consider applying **cube** twice to an integer to raise it to a 9th power:

```
-    (* find the ninth power of an integer *)
     val ninth = fn n => cube (cube n);
>    val ninth = fn : int -> int
```

**cube** is an **int** -> **int** function so **n** and the result must both be of type **int**.
For example:

```
-    ninth 3;
>    729 : int
```

because:

```
ninth 3
```

is like:

```
cube (cube 3) ==> cube 27 ==> 729
```

Now, compare the functions associated with **fourth** and **ninth**

```
fn n => sq (sq n)
fn s => cube (cube s)
```

These are almost the same apart from the function which is applied twice; **sq** in **fourth** and **cube** in **ninth**

We could abstract over this function:

```
fn f => fn (n:int) => f (f n);
```

**f**'s type is:

```
int -> int
```

because **n** is an integer and the result of the inner use of **f**:

```
(f n)
```

is the argument for the outer call of **f**:

```
f (f n)
```

**f**'s result type must be the same as its argument's. Thus, the new function is:

```
-    (* apply a function twice to an integer *)
     val twice = fn f => fn (n:int) => f (f n);
>    val twice = fn : (int –> int) –> int –> int
```

This is a function from a function from an integer to an integer, to a function from an integer to an integer.

We can use **twice** to find **4** to the fourth:

```
-    (twice sq) 4;
>    256 : int
```

First of all the function expression:

```
twice sq
```

is evaluated. **twice** is replaced giving:

```
(fn f => fn (n:int) => f (f n)) sq
```

**f** is associated with the argument giving:

```
fn (n:int) => sq (sq n)
```

The original function application is now:

```
(fn (n:int) => sq (sq n)) 4
```

**n** is associated with **4** giving:

```
sq (sq 4) ==> sq 16 ==> 256
```

We can use **twice** to define **fourth**:

```
-    val fourth = twice sq;
>    val fourth = fn : int –> int
```

**fourth** is like **twice** but with **f** set to **sq**:

```
-    fourth 3;
>    81 : int
```

We can use **twice** to define **ninth**:

```
-   val ninth = twice cube;
>   val ninth = fn : int -> int
```

**ninth** is like **twice** but with **f** set to **cube**:

```
-   ninth 2;
>   512 : int
```

## 3.11 Introducing polymorphism

Consider the function that doubles the result of applying a function to an integer:

```
-   val doublefunc = fn func => fn (n:int) => 2*func n;
>   val doublefunc = fn : (int -> int) -> int -> int
```

Here **func** must be a function that takes an integer argument and returns an integer result.

Suppose that we wanted **func** to be able to take an argument of any type and return an integer result. For example, we might want to find double the integer value of a real so **func** would be set to **real**. We might want to find double the length of a string so **func** would be set to **size**.

At present, **func** is applied to **n** and **n** is specified as **int** so we might try dropping the **int** requirement:

```
-   (* double the result of applying a function *)
    val doublefunc = fn func => fn n => 2*func n;
>   val doublefunc = fn : ('a -> int) -> 'a -> int
```

Now, the system tells us that **n** has type **'a** and **func** has type **'a -> int**

**'a**  is a type variable. Just as an integer bound variable can be associated with any integer value and a string bound variable can be associated with any string value, a type variable can be associated with any type.

Traditionally, Greek letters are used as the names of type variables:

$\alpha$   ==   alpha
$\beta$   ==   beta
$\gamma$   ==   gamma
$\delta$   ==   delta

. . .

However, most keyboards and displays do not support the Greek alphabet directly so quoted Roman letters are used to stand for the equivalent Greek letter in alphabetical order:

**'a**   ==   $\alpha$
**'b**   ==   $\beta$
**'c**   ==   $\gamma$
**'d**   ==   $\delta$

. . .

In **doublefunc**, **n** is not used as argument or operand for any type specific function or operation so it can be any type, say **'a**. **func** has **n** as argument, so **func**'s domain must be **'a** for consistency.

For example:

```
-    (* double the floor of a real *)
     val doublefloor = doublefunc floor;
>    val doublefloor = fn : real -> int
```

will double the integer value from a real value. Here, **func** is associated with the function from **floor**. **floor** is a:

```
real -> int
```

function and **func** is an:

```
'a -> int
```

function so for the types of **func** and **sq** to match, **'a** must be set to **real**. **n** is also of type **'a** in **doublefunc** so **n** must also be of type **real** in **doublefloor**.

For example:

```
-    doublefloor 3.3;
>    6 : int
```

**doublefloor** is like **doublefunc floor** so:

```
doublefloor 3.3 ==> (doublefunc floor) 3.3
```

Replacing **doublefunc** gives:

```
doublefunc floor ==> (fn func => fn n => 2*func n) floor ==>
fn n => 2*floor n
```

so:

```
(doublefunc floor) 3.3 ==>
(fn n => 2*floor n) 3.3 ==> 2*floor 3.3 ==> 6
```

Suppose we wanted a function to find double the length of a string. We could replace **func** with **size**:

```
-    (* double the size of a string *)
     val doublesize = doublefunc size;
>    val doublesize = fn : string -> int
```

Here, **func** is associated with the function from **size**. **size** is a:

```
string -> int
```

function and **func** is an:

```
'a -> int
```

function so for the types of **func** and **size** to match, **'a** must be set to **string**. **n** is also of type **'a** in **doublefunc** so **n** must also be of type **string** in **doublesize**.

For example:

```
-    doublesize "banyan";
>    12 : int
```

**doublesize** is like **doublefunc size** so:

```
doublesize "banyan" ==> (doublefunc size) "banyan"
```

Replacing **doublefunc** gives:

```
doublefunc size ==> (fn func => fn n => 2*func n) size ==>
fn n => 2*size n
```

so:

```
(doublefunc size) "banyan" ==>
(fn n => 2*size n) "banyan" ==> 2*size "banyan" ==> 12
```

In **doublefunc**, **n** is said to be a polymorphic variable. Polymorphic comes from the Greek and means "many forms". A polymorphic variable can be associated with an argument of any type. By extension, **func** could be said to be polymorphic because it can be associated with any function from an arbitrary type argument to an integer result. Thus, **doublefunc** could be said to be a polymorphic function, because its argument **func** is polymorphic.

It is important to distinguish polymorphism from overloading. A polymorphic function can be applied in some sense to argument values of any type. However, an overloaded operation can only be applied to operand values of a fixed variety of types. Overloading could be viewed as a restricted form of polymorphism. For overloading, the types of operands must be made explicit or be deducible from other uses. Polymorphism is far more general.

Let us look at another example. Consider:

```
-    val twice = fn f => fn (n:int) => f (f n);
>    val twice = fn : (int -> int) -> int -> int
```

Suppose we drop the requirement that **n** is integer:

```
-    (* apply a function twice *)
     val twice = fn f => fn n => f (f n);
>    val twice = fn : ('a -> 'a) -> 'a -> 'a
```

This is an extremely polymorphic function! First of all, **n** is not used in any typed operation so it can be any type, say **'a**. Next, **f** has **n** as argument so its domain must be of type **'a**. (**f n**) is an argument for **f** and we know that **f** has an **'a** argument so the result of (**f n**) must also be an **'a**. Hence, **f** must be an:

```
'a -> 'a
```

function. Finally, the result of **twice** is **f (f n)**. **f** returns an **'a** so **twice** must also return an **'a**. Thus, **twice** is a function from a function from some type to that type, to a function from that type to that type.

For example, we know that **plural** puts an **"s"** on the end of a string so to put two **"s"**s on the end of a string:

```
-      (* follow a string with "ss" *)
     val double_s = twice plural;
>    val double_s = fn : string -> string
```

In **twice**, **f** is an:

```
'a -> 'a
```

function and **plural** is a:

```
string -> string
```

function so for consistency, **'a** must be **string**. Hence in **double_s** both **n** and the result must be **string**.

For example:

```
-    double_s "lo";
>    "loss" : string
```

First of all:

```
double_s "lo" ==>
(twice plural) "lo"
```

Next:

```
twice plural ==>
(fn f => fn n => f (f n)) plural ==>
fn n => plural (plural n)
```

so:

```
(twice plural) "lo" ==>
(fn n => plural (plural n)) "lo" ==>
plural (plural "lo") ==> plural "los" ==> "loss"
```

## 3.12 Function composition function

We will now look at a very general polymorphic function. Consider applying function **f** to the result of applying function **g** to some value **x**. The only constraint is that the range of **g** must be the same as the domain of **f**: that is the result of **g** must be the same type as the argument of **f**:

```
-   (* apply f to the result of applying g *)
    val compose = fn f => fn g => fn x => f (g x);
>   val compose = fn : ('b -> 'c) -> ('a -> 'b) -> 'a -> 'c
```

No typed operations are performed on **x** so let us suppose it has arbitrary type **'a**.

**g** is applied to **x** so it must have domain **'a**. We do not know what sort of type **g** returns so let us suppose it is the arbitrary type **'b**. Note that we use a different type variable: we have no reason to assume that the domain and range of **g** are the same. Thus, **g** is an:

```
'a -> 'b
```

function. **f** is applied to **g**'s result so its domain must be **'b**. We do not know what sort of type **f** returns so let us suppose it is the arbitrary type **'c**.

Note that again we use a different type variable: we have no reason to suppose that **f**'s range is the same as either **g**'s domain or range. Thus, **f** is a:

```
'b -> 'c
```

function. Finally, **compose** returns whatever **f** returns so **compose**'s range is also **'c**.

For example, to convert the size of a string to a real:

```
-   ((compose real) size) "whisky";
>   6.0 : real
```

In compose, **f** is of type:

```
'b -> 'c
```

and **real** is of type:

```
int -> real
```

so **'b** must be **int** and **'c** must be **real**. Thus:

```
compose real ==>
(fn f => fn g => fn x => f (g x)) real ==>
fn g => fn x => real (g x)
```

which is:

```
('a -> int) -> 'a -> real
```

Now, in:

```
(compose real) size
```
**g** is of type:
```
'a -> int
```
and **size** is of type:
```
string -> int
```
so **'a** must be **string**.

Thus:
```
(compose real) size ==>
(fn g => fn x => real (g x)) size ==>
fn x => real (size x)
```
which is a:
```
string -> real
```
function. Finally:
```
((compose real) size) "whisky" ==>
(fn x => real (size x)) "whisky" ==>
real (size "whisky") ==> 6.0
```

Note that **compose** can be used with any two functions provided that the domain of the first is the same as the range of the second.

SML provides **compose** as the standard infix operator **o**:
```
( compose function1 ) function2 ==>
function1 o function2
```
For example:
```
-   (real o floor) 4.2;
>   4.0 : real
```
because:
```
(real o floor) 4.2 ==>
((compose real) floor) 4.2 ==>
real (floor 4.2) ==>
real 4 ==>
4.0
```

## 3.13 Scope

We need to be a bit clearer about precisely where we can use names. We saw above that for a function:
```
fn name => expression
```
the bound variable *name* is to be replaced in the body *expression*.

However, we have also seen that we can nest functions. Thus there might be problems if nested functions share the same bound variable. For example, in:
```
fn x => fn x => 2*x
```
the **x** in:
```
2*x
```
might at first sight appear to correspond to either the outer function's or the inner function's bound variable.

In programming languages, names are said to have scopes that determine where they can be referred to. In SML, the scope rule is that an outer bound variable is overriden by the introduction of an inner bound variable with the same name. That is, in:

```
fn name => expression
```

*name* is in scope in *expression* except where another function introduces the same *name* as a bound variable. Another way of expressing this is that a name in an expression corresponds to the bound variable of the innermost enclosing function to introduce it.

Thus, in

```
fn x => fn x => 2*x
```

the **x** in **2*x** is the inner function's **x**. Thus, in:

```
((fn x => fn x => 2*x) 2) 3
```

**x** should be set to **2** in:

```
fn x => 2*x
```

However, this function also introduces **x** overriding the outer function so there is nowhere corresponding to the outer **x** to be replaced. The **2** is discarded leaving:

```
(fn x => 2*x) 3 ==> 2*3 ==> 6
```

For example, consider:

```
(fn x => ((fn x => 2*x) 3)+x) 4
```

Here, the outer bound variable **x** is in **+x** in the body of the outer function but not in the body of the inner function. It is replaced by **4** giving:

```
((fn x => 2*x) 3)+4 ==> 2*3+4 ==> 10
```

It is generally safest to avoid nested introductions of the same bound variable name. Where they are unavoidable, look to the left from a use of a name to find the first place where it is introduced as a bound variable.

## 3.14 Illustrating function application

In the above worked examples of function applications we have:
- (a) evaluated the function expression to get a function
- (b) evaluated the argument expression to get a value
- (c) replaced all occurrences of the bound variable in the function's body with the argument value
- (d) evaluated the body

We are using this replacement of bound variables in function bodies with argument values as a way of illustrating or animating function applications. However it should not be thought that this is how SML systems actually implement function application. What they do is certainly equivalent to our approach but very different in practice.

Furthermore, while we have been exact so far about the order in which replacement and evaluation are carried out, as examples become larger we will become less rigorous. Sometimes we will delay evaluating parts of expressions in order to make what is going on more explicit. At other times, we will apparently evaluate different parts of an expression at the same time to simplify the presentation.

One of the pleasing properties of pure functional languages, like the SML subset we are studying here, is that some aspects of the order of evaluation need not be prescribed rigidly. For example, with arithmetic operators the order of operand expression evaluation is not important. Similarly, with nested function applications it is legitimate to evaluate all the argument expressions at the same time rather than in strict sequence as each nested layer is evaluated. Provided we are consistent in always evaluating function arguments before the function body then we will get the same result.

## 3.15  Testing

A vital aspect of programming is testing. You may think that a function looks all right on paper but testing it will often show up problems or inconsistencies. It is not good enough to check out a function with just one test case as this may not try out all the circumstances of its use. Of course, you cannot try a function will all possible argument values: there are an awful lot of strings and integers and reals. Instead, you should test each function with a representative sample of values. If a function consists of nested functions then you should try out different combinations of argument values for each layer.

Use the types of the arguments to guide testing. Check for limiting as well as typical cases. If the function has a string argument then check that it works with the empty string **""** as well as non-empty strings. For example, for:

```
-   val plural = fn word => word^"s";
>   val plural = fn : string -> string
```

we might try:

```
-   plural "hat";
>   "hats" : string
```

and:

```
-   plural "";
>   "s" : string
```

If a function has an integer argument then try it with **0** and negative values as well as positive values. For example, for:

```
-   val tax = fn sum => sum*25 div 100;
>   val tax = fn : int -> int
```

we might try:

```
-   tax 10000;
>   2500 : int
```

and:

```
-   tax 0;
>   0 : int
```

and:

```
-   tax ~2000;
>   ~500 : int
```

Again, for:

```
-    val endword = fn ending => fn word => word^ending;
>    val endword = fn : string -> string -> string
```

we might try:

```
-    (endword "fish") "ed";
>    "fished" : string
```

and:

```
-    (endword "push") "";
>    "push" : string
```

and:

```
-    (endword "") "ing";
>    "ing" : string
```

If a function has a boolean expression then try it with values to make the expression both true and false. For example, for:

```
-    val voter = fn age => age>=18;
>    val voter = fn : int -> bool
```

we might try:

```
-    voter 19;
>    true : bool
```

and:

```
-    voter 18;
>    true : bool
```

and:

```
-    voter 0;
>    false : bool
```

and:

```
-    voter ~19;
>    false : bool
```

You might also see what your function does with very big values as well as very small ones. For example, for:

```
-    val tax = fn sum => sum*25 div 100;
>    val tax = fn : int -> int
```

we might try:

```
-    tax 2000000000000000;
Error: integer too large
```

whoops . . . !

## 3.16 Summary

In this chapter we have focused on abstraction. First we considered how to associate names and values through global declarations, to use an SML system like a souped-up desk calculator. Next we looked at how to construct functions by generalizing expressions through name introduction. We then saw how to call functions to specialize the names. We next discussed the construction of functions that return functions as values as a way of introducing multiple abstraction points for values in expressions. This was then extended to higher order functions by abstracting over operations. Finally, we met polymorphism which enables the construction of very general functions for manipulating values of arbitrary type.

In the next chapter we are going to discuss pattern matching as a technique for structuring functions according to the information that they manipulate. We will also look at recursion as a means of dealing with a range of values.

## 3.17 Exercises

1) Identify the types of the following functions:
   a) `fn x => x div 2`
   b) `fn x => x/2.0`
   c) `fn x => x=2`
   d) `fn x => fn y => x mod y`
   e) `fn s1 => size s1*10`
   f) `fn s => s^"?"`
   g) `fn s => fn t => s^" "^t`
   h) `fn s1 => fn s2 => size s1<size s2`
   i) `fn b1 => fn b2 => not b1 orelse b2`
   j) `fn s => fn n => size s<=n`
   k) `fn x => fn y => floor x+y`
   l) `fn s => fn x => floor s*size x`
   m) `fn f => fn x => f x div x`
   n) `fn f => fn x => x orelse f x`
   o) `fn f => fn x => x/f x`
   p) `fn f => fn x => f x+size x`
   q) `fn f => fn x => not (f (floor x))`
   r) `fn f => fn x => 1+f x`
   s) `fn f => fn x => size (f x)`
   t) `fn f => fn x => not (f x)`
   u) `fn f => fn x => f (x+1)`
   v) `fn f => fn x => f (not x)`
   w) `fn f => fn x => f x`
   x) `fn f => fn x => fn y => (f x) y`
   y) `fn f => fn x => fn y => fn z => ((f x) y) z`
   z) `fn f => fn g => fn x => fn y => f x mod g y`
   A) `fn f => fn g => fn x => fn y => size (f x^g y)`
   B) `fn x => x`
   C) `fn x => fn y => x`
   D) `fn x => fn y => y`
2) Explain why the following functions are incorrectly formed:
   a) `fn x => x+x`
   b) `fn x => fn y => x*y`

c) `fn x => fn y => x>y`

d) `fn a => fn b => not a >= b`

e) `fn s1 => fn s2 => size s1^s2`

f) `fn x => size x andalso x`

g) `fn p => fn q => (not p) q`

h) `fn f => fn x => x*f x`

3) Write and test the following functions. Identify the type of each function:

a) find half of integer **x**

   − `half 4;`
   > `  2 : int`

b) find double real **y**

   − `double 2.1;`
   > `  4.2 : real`

c) join string **s** onto itself

   − `twice "very";`
   > `  "veryvery" : string`

4) Write and test the following functions. Identify the type of each function:

a) find net pay on gross pay **gross** after tax at 20%:

   − `net20 20000;`
   > `  16000 : int`

b) find net pay on gross pay **gross** after tax at 30%:

   − `net30 20000;`
   > `  14000 : int`

c) find net pay on gross pay **gross** after tax at **tax** %:

   − `(net 20) 20000;`
   > `  16000 : int`

d) use **net** from c) above to define functions which find tax at

   i) 20%

   ii) 30%

5) Write and test the following functions. Identify the type of each function:

a) put the string **"Happy "** before a string **s**:

   − `happy "Birthday";`
   > `  "Happy Birthday" : string`

b) put the string **"Merry "** before a string **s**:

   − `merry "Xmas";`
   > `  "Merry Xmas" : string`

c) put one string before another:

   − `(sbefore "Jolly ") "good!";`
   > `  "Jolly good!" : string`

d) use **sbefore** from c) above to define functions to put

   i) **"Merry "**

   ii) **"Happy "**

   before a string

6) Write and test the following functions. Identify the type of each function:

a) return a boolean to indicate whether or not string **s** comes before **neutral** in alphabetic order:

```
-   lessneutral "banana";
>   true : bool
```

b) return a boolean to indicate whether or not string **s** comes before **"zoo"** in alphabetic order:

```
-   lesszoo "zoo";
>   false : bool
```

c) return a boolean to indicate whether or not a second string comes before a first string:

```
-   (less "guava") "avocado";
>   true : bool
```

d) use **less** from c) above to define a function which returns a boolean to indicate whether or not a string comes before
   i) **"neutral"**
   ii) **"zoo"**

7) Write and test the following functions. Identify the type of each function:

a) for integer **n** return a tuple consisting of n and a boolean which indicates whether or not it is greater than 0:

```
-   (more0 22);
>   (22,true) : int * bool
```

b) for string **s** return a tuple consisting of **s** and its plural, found by adding **"s"** on the end:

```
-   (plural "goat");
>   ("goat","goats") : string * string
```

c) for integer **n** return a tuple consisting of **n**, its square and its cube:

```
-   powers 3;
>   (3,9,27) : int * int * int
```

8) Write and test the following functions. Identify the type of each function:

a) evaluate:

```
a*x*x+b*x+c
```

for integer values **a**, **b**, **c** and **x**:

e.g. **x*x+2*x+1** with **x=3** ==

```
-   (((quad 1) 2) 1) 3;
>   16 : int
```

b) use **quad** from a) above to define functions to return the values of
   i) **x*x+4*x+4**
   ii) **2*x*x+3*x-3**

for unknown **x**

9) Write and test the following functions. Identify the type of each function:

a) return a sentence formed by joining strings **article1**, **noun1**, **verb**, **article2** and **noun2** with a single space in between each string:

```
-   (((sentence "the") "cat") "sat on") "the") "mat"
>   "the cat sat on the mat" : string
```

b) use **sentence** from a) above to define functions to start sentences with:

i) **"the mouse ran to"**

ii) **"the cat ate"**

10) Write and test the following functions. Identify the type of each function:

a) return a boolean to indicate whether or not string **s** is longer than integer **l** characters:

  − **(longer 3) "huge";**

  > true : bool

b) return a boolean to indicate whether or a string is shorter than a second string:

  − **(shorter "long") "short";**

  > true : bool

using **longer** from a) above

11) Write and test the following functions. Identify the type of each function:

a) find if integer **i1** is less than or equal to integer **i2** without using <=:

  − **(less_or_eq 2) 3;**

  > true : bool

b) find if string **s1** is the same as string **s2** without using = or <>:

  − **(same "precise") "precise";**

  > true : bool

12) Write and test the following functions. Identify the type of each function:

a) find the real cost of **n** items at real price **p** with discount of **d** real per cent and additional sales tax of **t** real per cent:

  − **(((cost 5) 12.6) 20.0) 10.0;**

  > 55.44 : real

b) use the function from a) above to define a function to find the cost of an unknown number of items at unknown price and discount with additional sales tax of 12.5%

c) use the function from a) above to define a function to find the cost of an unknown number of items at unknown price and additional sales tax with discount of 15%

13) Write and test the following functions. Identify the type of each function:

a) check if real value **v1** is no more than **error** greater or less than real value **v2**:

  − **((close 12.01) 0.01) 12.00;**

  > true : bool

b) use the function from a) above to define a function to check if two real values are within 0.0005 of each other

# CHAPTER 4

# Pattern matching and recursion

## 4.1 Simplified notations

As you may have noticed, the full notations for associating names with function values and for calling functions are extremely long winded. We have used them so far to emphasize functions as values. We will now consider some simplifications. First of all, a function definition:

**val** *name1* = **fn** *name2* => *expression*

may be simplified. **val** is changed to **fun**, the = and **fn** are dropped, and => is replaced with = giving:

**fun** *name1 name2* = *expression*

For example, some of the functions from the previous chapter become:

```
-   fun tax sum = sum*25 div 100;
>   val tax = fn : int -> int

-   fun plural word = word^"s";
>   val plural = fn : string -> string

-   fun voter age = age >= 18;
>   val voter = fn : int -> bool

-   fun sq (x:int) = x*x;
>   val sq = fn : int -> int

-   fun taxdue tax = fn sum => sum*tax div 100;
>   val taxdue = fn : int -> int -> int
```

so:

```
-   fun taxdue tax sum = sum*tax div 100;
>   val taxdue = fn : int -> int -> int
```

Similarly:

```
-   fun endword ending word = word^ending;
>   val endword = fn : string -> string -> string

-   fun doublefunc func (n:int) = 2*func n;
>   val doublefunc = fn : (int -> int) -> int -> int
```

Note that **fun** is a shorthand for an association between a name and an explicit function value using **val**. The **val** form must be retained to associate a name and the value of an expression, even when the expression returns a function value. For example:

```
fun ending = endword "ing"
```

is incorrect because the expression:

```
endword "ing"
```

is not an explicit function value even though it returns one. The correct form is still:

```
-    val ending = endword "ing";
>    val ending = fn : string -> string
```

Function calls may also be simplified by dropping strict bracketing around function expressions. Thus:

( ( *function argument1* ) *argument2* ) *argument3*

becomes:

*function argument1 argument2 argument3*

which is evaluated from left to right.

For example:

```
-    endword "jump" "ing";
>    "jumping" : string
```

However, bracketing is essential when a function call or operator expression is an argument to another function. Consider:

```
sq sq 3
```

This is interpreted as:

```
(sq sq) 3
```

which fails because **sq** requires an integer rather than a function as its argument. Instead:

```
-    sq (sq 3);
>    81 : int
```

should be used.

## 4.2 Tables and functions

In Chapter 1, we looked at the use of tables to represent collections of things. In a table, each thing has a fixed number of properties across the rows. While a table might in principle be any size, in practice it consists of a fixed number of things at any given moment. Each thing is distinct and there is not necessarily any way of finding one of its properties from its other properties.

Consider the special case where the things are pairs of properties, for example cats and colours:

```
name        colour
Wallace     tabby
Mog         black
Spider      tabby
```

We can use this table to find the colour of a cat from its name. We look down the column of names until we find the required name and then look across the row to find the associated colour.

In Chapter 3 we looked at making functions which performed calculations on general values abstracted through bound variables. A table of pair associations is like a function in that we look up an argument value in one column to find the result value in another column. However, a table of associations is rather more restrictive than the sorts of functions we have considered so far. A function can find the result from arbitrary values through calculation whereas a table can only be used with specific values. That is, with a table we can find result values for individual cases but there is no general way to find the result for an arbitrary case. In particular, it is not clear what we should do when we get to the end of a column without finding the required value. In the above example, while a name could be absolutely any sequence of letters, we only know the associated colour in the three specific cases of "Wallace", "Mog" and "Spider". In general, there is no way of calculating a cat's colour from its name.

On the other hand, as yet we have no way of dealing with specific cases in SML functions. For example, consider finding the past tense for an English verb. We can often put "ed" on the end of a verb, for example "walked" for "walk" and "fished" for "fish". However, there are specific exceptions to this rule, for example, "stood" for "stand", "swam" for "swim" and "ate" for "eat". We could use a table to represent the special cases:

| verb | past |
|-------|-------|
| stand | stood |
| swim | swam |
| eat | ate |

but we do not have any obvious way of including the general case in a table.

## 4.3 Pattern matching

SML enables the use of functions to deal with individual as well as general cases through what is called pattern matching. In the last chapter, we saw that a function has the form:

> **fn** *name* => *expression*

A function may also be defined with a number of optional cases, each with a distinct pattern rather than a single bound variable:

> **fn** *pattern1* => *expression1* |
> *pattern2* => *expression2* |
> ...
> *patternN* => *expressionN*

To begin with, patterns may be constants or bound variables.

When the function is called, the argument is matched against each pattern in turn. When a match succeeds the corresponding expression is evaluated. For a constant pattern, the argument must have the same value for the match to succeed. A variable pattern will match any value and take on that value.

The patterns must all be of the same type and the expressions must all return the same type of value.

Note that there must be a case for every possible value of the pattern type. Usually, there will be a sequence of constant cases and then a variable case to match all the other values. If you miss out a possible case then the system will give an "exhaustiveness check" warning message but still allow you to use the function. If you call the function with an unknown case then the system will stop running the calling expression with an error message.

There is a simplified form of definition for multiple case functions:

**val** *name* = **fn** *pattern1* => *expression1* |
*pattern2* => *expression2* |
...
*patternN* => *expressionN*

becomes:

**fun** *name pattern1* = *expression1* |
*name pattern2* = *expression2* |
...
*name patternN* = *expressionN*

Pattern matching is a powerful programming technique which enables the structure of a function to reflect the structure of the data that it processes. This results in surprisingly small programs as conditional expressions are not needed to discriminate between different argument values. It also results in very readable programs because the program structure corresponds closely to the data.

## 4.4 Pattern matching with strings

For example, consider the table of past tenses:

| verb | past |
|------|------|
| stand | stood |
| swim | swam |
| eat | ate |

which augments the general rule of putting "ed" on the end of a verb. We can represent this in SML as a function from a string verb to a string past tense. We will have a constant pattern for each individual case in the table and a string bound variable for the general case:

```
-    (* find regular and irregular past tenses *)
     fun past "stand" = "stood" |
         past "swim" = "swam" |
         past "eat" = "ate" |
         past v = v^"ed";
>    val past = fn : string -> string
```

Consider:

```
-    past "eat";
>    "ate" : string
```

**"eat"** is matched with **"stand"** which fails. **"eat"** is matched with **"swim"** which fails. **"eat"** is matched with **"eat"** which succeeds so **"ate"** is returned.

Consider:

```
-    past "talk";
>    "talked" : string
```

**"talk"** is matched with **"stand"** which fails. **"talk"** is matched with **"swim"** which fails. **"talk"** is matched with **"eat"** which fails. Finally, the bound variable **v**, which matches anything, is set to **"talk"** so:

```
"talk"^"ed" ==> "talked"
```

is returned.

Now let us make a function for the table:

```
name        colour
Wallace     tabby
Mog         black
Spider      tabby
```

```
fun colour "Wallace" = "tabby" |
    colour "Mog" = "black" |
    colour "Spider" = "tabby" |
```

We need to deal with a cat name which is unknown to us. All the specific cases return a string value so we could match the unknown name to a bound variable and return a string message to say that we do not know that name:

```
-   (* find cat colour from name *)
    fun   colour "Wallace" = "tabby" |
          colour "Mog" = "black" |
          colour "Spider" = "tabby" |
          colour name = name^" unknown";
```

Consider:

```
-   colour "Fritz";
>   "Fritz unknown" : string
```

**"Fritz"** fails to match **"Wallace"**. **"Fritz"** fails to match **"Mog"**. **"Fritz"** fails to match **"Spider"**. **name** is bound to **"Fritz"** so:

```
"Fritz"^" unknown" ==> "Fritz unknown"
```

is returned.

As another example, consider UK traffic light sequences:

```
old           new
red           red & amber
red & amber   green
green         amber
amber         red
```

We can model light states as strings and the light sequence as a function from strings to strings:

```
-   (* find next traffic light state *)
    fun  change "red" = "red & amber" |
         change "red & amber" = "green" |
         change "green" = "amber" |
         change "amber" = "red" |
         change s = "illegal light: "^s;
>   val change = fn : string -> string
-   change "green";
>   "amber" : string
```

Again note the catch-all variable **s** in case of a string argument which is not a light state:

```
-   change "banana";
>   "illegal light: banana" : string
```

## 4.5 Raising exceptions

In Chapter 2 we met the idea of an exception as a way of changing the flow of evaluation, in particular to halt evaluation. When an exception is raised, the system will catch it, stop evaluation and display a message to say that the exception has happened. We can define our own exceptions and raise them when we want to halt evaluation.

At its simplest, an exception is defined by:

    –   **`exception`** *name* **`;`**

to which the system responds:

    >   exception *name*

Then to raise the exception:

    **`raise`** *name*

may be used in place of an expression. The system will stop evaluation and display:

    **`uncaught exception`** *name*

For example, we could define an exception for traffic lights:

    –   **`exception Bad_light;`**
    >   exception Bad_light

and, in the traffic light change function, raise it instead of having the catch all case:

```
–    (*traffic light change with exception *)
     fun   change "red" = "red & amber" |
           change "red & amber" = "green" |
           change "green" = "amber" |
           change "amber" = "red" |
           change s = raise Bad_light;
>    val change = fn : string –> string
```

Now, if **change** is called with an arbitrary string:

    –   **`change "concertina";`**
    uncaught exception Bad_light

evaluation stops.

There are also ways to catch a raised exception and continue processing, and to pass back information when raising an exception. This is known as handling an exception. The message **`uncaught exception`** means that there is not a user defined handler to catch the exception so the system ended up catching it. We will look at how to handle exceptions in a later chapter.

## 4.6 Wildcard pattern matching

Consider the table of cats and weights:

```
name       weight
Wallace    4.0
Mog        4.5
Spider     2.8
```

We could use this as the basis of a function to find the weight from a name:

```
fun  weight "Wallace" = 4.0 |
     weight "Mog" = 4.5 |
     weight "Spider" = 2.8 |
     ...
```
So far this function is:
```
string -> real
```
We need to decide what to do if the function is applied to an unknown name. We cannot return a string as all the specific cases return reals. Instead, we could raise an exception as above:
```
-   exception Cat;
>   exception Cat
-   (* find cat weight from name *)
    fun  weight "Wallace" = 4.0 |
         weight "Mog" = 4.5 |
         weight "Spider" = 2.8 |
         weight n = raise Cat;
>   val weight = fn : string -> real
```
Note the catch-all variable **n** in the last case. Here, the argument value is never subsequently used.

SML provides the wildcard pattern:
```
-
```
(underscore) which will match any argument value and effectively discard it. Here, we could use it instead of **n**:
```
-   (* cat weight with exception *)
    fun  weight "Wallace" = 4.0 |
         weight "Mog" = 4.5 |
         weight "Spider" = 2.8 |
         weight _ = raise Cat;
>   val weight = fn : string -> real
```
For example:
```
-   weight "Fritz";
    uncaught exception Cat
```
Here, **"Fritz"** fails to match **"Wallace"**, **"Mog"** and **"Spider"**. Finally, **"Fritz"** is matched by the wildcard pattern, ignored and the **Cat** exception is raised.

In general, if a bound variable in a pattern is not used on the right hand side of a function definition then it can be replaced by the wildcard pattern. Subsequently, during pattern matching the wildcard pattern will match any value in an argument in the corresponding position. That value is then ignored. In general a variable should only be used in a pattern if the value it will be matched with will be needed later on. Otherwise, the wildcard pattern should be used instead.

## 4.7 Pattern matching with booleans
The boolean type has the values **true** and **false** so we can define boolean functions of the form:

```
fn true => true option expression |
   false => false option expression
```

When such a function is applied to **true** then the value of the *true option expression* is returned. When it is applied to **false** the value of the *false option expression* is returned.

For example, consider the boolean negation operation, defined by the following truth table:

```
X       NOT X
true    false
false   true
```

We can write this as:

```
-   val NOT = fn true => false |
                 false => true;
>   val NOT = fn : bool -> bool
```

or:

```
-   fun NOT true = false |
       NOT false = true;
>   val NOT = fn : bool -> bool
```

Then, for:

```
-   NOT true;
>   false : bool
```

**true** matches **true** so **false** is returned. For:

```
-   NOT false;
>   true : bool
```

**false** does not match **true**. **false** matches **false** so **true** is returned.

In Chapter 2 we met the SML **andalso** conjunction operator which returns **true** for two **true** operands and **false** otherwise. We can express this with the following table:

```
X       Y       X andalso Y
false   false   false
false   true    false
true    false   false
true    true    true
```

Effectively, each thing in this table is a triple of an **X**, **Y** and **X AND Y** value. To use the table we need values for both **X** and **Y** and we have to find a row corresponding to both values to get the result of **X AND Y**.

We can write this as two cases for **X** each with two cases for **Y**:

```
-   val AND = fn false => (fn false => false |
                              true  => false) |
                 true  => (fn false => false |
                              true  => true);
>   val AND = fn : bool -> bool -> bool
```

Thus, if **AND** is applied to **false** then the first case for **Y** is applied:

```
-   AND false true;
>   false : bool
```

and if **AND** is applied to **true** then the second case is applied:

```
  -    AND true true;
  >    true : bool
```

This can be simplified to:

```
  -    (* logical conjunction *)
       fun AND false = (fn false => false |
                           true => false) |
           AND true = (fn false => false |
                          true => true);
  >    val AND = fn : bool -> bool -> bool
```

This can be simplified again:

```
  -    (* conjunction as table *)
       fun AND false false = false |
           AND false true  = false |
           AND true  false = false |
           AND true  true  = true;
  >    val AND = fn : bool -> bool -> bool
```

which is just like the table.

There is a further simplification. When **x** is `false`, the answer is always `false` and when **x** is `true` the answer is the same as **y**:

```
  -    (* conjunction through factorization *)
       fun AND false Y = false |
           AND true  Y = Y;
  >    val AND = fn : bool -> bool -> bool
```

Here, we have explicit cases for **x** and a catch-all bound variable for **y**.

Note that the system deduces that **y** is `bool`. Where the first case returns `false`, the second case returns **y** and the results of all function cases must have the same type.

Note that **y** is not used in the first case so it can be replaced by the wildcard pattern:

```
  -    fun AND false _ = false |
           AND true  Y = Y;
  >    val AND = fn : bool -> bool -> bool
```

In Chapter 2 we also looked at the boolean disjunction operator `orelse`. This returns `true` if either or both operands are `true` and `false` otherwise. We can express this with the following table:

| X | Y | X orelse Y |
|---|---|---|
| false | false | false |
| false | true | true |
| true | false | true |
| true | true | true |

This can be written as a function of two cases for **x** with two cases each for **y**:

```
  -    (* logical disjunction *)
       val OR = fn false => (fn false => false |
                                true => true) |
                   true  => (fn false => true |
                                true => true);
  >    val OR = fn : bool -> bool -> bool
  -    OR true false;
  >    true : bool
```

Once again, this can be simplified to:

```
-   (* disjunction as table *)
    fun OR false false = false |
        OR false true  = true |
        OR true  false = true |
        OR true  true  = true;
>   val OR = fn : bool -> bool -> bool
```

Now, note that if **x** is **false** then the answer is **y** and if **x** is **true** then the answer is **true**. Thus, we can again introduce a catch-all bound variable for **y**:

```
-   (* disjunction through factorisation *)
    fun OR false Y = Y |
        OR true  Y = true;
>   val OR = fn : bool -> bool -> bool
```

Again, note that **y** is not used in the second case so it can be replaced by the wildcard pattern:

```
-   fun OR false Y = Y |
        OR true  _ = true;
>   val OR = fn : bool -> bool -> bool
```

## 4.8 Recursion with integers

As we discussed in Chapter 1, recursion is used in functional languages, for repetitive processing of data. Recursion is based on a function invoking itself, which in turn creates new instances of the bound variables with new values.

In a recursive function, it is useful to distinguish base cases from recursion cases. For a base case, some property of the arguments is satisfied, recursion stops and a value is returned. For a recursion case, that property is not satisfied and the function is called again to process some modification of its arguments. The simplest property for an argument to have is that it is some value. Thus, pattern matching with constants can often be used for base cases. For a recursion case, arguments are modified and reused. Thus for recursion case patterns of bound variables are often used.

Recursion is usually defined over a range of values and some of the values, typically at the top or bottom of the range, are nominated as the base cases which terminate the recursion. Thus, for recursion to terminate there must be at least one base case.

To begin with, we will look at recursion with integer values. Consider the non-negative integers starting at **0**:

```
0 1 2 3 4 5 6 7 8 9 10 ...
```

In this sequence, each value is one more than the one before it. That is each value is the successor of the one before it. Now, note that:

```
1 == 1+0
2 == 1+1 == 1+1+0
3 == 1+2 == 1+1+1 == 1+1+1+0
4 == 1+3 == 1+1+2 == 1+1+1+1 == 1+1+1+1+0
...
```

In general, any positive number is a finite number of successors of 0. We can use this to give a formal definition of a (non-negative) integer:

```
0  is an integer
1+N  is an integer if N is an integer
```

Thus:

```
1 == 1+0 is an integer
2 == 1+1 is an integer
3 == 1+2 is an integer
. . .
```

This is a recursive definition: being an integer is defined in terms of being an integer with **0** as the base case. Many algorithms involving integers can be defined recursively in terms of a base case for **0** and a recursion case for a positive value. Then, an important component of a typical recursion case is to take the predecessor of the positive value and call the function again. Thus, by repeatedly subtracting **1** the base case is reached.

In general, to do something **0** times do not do it, and to do something **N** times do it once and then do it **N-1** times. We can express this as:

```
fun  name1 0 =  base case expression |
     name1 name2 = recursion case expression using name2 - 1
```

For example, consider finding the sum of the first **n** numbers. The sum of the first **0** numbers is **0**. The sum of the first **n** numbers is **n** added to the sum of the first **n-1** numbers:

```
-    (* sum integers from 1 to n *)
     fun sum 0 = 0 |
         sum n = n+sum (n-1);
>    val sum = fn : int -> int
```

**n** must be an integer because the pattern **0** is an integer. The result is an integer because the result of the base case, **0**, is an integer. Thus:

```
-    sum 4;
>    10 : int
```

because:

```
sum 4 ==> 4+sum 3 ==> 4+3+sum 2 ==> 4+3+2+sum 1 ==>
4+3+2+1+sum 0 ==> 4+3+2+1+0 ==> 10
```

Consider finding **2** to the power **n**. **2** to the **0** is **1**. For **2** to the **n**, multiply **2** by **2** to the **n-1**:

```
-    (* 2 to the power n *)
     fun power2 0 = 1 |
         power2 n = 2*power2 (n-1);
>    val power2 = fn : int -> int
```

**n** must be an integer because the pattern **0** is an integer. The function returns an integer because the base case, **1**, is an integer.

Thus:

```
-    power2 3;
>    8 : int
```

because:

```
power2 3 ==> 2*power2 2 ==> 2*2*power2 1 ==>
2*2*2power2 0 ==> 2*2*2*1 ==> 8
```

This function can be generalized to find the value of any number to the power of another number. For **x** to the power **n**, **x** to the **0** is **1** and **x** to the **n** is **x** times **x** to the **n-1**: Thus, we can replace **2** with **x**:

```
-    (* x to the power n *)
     fun power x 0 = 1 |
         power x n = x*power x (n-1);
>    val power = fn : int -> int -> int
```

The function returns an integer because the base case, **1**, is an integer. **n** must be an integer because the pattern **0** is an integer. **x** must be an integer because **power** must return an integer and **x** is multiplied by **power**'s result.

Note that **x** is not used in the base case so it can be replaced by the wildcard pattern:

```
-    fun power _ 0 = 1 |
         power x n = x*power x (n-1);
>    val power = fn : int -> int -> int
```

For example:

```
-    power 4 4;
>    256 : int
```

because:

```
power 4 4 ==> 4*power 4 3 ==> 4*4power 4 2 ==>
4*4*4*power 4 1 ==> 4*4*4*4*power 4 0 ==> 4*4*4*4*1 ==> 256
```

We can use **power** to define functions to find powers of given integers, for example **3**:

```
-    val power3 = power 3;
>    val power3 = fn : int -> int
```

**power3** is like **power** with **x** set to **3**;

```
-    power3 3;
>    27 : int
```

Consider multiplying **x** by **y**. **x** times **0** is **0**. **x** times **y** is **x** added to **x** times **y-1**:

```
-    (* multiply integers through addition *)
     fun mult x 0 = 0 |
         mult x y = x+mult x (y-1);
>    val mult = fn : int -> int -> int
```

The function must return an integer because the base case, **0**, is an integer. **y** must be an integer because the pattern **0** is an integer. **x** is an integer because it is added to the result of the function.

Note that **x** is not used in the base case so it can be replaced by the wildcard pattern:

```
-    fun mult _ 0 = 0 |
         mult x y = x+mult x (y-1);
>    val mult = fn : int -> int -> int
```

Thus:

```
-    mult 5 2;
>    10 : int
```

because:

```
mult 5 2 ==> 5+mult 5 1 ==> 5+5+mult 5 0 ==> 5+5+0 ==> 10
```

We can use **mult** to define functions to multiply by specific integers, for example **3**:

```
-    (* multiply by 3 *)
     val threetimes = mult 3;
>    val threetimes = fn : int -> int
```

**threetimes** is like **mult** with **x** set to **3**:

```
-    threetimes 8;
>    24 : int
```

Consider adding **x** and **y**. **x** plus **0** is **x**. **x** plus **y** is one more than **x** plus **y-1**:

```
-    (* add integers through incrementing and decrementing *)
     fun add x 0 = x |
         add x y = 1+add x (y-1);
>    val add = fn : int -> int -> int
```

The function returns an integer because in the recursion case **1** is added to the function value. **y** is an integer because the pattern **0** is an integer. **x** is an integer because it is returned from the base case and must have the same type as the recursion case.

Thus:

```
-    add 4 3;
>    7 : int
```

because:

```
add 4 3 ==> 1+add 4 2 ==> 1+1+add 4 1 ==> 1+1+1+add 4 0 ==>
1+1+1+4 ==> 7
```

We can use **add** to define functions to add specific integers to other integers, for example **5**:

```
-    (* add 5 *)
     val add5 = add 5;
>    val add5 = fn : int -> int
```

**add5** is like **add** with **x** set to **5**:

```
-    add5 6;
>    11 : int
```

## 4.9 Generalizing summing integer sequences

Consider the function to find the sum of the squares of the first **n** integers. The sum of the squares of the first **0** integers is **0**. The sum of the squares of the first **n** integers is **n** squared plus the sum of the squares of the first **n-1** integers:

```
-    (* sum of squares from 1 to n *)
     fun sumsq 0 = 0 |
         sumsq n = sq n+sumsq (n-1);
>    val sumsq = fn : int -> int
-    sumsq 3;
>    14 : int
```

because:

```
sumsq 3 ==> sq 3+sumsq 2 ==> sq 3+sq 2+sumsq 1 ==>
sq 3+sq 2+sq 1+sumsq 0 ==> sq 3+sq 2+sq 1+0 ==>
9+4+1+0 ==> 14
```

Consider the function to find the sum of the doubles of the first **n** integers.
The sum of the doubles of the first **0** integers is **0**. The sum of the doubles of the
first **n** integers is **n** doubled plus the sum of the doubles of the first **n-1** integers.

```
-    (* double an integer *)
     fun double x = 2*x;
>    val double = fn : int -> int

-    (* sum of doubles from 1 to n *)
     fun sumdouble 0 = 0 |
         sumdouble n = double n+sumdouble (n-1);
>    val sumdouble = fn : int -> int
-    sumdouble 3;
>    12 : int
```

because:

```
sumdouble 3 ==> double 3+sumdouble 2 ==>
double 3+double 2+sumdouble 1 ==>
double 3+double 2+double 1+sumdouble 0 ==>
double 3+double 2+double 1+0 ==> 6+4+2+0 ==> 12
```

These functions are the same apart from the function applied to the argument **n**. **sumsq** uses **sq** and **sumdouble** use **double**; both are of type:

```
int -> int
```

We can generalize **sumsq** and **sumdouble** to a function which finds the sum of
applying an arbitrary **int -> int** function to the first **n** integers:

```
-    (* sum function f from 1 to n *)
     fun sumfunc f 0 = 0 |
         sumfunc f n = f n+sumfunc f (n-1);
>    val sumfunc = fn : (int -> int) -> int -> int
```

This function returns an integer because **0** is an **int**. **n** must be an integer
because it has the same type as the pattern **0** and because **1** is taken from it.
Thus **f** must be an **int -> int** function because it is applied to the integer **n**
and it must return an integer for the addition in the recursion case because
**sumfunc** returns an integer in the recursion case.

Note that **f** is not used in the base case so it could be replaced by the
wildcard pattern:

```
-    fun sumfunc _ 0 = 0 |
        sumfunc f n = f n+sumfunc f (n-1);
>    val sumfunc = fn : (int -> int) -> int -> int
```

For example:

```
-    sumfunc sq 3;
>    14 : int
```

because:

```
sumfunc sq 3 ==> sq 3+sumfunc sq 2 ==>
sq 3+sq 2+sumfunc sq 1 ==> sq 3+sq 2+sq 1+sumfunc sq 0 ==>
sq 3+sq 2+sq 1+0 ==> 9+4+1+0 ==> 14
```

Also:

```
-    sumfunc double 3;
>    12 : int
```

because:

```
sumfunc double 3 ==> double 3+sumfunc double 2 ==>
double 3+double 2+sumfunc double 1 ==>
double 3+double 2+double 1+sumfunc double 0 ==>
double 3+double 2+double 1+0 ==> 6+4+2+0 ==> 12
```

We can use **sumfunc** to define **sumsq**. **sumsq** is like **sumfunc** with **f** set to **sq**:

```
-   val sumsq = sumfunc sq;
>   val sumsq = fn : int -> int
```

Note that **sumfunc** is a:

```
(int -> int) -> int -> int
```

function and **sq** is a:

```
int -> int
```

function so:

```
sumsq == sumfunc sq : int -> int
```

Now:

```
-   sumsq 3;
>   14 : int
```

because:

```
sumsq 3 ==> sumfunc sq 3 ==> ... ==> 14
```

Similarly, we can define **sumdouble** to be like **sumfunc** with **f** set to **double**:

```
-   val sumdouble = sumfunc double;
>   val sumdouble = fn : int -> int
-   sumdouble 3;
>   10 : int
```

**sumfunc** is another higher order function because it takes a function as argument and returns a function as result.

## 4.10 Conditional expression

Pattern matching is used to discriminate between values but can only identify their presence or absence. When other properties must be checked, the conditional expression is used. This has the form:

```
if    expression1
then  expression2
else  expression3
```

*expression1* must return a boolean value. *expression2* and *expression3* must return values of the same type.

If *expression1* is **true** then the value of *expression2* is returned. If *expression1* is **false** then the value of *expression3* is returned.

For example, suppose we want to find the absolute value of an integer, that is the value without regard for whether it is negative. If it is greater than or equal to zero then leave it alone. Otherwise negate it to make it positive:

```
-   (* absolute value of an integer *)
    fun abs x = if x >=0
                then x
                else ~x;
>   val abs = fn : int -> int
```

**x** is integer because it is compared with **0**.
Thus:

```
-    abs ~3;
>    3 : int
```

**abs** is provided as a standard SML function.

For example, to find the longer of strings **s1** and **s2**, we compare their sizes. If the first string is longer than the second then we return the first. Otherwise we return the second string:

```
-    (* longer of two strings *)
     fun max s1 s2 = if size s1>size s2
                     then s1
                     else s2;
>    val max = fn : string -> string -> string
```

Note that **size** has a string argument so **s1** and **s2** must be strings. Note that **size** returns an integer so **>** must be integer comparison.

Thus:

```
-    max "big" "small";
>    "small" : string
```

## 4.11 Conditional expressions and boolean values

This is a good place to reiterate that the result of a boolean expression is a boolean value. Thus there is no need to test a boolean expression to return explicitly a boolean value. For example, in:

```
fun positive n = if n>0
                 then true
                 else false
```

whenever **n** is greater than **0** then **n>0** is **true** and whenever **n** is not greater than **0** then **n>0** is **false** so the conditional expression is redundant. Hence:

```
-    (* is integer n positive? *)
     fun positive n = n>0;
>    val positive = fn : int -> bool
```

is all that is needed.

There is never any need to build a conditional expression which returns **true** from the then case and **false** from the else case. Instead, the boolean expression alone will do. In general:

```
if   boolean expression
then true
else false
```

is the same as:

*boolean expression*

Similarly:

```
if boolean expression
then false
else true
```

is the same as:

> **not** ( *boolean expression* )

## 4.12 Pattern matching with reals

As we saw in Chapter 2, real arithmetic is not precise and comparison of real values is unreliable. Similarly, pattern matching with real values, though allowed in SML, is not recommended. For example, pattern matching with a case for **0.0** may not succeed even when a value is so small that it might as well be zero.

Instead, conditional expressions may be used with reals to test whether potential result values are within acceptable error ranges of a required value. In particular, conditional expressions should used for recursion with real values.

For example, consider finding the sum of all the reals between **n** and **0.0** in steps of **0.1**. Each time, **n** is added to the result of finding the sum from **0.0** to **0.1** less than **n**:

```
-    (* bad attempt to sum from 0.0 to n by pattern matching
     0.0 *)
     fun rsum 0.0 = 0.0 |
         rsum n = n+rsum (n-0.1);
>    val rsum = fn : real -> real
```

The recursion is supposed to stop when the argument is **0.0**.

Running:

```
-    rsum 8.0;
```

on the SML system I use . . . it runs out of memory! Because of inaccuracies in real arithmetic, **n** is never exactly **0.0** and so recursion continues with **n** becoming more and more negative.

Instead, an explicit test should be used, for example to see if **n** is equal to or less than **0.00000000000005**:

```
-    (* sum from 0.0 to n with acceptable bound for 0.0 *)
     fun rsum n = if n<=0.000000000000005
                  then 0.0
                  else n+rsum (n-0.1);
>    val rsum = fn : real -> real
```

Now, running:

```
-    rsum 8.0;
>    324.000000000001 : real
```

the answer should be **324.0** so an error of **0.000000000001** has accumulated. By printing out values of **n** as the calculation proceeds (a technique we will look at in a later chapter) we get the series:

```
8.0 7.9 7.8 7.7 7.6 7.5 7.4 7.3 7.2 7.1 7.0 6.9 6.8  ...
6.50000000000001 6.40000000000001   6.30000000000001   ...
1.00000000000001 0.900000000000012 0.800000000000012 ...
0.200000000000012 0.100000000000012 1.16850973341798E-14
```

so the value of **n** drifts more and more as the error from **n-0.1** mounts up. The last term is effectively **0.00000000000001**, close to **0.0** but not close enough for the pattern match in our first attempt at **rsum**.

## 4.13 More testing

In the last chapter we wrote functions which carried out simple calculations. Testing them involved trying out representative test cases. We have now seen a number of ways of structuring functions by cases and with conditional expressions. When testing such functions, it is important to ensure that they behave correctly on all possible paths through them.

Thus, when you are testing a simple case structured function, you should really try it with argument values for every case. If there are a lot of cases for which the action is similar then try out a small set of them. If the function has a catch all case or an exception case then check these out as well.

For example, to test:

```
-   fun past "stand" = "stood" |
        past "swim" = "swam" |
        past "eat" = "ate" |
        past v = v^"ed";
>   val past = fn : string -> string
```

We might try the typical cases:

```
-   past "stand";
>   "stood" : string

-   past "eat";
>   "ate" : string
```

and the special case:

```
-   past "walk";
>   "walked" : string
```

Again, to test:

```
-   fun OR false Y = Y |
        OR true _ = true;
>   val OR = fn : bool -> bool -> bool
```

we might try:

```
-   OR false false;
>   false : bool
```

and:

```
-   OR true true;
>   true : bool
```

We have seen that recursive functions have base and recursion cases. Thus, you should test a recursive function with values to test all the base and recursion cases.

For example, to test:

```
-   fun power x 0 = 1 |
        power x n = x*power x (n-1);
>   val power = fn : int -> int -> int
```

we might try the recursion cases:

```
-   power 2 3;
>   8 : int
```

and:

```
-    power 0 3;
>    0 : int
```

and the base case:

```
-    power 3 0;
>    1 : int
```

We might try:

```
-    power 0 0;
>    1 : int
```

Do we want 0 to the power of 0 to be 1...?

We also looked at the use of conditional expressions. When a function has conditional expressions it should be tested with different values that will make the condition both true and false. If the function has nested conditional expressions then test values should be chosen to try out all possible paths.

For example, for:

```
-    fun max s1 s2 = if size s1>size s2
                     then s1
                     else s2;
>    val max = fn : string -> string -> string
```

we might try:

```
-    max "enormous" "tiny";
>    "enormous" : string
```

where the condition is true, and:

```
-    max "big" "small";
>    "small" : string
```

where the condition is false. We could also try empty string arguments:

```
-    max "" "huge";
>    "huge" : string

-    max "vast" "";
>    "vast" : string
```

We might also try arguments of the same size:

```
-    max "tiny" "vast";
>    "vast" : string
```

Here, do we really want the second argument as the result...?

Thus, testing throws up effects that we may not have considered when we wrote the function.


## 4.14 Summary

In this chapter we looked at how to use pattern matching to identify different cases for a function's argument, in particular to represent simple association tables as case structured functions. We saw how the wildcard pattern is used to ignore unknown cases. We then considered pattern matching on booleans and saw how to represent tables where one of two columns is consulted to return a result from the other. We discussed recursion as a way of repeating an activity by referring to a function through an associated name in that function's body. In particular, we looked at processing descending ranges of integers. We constructed base cases for constants when repetition stops and recursion cases where an argument is modified before being passed to the next stage. Finally, we met the conditional expression which is used when properties other than specific values are needed to distinguish cases.

The tables we represented in this chapter were of fixed size. In the next chapter we will meet the list type which we can use to represent collections of varying size.

## 4.15 Exercises

1) Identify the types of the following functions:

a) ```
fun f1 "a" = 1 |
    f1 "b" = 2 |
    f1 c = 0
```

b) ```
fun f2 0 = "zero" |
    f2 1 = "one" |
    f2 n = "???"
```

c) ```
fun f3 1 = ("one",1.0) |
    f3 2 = ("two",2.0) |
    f3 n = ("???",0.0)
```

d) ```
fun f4 1 1 = true |
    f4 2 2 = true |
    f4 n1 n2 = false
```

e) ```
fun f5 "one" 1 = "o" |
    f5 "one" 2 = "n" |
    f5 "one" 3 = "e" |
    f5 s n = "?"^s^"?"
```

f) ```
fun f6 1 = 1 |
    f6 n = f6 (n-1)
```

g) ```
fun f7 m 0 = m |
    f7 m n = f7 m (n-1)
```

h) ```
fun f8 _ _ s3 0 = s3 |
    f8 s1 s2 s3 n = f8 s1 s2 (s3^s2^s1) (n-1)
```

i) ```
fun f9 x = if x<1
           then "small"
           else "big"
```

j) ```
fun f10 x = if x>0.0
            then (x,"pos")
            else (x,"not pos")
```

k) ```
fun f11 x y = if x<y
              then x
              else f11 (x-0.1) y
```

2) Explain why the following functions are badly formed:

a) ```
fun f1 1 = "one" |
    f1 1.0 = "one" |
    f1 n = "not one"
```

b) ```
fun f2 1 = "true" |
    f2 n = false
```

c) ```
fun f3 "real"   = 1.0 |
    f3 "int"    = 1 |
    f3 "string" = "one" |
    f3 n = false
```

d) ```
fun f4 x y = if x>y
                then "yes"
                else "no"
```

e) ```
fun f5 x  = if x>3
                then true
                else "no"
```

f) ```
fun f6 x y = if x<y
                then x
                else f6 (x-y) y
```

g) ```
fun f7 x y 0 = x |
    f7 x y z = f7 (x-y) y (z-1)
```

3) Write and test the following functions. Identify the type of each function:

a) In general, the plural of an English word is found by following it with "s". However, there are a number of exceptions, for example:

| singular | plural |
|---|---|
| sheep | sheep |
| mouse | mice |
| fish | fish |
| datum | data |
| louse | lice |

Write a case structured function **plural** which given a string word returns it with "s" on the end, unless it is one of the above special cases in which case the appropriate plural should be returned.

b) The following table might be used to translate between English and Spanish colour words:

| English | Spanish |
|---|---|
| black | negra |
| white | blanca |
| red | roja |
| yellow | amarilla |
| blue | azul |
| green | verde |

Write case structured functions to convert colour words from:

i)  English to Spanish
ii) Spanish to English

In both cases, how do you deal with an unknown colour word?

c) The following table might be used to find the number of legs for various creatures:

| animal | legs |
|---|---|
| whale | 0 |
| swan | 2 |
| drunk | 0 |

```
goat      4
spider    8
ant       6
Silver    1
```

Write a case structured function to return the number of legs for a given creature. How do you deal with an unknown creature?

4) Write and test the following functions. Identify the type of each function:

a) The truth table for the boolean IMPLIES operator is

```
X        Y        X IMPLIES Y
false    false    true
false    true     true
true     false    false
true     true     true
```

Write a case structured function for IMPLIES
i)  with 4 cases directly from the truth table
ii) with 2 cases by finding a pattern within the truth table

b) The truth table for the boolean NAND operator is

```
X        Y        X NAND Y
false    false    true
false    true     true
true     false    true
true     true     false
```

Write a case structured function for NAND
i)  with 4 cases directly from the truth table
ii) with 2 cases by finding a pattern within the truth table

5) Write and test the following functions. Identify the type of each function:

a) The first 7 terms of the factorial sequence are:

```
n   0   1   2   3   4    5    6   ...
n!  1   1   2   6   24  120  720 ...
```

In general, $n$ factorial is $n$ times $n-1$ factorial:

```
0! == 1
n! == n*(n-1)!
```

Write a function to calculate $n$ factorial for arbitrary non-negative integer $n$. Do not use a conditional expression.

b) Consider $x-y$. If $y$ is zero then the result is $x$. Otherwise the result is the difference between the predecessor of $x$ and the predecessor of $y$:

```
x-0 == x
x-y == (x-1)-(y-1)
```

```
9-6 == 8-5 == 7-4 == 6-3 == 5-2 == 4-1 == 3-0 == 3
```

Given:

```
-   fun pred n = n-1;
>   val pred = fn : int -> int
```

write a recursive function to subtract one integer from another, without using $-$ other than for subtracting $1$. Do not use a conditional expression.

c) The first 10 terms of the Fibonacci series are:

| n     | 0 | 1 | 2 | 3 | 4 | 5 | 6 | 7  | 8  | 9  | 10 | ... |
|-------|---|---|---|---|---|---|---|----|----|----|----|-----|
| fib n | 0 | 1 | 1 | 2 | 3 | 5 | 8 | 13 | 21 | 34 | 55 | ... |

In general, the **n**th term is found by adding together the **n−1**th and **n−2**th terms. Write a recursive function to return the **n**th term of the Fibonacci series for non-negative integer **n**. Do not use a conditional expression.

6) Write and test the following functions. Identify the type of each function:

a) Write a recursive function to join string s onto itself non-negative integer n times:

```
-    sjoin 3 "very";
>    "veryveryvery" : string
```

Do not use a conditional expression.

b) Use **sjoin** from a) above to define a function to join a string onto itself the same number of times as its length:

```
-    ljoin "huge";
>    "hugehugehugehuge" : string
```

c) Write a function to join string **s1** onto the end of string **s2** integer **n** times:

```
-    rjoin "!" "Help" 3;
>    "Help!!!" : string
```

If **n** is **0** then return **s2**. Otherwise join **s1** onto the result of joining **s1** onto the end of **s2 n−1** times.

7) Use the following function

```
fun sumfunc _ 0 = 0 |
    sumfunc f n = f n+sumfunc f (n-1)
```

to define functions to find the sum of the first **n**

a) cubes
b) factorials
c) integers

8) Write and test the following functions. Identify the type of each function:

a) Write a function to find the bigger of two integers:

```
-    max 4 5;
>    5 : int
```

b) Write a function to find the biggest of three reals:

```
-    max3 1.2 3.4 3.2;
>    3.4 : real
```

9) Write a function of an integer **n** which returns a string as follows:

```
n < 0 == "negative"
n = 0 == "zero"
n > 0 == "positive"
```

Identify the function's type.

10) Write and test the following functions. Identify the type of each function:

a) Write a function to divide integer **x** by integer **y**, by repeated subtraction and addition of **1**, given that:

```
x DIV 0 == error
x DIV y == 1+(x-y) DIV y if x>=y
         == 0              if x<y
```

```
9 DIV 2 == 1+7 DIV 2 == 1+1+5 DIV 2 == 1+1+1+3 DIV 2 ==
1+1+1+1+1 DIV 2 == 1+1+1+1+0 == 4
```

For example:

```
-   DIV 12 5;
>   2 : int
```

Do not use **div**.

b)  Write a function to find the remainder on dividing integer **x** by integer **y** without using **mod** or **div**:

```
-   MOD 15 4;
>   3 : int
```

Each time, subtract **y** from **x** until **x** is smaller than **y**:

```
15 MOD 4 == 11 MOD 4 == 7 MOD 4 == 3 MOD 4 == 3
```

11) Write and test the following functions. Identify the type of each function:

a)  Write a function which given two strings repeatedly joins spaces onto the end of the first to make it the same length as the second:

```
-   extend_space "cat" "catamaran";
>   "cat      " : string
```

b)  Write a function which given three strings repeatedly joins the first onto the end of the second to make it at least the same length as the third:

```
-   extend "." "cat" "catapult";
>   "cat....." : string
```

You may assume that the first string has only one letter.

c)  Use the function from b) to define the function from a).

# CHAPTER 5

# Introducing lists

## 5.1 Introduction

In Chapter 1 we saw that models are made out of variable sized collections of things and that things are fixed size groups of properties. In the last three chapters we have looked at how we can represent properties as values from basic types and how we can start to use operations on basic types to build functions which serve as methods for the things so represented. In this and the next chapter we are going to discuss the representation of variable sized collections of things with single properties. In Chapter 7, we will at last be able to manipulate collections of multi-property things.

## 5.2 Basic list values

SML provides the list type as one way of representing collections. A list is a variable length sequence of elements which are all of the same type. We can think of a list as being made up of cells with two fields:

known as the head and the tail. If the head is a value of any type then the tail must be a list with elements of the same type as the head value.

Lists always end with the empty list, also known as the null list, which is written as:

**nil**

or:

**[]**

Lists are formed using the infix constructor operator **::**, sometimes called "cons". For:

*expression1* **::** *expression2*

*expression2* must be a list of the same type as *expression1*.

**::** has greater precedence than comparison operators and less precedence than arithmetic operators and function calls. Thus, the latter need not be bracketed when used to make list elements. For example:

    `1::[]`

which we could draw as the cell:

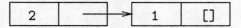

is an integer list with `1` in the head and the empty list in the tail. Similarly:

    `2::(1::[])`

which we could draw as:

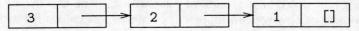

is an integer list with `2` in the head and the integer list `1::[]` in the tail. Thus:

    `3::(2::(1::[]))`

which we could draw as:

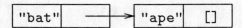

is an integer list with `3` in the head and the integer list `2::(1::[])` in the tail.
    Also:

    `"ape"::[]`

drawn as:

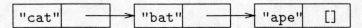

is a string list with `"ape"` in the head and `[]` in the tail. Similarly:

    `"bat"::("ape"::[])`

drawn as:

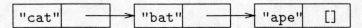

is a string list with `"bat"` in the head and the string list `"ape"::[]` in the tail.
Thus:

    `"cat"::("bat"::("ape"::[]))`

drawn as:

is a string list with `"cat"` in the head and the string list `"bat"::("ape"::[])`
in the tail.
    There are two simplifications to the list notation. First of all, if the tail of a list
is a list then it need not be bracketed so:

    *expression1* `::` ( *expression2* `::` *expression3* )

simplifies to:

*expression1* :: *expression2* :: *expression3*

For example:

```
3::(2::(1::[]))
```

simplifies to:

```
3::2::1::[]
```

and:

```
"cat"::("bat"::("ape"::[]))
```

simplifies to:

```
"cat"::"bat"::"ape"::[]
```

Secondly, lists that end in the empty list may be written within square brackets, with elements separated by commas, without the empty list at the end. Thus:

*expression1* :: *expression2* :: ... :: *expressionN* :: []

may be written as:

[ *expression1* , *expression2* , ... , *expressionN* ]

For example:

```
1::2::3::[]
```

is the same as:

```
[1,2,3]
```

and:

```
"cat"::"bat"::"ape"::[]
```

is the same as:

```
["cat"::"bat"::"ape"]
```

SML systems print list values using the [...] form.

Lists can be made of elements of any type including tuples, functions and lists. For example, the list of names:

```
[("Donald","Duck"),("Mickey","Mouse"),("Pluto","Pup")]
```

is a list of **string * string** tuples. Also:

```
[fn (x:int) => x*x,fn (x:int) => x*x*x,fn (x:int) => x*x*x*x]
```

is a list of **int -> int** functions. And:

```
[[1,1,1],[2,4,8],[3,9,27]]
```

drawn as:

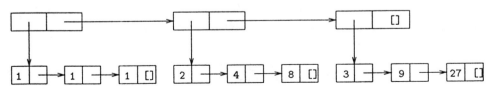

is a list of integer lists of numbers and their powers:

Note that:

[ *expression* ]

is a one element list of the same type as *expression*. For example:

    ["dog"]

drawn as:

    ┌──────────┬───────┐
    │ "dog"    │  []   │
    └──────────┴───────┘

is a string list with one element.

The list type is a polymorphic type; that is lists may have any type as element. Suppose `'a` is any type. Then a list of that type of element has type:

    'a list

`list` is the type constructor for lists.

`::`'s type is:

    -   (op ::);
    >   fn : ('a * 'a list) -> 'a list

so `::` takes one argument of any type `'a` and another argument of a list of that type, `'a list`, and returns a list of that type.

For example, an integer list:

    -   1::2::3::[];
    >   [1,2,3] : int list

a string list:

    -   "a"::"b"::"c"::[];
    >   ["a","b","c"] : string list

and a list of tuples of integers and strings:

    -   [(1,"one"),(2,"two"),(3,"three")];
    >   [(1,"one"),(2,"two"),(3,"three")] : (int * string) list

Note that because the list element type is a tuple it is bracketed in the type expression: `list` has greater precedence in type expressions than `*`. In contrast:

    int * string list

is a tuple of an integer and a string list, for example:

    -   (1,["yes","ja","si"]);
    >   (1,["yes","ja","si"]) : int * string list

For example, a list of integer to integer functions:

    -   [fn (x:int) => x*x,fn (x:int) => x*x*x,
        fn (x:int) => x*x*x*x];
    >   (int -> int) list

Note that again the function element type is bracketed because `list` has greater precedence than `->` in type expressions. In contrast:

    int -> int list

is a function from a function to an integer list, for example:

    -   (* construct list with three integer x *)
        fun three (x:int) = [x,x,x];
    >   val three = fn : int -> int list
    -   three 3;
    >   [3,3,3] : int list

For example, a list of integer lists:

```
-   [[1,1,1],[2,4,8],[3,9,27]];
>   [[1,1,1],[2,4,8],[3,9,27]] : int list list
```

So far we have concentrated on lists with values as elements. Lists may have expressions as elements, not just values, so long as those expressions all return the same types. Like `::`, the `,` in the bracketed list notation has lower precedence than arithmetic expressions and function calls so they need not be bracketed. For example:

```
-   [2.0,2.0*2.0,2.0*2.0*2.0,2.0*2.0*2.0*2.0];
>   [2.0,4.0,8.0,16.0] : real list
```

Again:

```
-   [size "fish",floor 42.24,sq 3];
>   [4,42,9] : int list
```

Note that some SML systems may not display all of very long lists. For example, on the system I use:

```
-   [1,2,3,4,5,6,7,8,9,0,1,2,3,4,5,6,7,8,9,0];
>   [1,2,3,4,5,6,7,8,9,0,1,2,...] : int list
```

only the first 12 elements are displayed.

## 5.3 Pattern matching with lists

A formal definition of a list is:

[] is a list
if *expression1* is an `'a` and *expression2* is an `'a list`
then *expression1* `::` *expression2* is an `'a list`

For recursive functions of lists we can now use `[]` for the base case and recursion cases with list patterns. These are formed from `::` or `[...,...]` with constants, lists and names.

**fun** *name* `[]` = *base case* |
    *name* ( *head* `::` *tail* ) = *recursion case* using *head* and *tail*

Here, *head* and *tail* are both constants or names or list patterns.

For matching a list pattern, the argument must have the same structure as the pattern, with constants in the same positions. Names in the list pattern match with and are set to values in the argument in the same position.

To begin with we will use patterns of the form:

`h::t`

so `h` will match the head of a list argument and `t` will match the tail.

Note that a list pattern using `::` must be bracketed.

For example, consider finding the length of a list. The empty list has zero length. Otherwise, the length is one more than the length of the tail:

```
-   (* length of list *)
    fun length [] = 0 |
        length (h::t) = 1+length t;
>   val length = fn : 'a list -> int
```

This is a polymorphic function: it will find the length of a list of any type. No operations are performed on the list elements apart from pattern matching so the list's type is irrelevant.

Note that **h** is not used in the recursion case so it can be replaced by the wildcard pattern:

```
-    fun length [] = 0 |
         length (_::t) = 1+length t;
>    val length = fn : 'a list -> int
```

For example:

```
-    length ["c","b","a"];
>    3 : int
```

because:

```
length ["c","b","a"] ==> match _ with "c"
                              take t as ["b","a"]
1+length ["b","a"] ==> match _ with "b"
                            take t as ["a"]
1+1+length ["a"] ==> match _ with "a"
                          take t as to []
1+1+1+length [] ==>

1+1+1+0 ==> 3
```

Consider, for example, adding the elements of an integer list together. The sum of the elements of an empty list is **0**. The sum of the elements of a non-empty list is the head added to the sum of the tail:

```
-    (* sum an integer list *)
     fun sum [] = 0 |
         sum (h::t) = h+sum t;
>    val sum = fn : int list -> int
```

**sum** returns an integer because **0** is integer. The argument is an integer list because **h** is an integer because **h** is added to the result of **sum**.

For example:

```
-    sum [9,7,5,3];
>    24 : int
```

because:

```
sum [9,7,5,3] ==> take h as 9
                       take t as [7,5,3]
9+sum [7,5,3] ==> take h as 7
                       take t as [5,3]
9+7+sum [5,3] ==> take h as 5
                       take t as [3]
9+7+5+sum [3] ==> take h as 3
                       take t as []
9+7+5+3+sum [] ==>

9+7+5+3+0 ==> 24
```

Consider, for example, counting how often **0** appears in an integer list. If the list is empty then **0** appears **0** times. Otherwise, if **0** is the head then add **1** to the count for the tail. Otherwise, count **0** in the tail:

```
-    (* count 0 in an integer list *)
     fun count0 [] = 0 |
         count0 (0::t) = 1+count0 t |
         count0 (h::t) = count0 t;
>    val count0 = fn : int list -> int
```

The argument is an integer list because 0 in 0::t is an integer. The result is an integer because the base case is 0.

Note that h is not used in the second recursion case so it can be replaced by the wildcard pattern:

```
-    fun count0 [] = 0 |
         count0 (0::t) = 1+count0 t |
         count0 (_::t) = count0 t;
>    val count0 = fn : int list -> int
```

For example:

```
-    count0 [1,0,2,0,0,1];
>    3 : int
```

because:

```
count0 [1,0,2,0,0,1] ==> match _ with 1
                              take t as [0,2,0,0,1]

count0 [0,2,0,0,1] ==> match 0
                              take t as [2,0,0,1]

1+count0 [2,0,0,1] ==> match _ with 2
                              take t as [0,0,1]

1+count0 [0,0,1] ==> match 0
                              take t as [0,1]

1+1+count0 [0,1] ==> match 0
                              take t as [1]

1+1+1+count0 [1] ==> match _ with 1
                              take t as []

1+1+1+count0 [] ==>

1+1+1+0 ==> 3
```

## 5.4 Equality types

Consider counting how often value v appears in a list. v appears in the empty list 0 times. If the head of the list is v then add 1 to the count of v in the tail. Otherwise, count v in the tail:

```
-    (* count value in list *)
     fun count v [] = 0 |
         count v (h::t) = if v=h
                             then 1+count v t
                             else count v t;
>    val count = fn : ''a -> ''a list -> int
```

Here, the type involves the variable ''a rather than the usual 'a.

In length above, we saw that no operations were performed on the list elements so they could be any type. We represented such a polymorphic type with an 'a. Here, the operation performed on v and h is an equality comparison with =. Hence, v and h must be the same type and that type may be any for which equality is defined – an equality type. This is a slight restriction on a polymorphic type and so the variable is written with two primes in front of the alphabetic identifier instead of one prime for a fully polymorphic type. Hence the use of `''a` in the type here:

```
''a -> ''a list -> int
```

For example:

```
-   count "ash" ["oak","ash","elm","ash","oak"];
>   2 : int
```

because:

```
count "ash" ["oak","ash","elm","ash","oak"] ==>
 take h as "oak"
 take t as ["ash"...]
count "ash" ["ash","elm","ash","oak"] ==>
 take h as "ash"
 take t as ["elm"...]
1+count "ash" ["elm","ash","oak"] ==>
 take h as "elm"
 take t as ["ash","oak"]
1+count "ash" ["ash","oak"] ==> take h as "ash"
                                take t as ["oak"]
1+1+count "ash" ["oak"] ==> take h as "oak"
                            take t as []
1+1+count "ash" [] ==>
1+1+0 ==>2
```

This is a polymorphic function and may be used to count occurrences of any type of value in a list of appropriate type. It may also be used to define functions to count specific values in lists of specific types. For example, to count `0` in integer lists:

```
-   val count0 = count 0;
>   val count0 = fn : int list -> int
```

`count0` is like `count` with `v` set to `0`.

Note that the type `''a` in `count` has been specialized to `int`, an equality type, in `count0`. `v` has been associated with an integer value. `v` was of type `''a` so all occurrences of `''a` must become `int` for consistency. Similarly, in:

```
-   (* count "ash" in string list *)
    val countash = count "ash";
>   val countash = fn : string list -> string
```

to count occurrences of `"ash"`, `''a` has been specialized to `string`.

## 5.5 General list operations

There are a number of useful general list operations which we will now consider. These are polymorphic and form the basis of many list functions.

### 5.5.1 Add to end of list

Consider adding a value to the end of a list. For example:

```
-    add 5 [1,2,3,4];
>    [1,2,3,4,5] : int list
```

To add a value to an empty list, make a new list with the value as the only element. Otherwise, put the head of the list onto the front of adding the value to the end of the tail of the list:

```
-    (* put value on the end of list *)
     fun add v [] = [v] |
         add v (h::t) = h::add v t;
>    val add = fn : 'a -> 'a list -> 'a list
```

Suppose **v** is of unknown type **'a**. Then the result of **add** is an **'a list** because the base case returns a list with **v** as head. Then **h** must be of type **'a** because it is joined onto the front of the result of **add** so the list argument is an **'a list**.

For example:

```
-    add "d" ["a","b","c"];
>    ["a","b","c","d"] : string list
```

because:

```
add "d" ["a","b","c"] ==> take h as "a"
                              take t as ["b","c"]

"a"::add "d" ["b","c"] ==> take h as "b"
                              take t as ["c"]

"a"::"b"::add "d" ["c"] ==> take h as "c"
                              take t as []

"a"::"b"::"c"add "d" [] ==>

"a"::"b"::"c"::["d"] ==>

"a"::"b"::["c","d"] ==>

"a"::["b","c","d"] ==>

["a","b","c","d"]
```

This is a common technique: the list is unwound to the required point and then wound back up again.

### 5.5.2 Append two lists end to end

Consider joining two lists end to end:

```
-    append [1,2,3] [4,5,6];
>    [1,2,3,4,5,6] : int list
```

Just using **::** will not work. In:

```
[1,2,3]::[4,5,6]
```

the head is an **int list** and so is the tail. Instead, we have to unwind the head and join it from the back onto the tail:

```
append [1,2,3] [4,5,6] ==>

1::append [2,3] [4,5,6] ==>

1::2::append [3] [4,5,6] ==>

1::2::3::append [] [4,5,6] ==>

1::2::3::[4,5,6] ==>
```

```
1::2::[3,4,5,6] ==>
1::[2,3,4,5,6] ==>
[1,2,3,4,5,6]
```

If the first list is empty then return the second list. Otherwise join the head of the first onto the result of appending the tail of the first onto the second:

```
-    (* append a list onto the end of another *)
     fun append [] 12 = 12 |
         append (h::t) 12 = h::append t 12;
>    val append = fn : 'a list -> 'a list -> 'a list
```

Suppose the first argument is an **'a list**. Then **h** is of type **'a** so the result is an **'a list** because **h** is joined onto it. **12** must also be an **'a list** because it is the base case result. For example:

```
append ["a","b","c"] ["d","e","f"] ==> take h as "a"
                                       take t as ["b","c"]
"a"::append ["b","c"] ["d","e","f"] ==> take h as "b"
                                        take t as ["c"]
"a"::"b"::append ["c"] ["d","e","f"] ==> take h as "c"
                                         take t as []
"a"::"b"::"c"::append [] ["d","e","f"] ==>
"a"::"b"::"c"::["d","e","f"] ==>
"a"::"b"::["c","d","e","f"] ==>
"a"::["b",c,"d","e","f"] ==>
["a","b","c","d","e","f"]
```

SML systems provide the append function as the infix operator **@**:

```
-    op @;
>    fn : 'a list * 'a list -> 'a list
```

For example:

```
-    ["alpha","beta"]@["gamma","delta","epsilon"];
>    ["alpha","beta","gamma","delta","epsilon"] : string list
```

**@** is a function and may not appear in patterns. In contrast, **::** is a constructor and may appear in patterns.

Expressions containing bracketed sequences of **@** may be simplified by dropping the brackets:

```
( value1 @ value2 ) @ value3 ==>
value1 @ value2 @ value3
```

For example:

```
-    [1,2,3]@[4,5,6]@[7,8,9];
>    [1,2,3,4,5,6,7,8,9] : int list
```

**@** has the same precedence as the list constructor **::**.

### 5.5.3 Insert before value in list

Consider inserting value **v1** before the first occurrence of value **v2** in a list:

```
-    insertb "c" "d" ["a","b","d"];
>    ["a","b","c","d"] : string list
```

If the list is empty then there are no occurrences of **v2**. If the list starts with **v2** then put **v1** on the front of the list. Otherwise put the head of the list onto the result of inserting **v1** before the first occurrence of **v2** in the tail of the list:

```
-   (* insert value v1 before value v2 in list *)
    fun insertb v1 v2 [] = [] |
        insertb v1 v2 (h::t) = if h=v2
                               then v1::h::t
                               else h::insertb v1 v2 t;
>   val insertb = fn : ''a -> ''a -> ''a list -> ''a list
```

No operations are performed on **h** and **v2** apart from an equality comparison. Hence they must be equality types, say **''a**. Then the result must be a **''a** **list** because **h** is at the start of a result list. **v1** must be of type **''a** because it is in that result list and starts a result list. Thus **h::t** must be a **''a** **list** because it starts with a **''a**.

Note that **v1** and **v2** are not used in the base case so they can be replaced by the wildcard pattern:

```
-   fun insertb _ _ [] = [] |
        insertb v1 v2 (h::t) = if h=v2
                               then v1::h::t
                               else h::insertb v1 v2 t;
>   val insertb = fn : ''a -> ''a -> ''a list -> ''a list
```

For example:

```
-   insertb 3 4 [1,2,4];
>   [1,2,3,4] : int list
```

because:

```
insertb 3 4 [1,2,4] ==> take h as 1
                        take t as [2,4]

1::insertb 3 4 [2,4] ==> take h as 2
                         take t as [4]

1::2::insertb 3 4 [4] ==> take h as 4
                          take t as []

1::2::3::4::[] ==>

[1,2,3,4]
```

Consider inserting value **v1** before all occurrences of value **v2** in a list:

```
-   insertball 0 1 [1,2,1,3];
>   [0,1,2,0,1,3] : int list
```

If the list is empty then there are no occurrences of **v2**: **v2** and **v1** can be replaced by the wildcard pattern. If the list starts with **v2** then insert **v1** after all occurrences of **v2** in the tail of the list and put **v1** and **v2** on the front of the new list. Otherwise, put the head of the list onto the result of inserting **v1** before all occurrences of **v2** in the tail of the list:

```
-   (* insert v1 before all v2 in list *)
    fun insertball _ _ [] = [] |
        insertball v1 v2 (h::t) =
            if h=v2
            then v1::h::insertball v1 v2 t
            else h::insertball v1 v2 t;
>   val insertball = fn : ''a -> ''a -> ''a list -> ''a list
```

For example:
```
-   insertball "a" "b" ["b","c","d","b"];
>   ["a","b","c","d","a","b"] : string list
```
because:
```
insertball "a" "b" ["b","c","d","b"] ==>
 take h as "b"
 take t as ["c","d","b"]
"a"::"b"::insertball "a" "b" ["c","d","b"] ==>
 take h as "c"
 take t as["d","b"]
"a"::"b"::"c"::insertball "a" "b" ["d","b"] ==>
 take h as "d"
 take t as ["b"]
"a"::"b"::"c"::"d"::insertball "a" "b" ["b"] ==>
 take h as "b"
 take t as []
"a"::"b"::"c"::"d"::"a"::"b"::insertball "a" "b" [] ==>
"a"::"b"::"c"::"d"::"a"::"b"::[] ==>
["a","b","c","d","a","b"]
```

### 5.5.4 Delete value from list
Consider deleting value **v** from a list of appropriate type:
```
-   delete 3 [1,2,3,4];
>   [1,2,4] : int list
```
If the list is empty then nothing can be deleted so return the empty list. Otherwise, if **v** is the head of the list then return the tail. Otherwise, put the head onto the result of deleting **v** from the tail:
```
-   (* delete value from list *)
    fun delete _ [] = [] |
        delete v (h::t) = if v=h
                          then t
                          else h::delete v t;
>   val delete = fn : ''a -> ''a list -> ''a list
```
**v** and **h** are compared for equality so they must be equality types, say `''a`. The list must be of type `''a list` and the result must be of type `''a list` because **t** must be of type `''a list`. For example:
```
delete 3 [1,2,3,4] ==> take h as 1
                       take t as [2,3,4]
1::delete 3 [2,3,4] ==> take h as 2
                        take t as [3,4]
1::2::delete 3 [3,4] ==> take h as 3
                         take t as [4]
1::2::[4] ==> 1::[2,4] ==> [1,2,4]
```
Consider deleting all occurrences of value **v** in a list:
```
-   deleteall 0 [1,0,2,0,3];
>   [1,2,3] : int list
```

If the list is empty then there are no occurrences. If the list starts with **v** then delete all occurrences in the tail. Otherwise, put the head onto the result of deleting all occurrences of **v** in the tail:

```
-    (* delete all occurrences of value from list *)
     fun deleteall _ [] = [] |
         deleteall v (h::t) = if v=h
                             then deleteall v t
                             else h::deleteall v t;
>    val deleteall = fn : ''a -> ''a list -> ''a list
```

For example:

```
-    deleteall "a" ["a","b","a","c","a"];
>    ["b","c"] : string list
```

because:

```
deleteall "a" ["a","b","a","c","a"] ==>
  take h as "a"
  take t as ["b","a","c","a"]
 deleteall "a" ["b","a","c","a"] ==>
  take h as "b"
  take t as ["a","c","a"]
 "b"::deleteall "a" ["a","c","a"] ==>
  take h as "a"
  take t as ["c","a"]
 "b"::deleteall "a" ["c","a"] ==>
  take h as "c"
  take t as ["a"]
 "b"::"c"::deleteall "a" ["a"] ==>
  take h as "a"
  take t as []
 "b"::"c"::deleteall "a" [] ==>
 "b"::"c"::[] ==>["b","c"]
```

## 5.5.5 Replace value in list

Consider replacing value **v1** with value **v2** in a list:

```
-    replace "c" "C" ["A","B","c","D"];
>    ["A","B","C","D"] : string list
```

If the list is empty then there is nothing to replace so return the empty list. If the head of the list is **v1** then put **v2** onto the tail of the list. Otherwise put the head onto the result of replacing **v1** with **v2** in the tail:

```
-    (* replace v1 with v2 in list *)
     fun replace _ _ [] = [] |
         replace v1 v2 (h::t) = if v1=h
                              then v2::t
                              else h::replace v1 v2 t;
>    val replace = fn : ''a -> ''a -> ''a list -> ''a list
```

**v1** and **h** are compared for equality so they must be equality types, say ''**a**. The list argument is of type ''**a list**. The result must be of type ''**a list** because **h** is put onto it. **v2** must be of type ''**a** because it is put on the front of **t** which is of type ''**a list**. For example:

```
-   replace "saw" "ate" ["the","cat","saw","the","rat"];
>   ["the","cat","ate","the","rat"] : string list
```

because:

```
replace "saw" "ate" ["the","cat","saw","the","rat"] ==>
  take h as "the"
  take t as ["cat","saw","the","rat"]

"the"::replace "saw" "ate" ["cat","saw","the","rat"] ==>
  take h as "cat"
  take t as ["saw","the","rat"]

"the"::"cat"::replace "saw" "ate" ["saw","the","rat"] ==>
  take h as "saw"
  take t as ["the","rat"]

"the"::"cat"::"ate"::["the","rat"] ==>

"the"::"cat"::["ate","the","rat"] ==>

"the"::["cat","ate"::"the","rat"] ==>

["the","cat","ate","the","rat"]
```

Consider replacing all occurrences of value **v1** with value **v2** in a list:

```
-   replaceall 0 9 [1,0,2,0,3];
>   [1,9,2,9,3] : int list
```

If the list is empty then there are no occurrences to replace. If the list starts with **v1** then put **v2** onto the result of replacing all **v1** with **v2** in the tail. Otherwise put the head onto the result of replacing all **v1** in the tail with **v2**:

```
-   (* replace all v1 with v2 in list *)
    fun replaceall _ _ [] = [] |
        replaceall v1 v2 (h::t) = if h=v1
                                  then v2::replaceall v1 v2 t
                                  else h::replaceall v1 v2 t;
>   val replaceall = fn : ''a -> ''a -> ''a list -> ''a list
```

For example:

```
-   replaceall "a" "@" ["a","b","a","c"];
>   ["@","b","@","c"] : string list
```

because:

```
replaceall "a" "@" ["a","b","a","c"] ==>
 take h as "a"
 take t as ["b","a","c"]

"@"::replaceall "a" "@" ["b","a","c"] ==>
 take h as "b"
 take t as ["a","c"]

"@"::"b"::replaceall "a" "@" ["a","c"] ==>
 take h as "a"
 take t as ["c"]

"@"::"b"::"@"::replaceall "a" "@" ["c"] ==>
 take h as "c"
 take t as []

"@"::"b"::"@"::"c"::replaceall "a" "@" [] ==>

"@"::"b"::"@"::"c"::[] ==>

["@","b","@","c"]
```

## 5.6 Explicit list element selection

As we have seen, list elements are selected by pattern matching. However, it is sometimes convenient to access the head or tail of a list explicitly. We can define list head and tail selection functions ourselves through list pattern matching.

We know that an empty list does not have a head or tail. We can define an exception:

```
-    exception Hd;
>    exception Hd
```

to cater for taking the head of an empty list. Now, for the head of a list:

```
-    (* head of list *)
     fun hd (h::_) = h |
         hd [] = raise Hd;
>    val hd = fn : 'a list -> 'a
```

we either select it through pattern matching on a non-empty list or raise the exception for an empty list. For example:

```
-    hd [1,2,3];
>    1 : int
```

Similarly, for the tail of a list:

```
-    exception Tl;
>    exception Tl
```

```
-    (* tail of list *)
     fun tl (_::t) = t |
         tl [] = raise Tl;
>    val tl = fn : 'a list -> 'a list
```

we either select it through pattern matching or raise the exception for an empty list. For example:

```
-    tl [1,2,3];
>    [2,3] : int list
```

`hd` and `tl` may be nested to select inner elements. For example, to select the second element in a list:

```
-    hd (tl [3,2,1]);
>    2 : int
```

The tail of [3,2,1] is [2,1] so the head of the tail of [3,2,1] is 2. Similarly, drop the first two elements from a list:

```
-    tl (tl [3,2,1]);
>    [1] : int list
```

The tail of [3,2,1] is [2,1] so the tail of the tail is [1]. To take the third element in a list:

```
-    hd (tl (tl [3,2,1]));
>    1 : int
```

The tail of the tail of [3,2,1] is [1] so its head is 1. Again, drop the first three elements from a list:

```
-    tl (tl (tl [3,2,1]));
>    [] : int list
```

Note that [] can end any list but here the list is of type **int list** so in this context [] is of type **int list** as well.

In general it is clearer to use pattern matching rather than **hd** and **tl**. First of all, the structure of the list can be read off from the pattern. Secondly, the nested use of **hd** and **tl** is hard to read.

For example, suppose we have a list of lists and we want to find the second element of the second list. Compare:

```
-    fun element_2_2 l = hd (tl (hd (tl l)));
>    val element_2_2 = fn : 'a list list -> 'a
```

with:

```
-    fun element_2_2 (_::(_::e::_)::_) = e;
>    val element_2_2 = fn : 'a list list -> 'a
```

In the second case the element of interest is clearly identified, as is the surrounding structure.

## 5.7 Indexed list access

Sometimes it is useful to be able to access elements by specifying their position relative to the start of a list. For example, if we have a list of things in order and we want to find the first or the second or the third and so on. Consider the list:

[ *value1* , *value2* , *value3* , *value4* , ... ]

Consider finding each element using **hd** and **tl**. To find the first:

**hd** [ *value1* , *value2* , *value3* , *value4* , ... ] ==>
*value1*

To find the second:

**hd** (**tl** [ *value1* , *value2* , *value3* , *value4* , ... ]) ==>
*value2*

To find the third:

**hd** (**tl** (**tl** [ *value1* ,
*value2* , *value3* , *value4* , ... ])) ==>
*value3*

To find the fourth:

**hd** (**tl** (**tl** (**tl** [ *value1* ,
*value2* , *value3* , *value4* , ... ]))) ==>
*value4*

In general, the first element in a list is the head. Otherwise, to find the **i**th value in a list, take the tail **i-1** times and then take the head:

```
-    fun find 1 (h::_) = h |
         find i (_::t) = find (i-1) t |
```

Note that the head is ignored in the recursion case and the tail is ignored in the base case.

So far, this function is of type:

```
int -> 'a list -> 'a
```

**i** and **1** are both integers. Suppose **h::t** is an **'a list**. Then the result is an **'a**.

However, this function is incomplete: there is no case for an empty list! An empty list does not have an **i**th element so some value must be returned to indicate failure. Alas, there is no value which is that of all types **'a**. We have to be more specific about the type of list. Suppose it is an integer list. We could return ~1 to indicate failure, assuming that ~1 is not in the list:

```
-   (* find ith in integer list *)
    fun findi 1 (h::_) = h |
        findi i (_::t) = findi (i-1) t |
        findi _ [] = ~1;
>   val findi = fn : int -> int list -> int
```

The last case returns an integer so all cases must return integers so **h** must be an integer so the list argument must be an integer list.

Note that the index value is ignored in the last case.

Similarly, for a string list, we supply a string value for when we reach the end of the list:

```
-   (* find ith in string list *)
    fun finds 1 (h::_) = h |
        finds i (_::t) = finds (i-1) t |
        finds _ [] = "fail";
>   val finds = fn : int -> string list -> string
```

Now, the last case returns a string so all cases must return strings so **h** must be a string so the list argument must be a string list.

For example:

```
-   findi 3 [1,4,9,16];
>   9 : int
```

because:

```
findi 3 [1,4,9,16] ==>
findi 2 [4,9,16] ==>
findi 1 [9,16] ==>
9
```

And:

```
-   finds 4 ["apple","banana","cherry"];
>   "fail" : string
```

because:

```
finds 4 ["apple","banana","cherry"] ==>
finds 3 ["banana","cherry"] ==>
finds 2 ["cherry"] ==>
finds 1 [] ==>
"fail"
```

Note that these functions have both a specific type and a list bound variable. Thus, there must be enough cases to satisfy all possible combinations of values of that type and lists.

An alternative to returning a typed failure value is to define an exception:

```
-   exception Find;
>   exception Find
```

and then make a general function which raises an exception if the required value is not found:

```
-   (* find ith in list *)
    fun find 1 (h::_) = h |
        find i (_::t) = find (i-1) t |
        find _ [] = raise Find;
>   val find = fn : int -> 'a list -> 'a
```

Now there is no restriction on the type of or the values in the list.

Consider deleting the `i`th in a list:

```
-    idelete 3 [1,4,8,16];
>    [1,4,16] : int
```

The empty list has no `i`th element, so ignore the index. To delete the first element, ignore the head and return the tail. Otherwise, put the head onto the result of deleting the `i-1`th in the tail:

```
-    (* delete ith in list *)
     fun idelete _ [] = [] |
         idelete 1 (_::t) = t |
         idelete i (h::t) = h::idelete (i-1) t;
>    val idelete = fn : int -> 'a list -> 'a list
```

This is a polymorphic function. Suppose `h::t` is an `'a list`. Then `t` is an `'a list` and so is the result. For example:

```
-    idelete 3 ["a","b","z","d"];
>    ["a","b","d"] : string list
```

because:

```
idelete 3 ["a","b","z","d"] ==>
"a"::idelete 2 ["b","z","d"] ==>
"a"::"b"::idelete 1 ["z","d"] ==>
"a"::"b"::["d"] ==>
["a","b","d"]
```

Consider inserting a value `v` before the `i`th element in a list:

```
-    iinsertb 3 "c" ["a","b","d"];
>    ["a","b","c","d"] : string list
```

If the list is empty then it has no `i`th element: the index and value can be ignored. Otherwise, to insert before the first element, put the value on the front of the list. Otherwise, put the first element onto the front of the result of inserting before the `i-1`th element in the list:

```
-    (* insert before ith in list *)
     fun iinsertb _ _ [] = [] |
         iinsertb 1 v l = v::l |
         iinsertb i v (h::t) = h::iinsertb (i-1) v t;
>    val iinsertb = fn : int -> 'a -> 'a list -> 'a list
```

This is a polymorphic function. If the list argument `l` is an `'a list` then `v` is an `'a` because it is put on the front of `l`. The result is also an `'a list` because `v` is put on the front of `l`. For example:

```
-    iinsertb 3 3 [1,2,4];
>    [1,2,3,4] : int list
```

because:

```
iinsertb 3 3 [1,2,4] ==>
1::iinsertb 2 3 [2,4] ==>
1::2::iinsertb 1 3 [4] ==>
1::2::3::[4] ==>
[1,2,3,4]
```

Consider replacing the ith element in a list with value **v**:

```
-    ireplace 3 "c" ["a","b","?","d"];
>    ["a","b","c","d"] : string list
```

If the list is empty then there is nothing to replace. If **i** is one then replace the head of the list with **v**. Otherwise put the head onto the result of replacing the **i-1**th in the tail:

```
-    (* replace ith in list *)
     fun ireplace _ _ [] = [] |
         ireplace 1 v (_::t) = v::t |
         ireplace i v (h::t) = h::ireplace (i-1) v t;
>    val ireplace = fn : int -> 'a -> 'a list -> 'a list
```

If the list is an **'a list** then **t** is an **'a list** and **v** must be an **'a** because it is joined onto **t**. The result is an **'a list** because **v::t** is an **'a list**. For example:

```
-    ireplace 3 true [true,true,false,true];
>    [true,true,true,true] : bool list
```

because:

```
ireplace 3 true [true,true,false,true] ==>
true::ireplace 2 true [true,false,true] ==>
true::true::ireplace 1 true [false,true] ==>
true::true::true::[true] ==>
[true,true,true,true]
```

An alternative way to replace the ith in a list is to delete the ith and then insert before the ith:

```
-    fun ireplace i v l = iinsertb i v (idelete i l);
>    val replace = fn : int -> 'a -> 'a list -> 'a list
```

However, this is less efficient than the first version as the list must be scanned twice: once to delete the element and once to insert the new one.


## 5.8 Testing list functions

We have seen that a typical function to process a list has one or more base cases and one or more recursion cases. To try and ensure that every path through the function works then, as for integer recursive functions, we should test list functions with values for all the base and recursion cases. For example, for:

```
-    fun append [] l2 = l2 |
         append (h1::t1) l2 = h1::append t1 l2;
>    val append = fn : 'a list -> 'a list -> 'a list
```

we might try the base case:

```
-    append [] [1,2,3];
>    [1,2,3] : int list
```

and the recursion case:

```
-    append [1,2,3] [4,5,6];
>    [1,2,3,4,5,6] : int list
```

Or, for:

```
-    fun ireplace _ _ [] = [] |
         ireplace 1 v (_::t) = v::t |
         ireplace i v (h::t) = h::ireplace (i-1) v t;
>    val ireplace = fn : int -> 'a -> 'a list -> 'a list
```

we might try the base cases:

```
-    ireplace 3 "cat" [];
>    [] : string list
```

and:

```
-    ireplace 1 "ant" ["ape","bat","cat"];
>    ["ant","bat","cat"] : string list
```

and the recursion case:

```
-    ireplace 3 "cow" ["ape","bat","cat","dog"];
>    ["ape","bat","cow","dog"] : string list
```

If we try:

```
-    ireplace 0 0 [1,2,3,4];
>    [1,2,3,4] : int list
```

then we may be surprised but relieved to find that recursion stops when the list is empty rather than it continuing for ever with i getting more and more negative . . .

## 5.9 Summary

In this chapter we have met the list as a way of representing variable length sequences of the same type. We have looked at how to construct list patterns for recursion over lists and met a variety of general purpose list functions.

In the next chapter, we are going to consider further techniques for list processing. In particular, we will construct a number of higher order functions for lists.

## 5.10 Exercises

1) Identify the types of the following expressions:
   a) [2,4,6,8]
   b) [2.2,4.4,6.6,8.8]
   c) [fn s => s^"s",fn s => s^"ed",fn s => s^"ing"]
   d) [true]
   e) [(1,1.0,"one"),(2,2.0,"two"),(3,3.0,"three")]
   f) [(1,(1.0,"one")),(2,(2.0,"two")),(3,(3.0,"three"))]
   g) [[1.0,1.0],[2.0,4.0],[3.0,9.0]]
   h) [[[1,1],[2,4],[3,9]],[[1,1],[2,8],[3,27]]]
   i) [("Pat",["Patricia","Patrick"]),
        ("Jo",["Josephine","Joseph"])]
   j) [[("a",1),("b",2)],[("c",3),("d",4)]]
   k) [(1,[(2,2),(3,3)]),(2,[(2,4),(3,6)])]
   l) [[1.0,2.0,3.0]] m) [1,2,3]::[[4,5,6]]

2) Explain why the following expressions are badly formed:
   a) `[1,2,3.0]`
   b) `[true,"false",true]`
   c) `[(1,1),(2,4.0),(3,9)]`
   d) `[fn x => x+1,fn x => x+1.0,fn x => x^"1"]`
   e) `[1,2,3]::4`
   f) `["a","b","c"]::["d","e","f"]`

3) Identify the types of the following functions:
   a) `fun f1 [] = 0 |`
      `     f1 (h::t) = 2*h+f1 t`
   b) `fun f2 [] = 0.0 |`
      `     f2 (h::t) = h+f2 t`
   c) `fun f3 [] = [] |`
      `     f3 (0::t) = 0::(f3 t) |`
      `     f3 (_::t) = f3 t`
   d) `fun f4 [] = [] |`
      `     f4 ("a"::t) = true::f4 t |`
      `     f4 (_::t) = false::f4 t`
   e) `fun f5 [] = "" |`
      `     f5 (h::t) = h^h^f5 t`
   f) `fun f6 [] = (0.0,0.0) |`
      `     f6 (h::t) = (h,h/2.0)::f6 t`
   g) `fun f7 [] = [] |`
      `     f7 (h::t) = (h,h)::f7 t`
   h) `fun f8 [] = [] |`
      `     f8 (h::t) = [h]::f8 t`

4) Explain why the following functions are badly formed:
   a) `fun f1 [] = [] |`
      `     f1 (h::t) = h*h::f1 t`
   b) `fun f2 v [] = v |`
      `     f2 v (h::t) = v+h::f2 t`
   c) `fun f3 [] = [] |`
      `     f3 (h::t) = [h]::f3 [t]`
   d) `fun f4 [] = [] |`
      `     f4 (0::t) = f4 t |`
      `     f4 (h::t) = h/2.0::f4 t`
   e) `fun f5 [] = [] |`
      `     f5 (h::t) = [h]::[f5 t]`

5) Write and test the following functions. Identify the type of each function:
   a) return a list of the first n integers in descending order:
      ```
      -   intlist 5;
      >   [5,4,3,2,1] : int list
      ```
   b) return a list of the first n squares in descending order:
      ```
      -   sqlist 5;
      >   [25,16,9,4,1] : int list
      ```
   c) return a list of tuples of the first n integers and their squares in descending order:

– `intsqlist 5;`
> [(5,25),(4,16),(3,9),(2,4),(1,1)] : (int * int) list

d) return a list of **n** occurrences of string s:

– `repeat 5 "very";`
> ["very","very","very","very","very"] : string list

6) Write and test the following functions. Identify the type of each function:

a) conjoin all elements of a boolean list together. If the list is empty then return true. Otherwise conjoin the head onto the result of conjoining the tail:

– `andlist [true,false,true,true,false];`
> false : bool

b) join all elements of a string list end to end. If the list is empty then return the empty string. Otherwise join the head onto the result of joining together the tail:

– `sjoin ["many","happy","returns"];`
> "manyhappyreturns" : string

c) join all elements in a string list end to end with spaces in between:

– `spjoin ["many","happy","returns"];`
> "many happy returns" : string

The function should have cases for an empty list, a one element list and several elements in the list. It should only put a space after a string if it is not the last element in the list.

7) Write and test the following functions. Identify the type of each function:

a) count how many elements of an integer list are positive

– `poscount [1,0,2,~3,4];`
> 3 : int

b) count how many elements of a string list have more than 3 characters:

– `more3 ["cat","goat","dog","horse"];`
> 2 : int

c) count how many elements of an arbitrary list have elements with property **p**. If the list is of type **'a** then **p** is an **'a -> bool** function:

– `countprop (fn r => r<0.0) [1.1,~2.2,3.3,~4.4];`
> 2 : int

d) use the function from c) to define the functions from a) and b)

8) Write and test the following functions. Identify the type of each function:

a) check whether all elements of an integer list are non-zero
b) check whether all elements of a string list have at least 4 letters
c) check whether all elements of an arbitrary list have property **p**
d) use the function from c) to define the functions from a) and b)

9) Write and test the following functions. Identify the type of each function:

a) check whether at least one element of an integer list is bigger than 42
b) check whether at least one element of a string list is **"banana"**
c) check whether at least one element of an arbitrary list has property **p**
d) use the function from c) to define the functions from a) and b)

10) Write and test the following functions. Identify the type of each function:

a) delete the last in a list. If the list is empty, return the empty list. If the list has one element, return the empty list. Otherwise put the head onto the result of deleting the last in the tail:

- `dellast [5,4,3,2,1];`
- `> [5,4,3,2] : int list`

b) insert value **v1** after the first occurrence of value **v2** in a list:

- `inserta "d" "c" ["a","b","c","e"];`
- `> ["a","b","c","d","e"] : string list`

c) insert value **v1** after all occurrences of value **v2** in a list:

- `insertaall 1 0 [0,0,0];`
- `> [0,1,0,1,0,1] : int list`

11) Write and test the following functions. Identify the type of each function:

a) return the position of a value in a list:

- `pos "c" ["a","b","c","d"];`
- `> 3 : int`

If the list does not contain the value then return 1. Thus, its position will be one more than the length of the list:

- `pos 99 [1,2,3,4];`
- `> 5 : int`

b) insert value **v1** after the **i**th element of a list:

- `iinserta "@" 3 ["a","b","c","d"];`
- `> ["a","b","c","@","d"] : string list`

# CHAPTER 6
# List higher order functions

## 6.1 Accumulation variables

Sometimes it is necessary to pass intermediate information from stage to stage in a recursion.

For example, consider finding the biggest in an integer list. Here, we have to keep track of the biggest so far. If the list is empty then the biggest is the biggest so far. If the head is bigger than the biggest so far then the biggest so far becomes the head for finding the biggest in the tail. Otherwise, the biggest so far remains the same for finding the biggest in the tail:

```
-    (* find biggest in integer list given biggest so far *)
     fun max1 (bsf:int) [] = bsf |
         max1 bsf (h::t) = if h>bsf
                           then max1 h t
                           else max1 bsf t;
>    val max1 = fn : int -> int list -> int
```

Assuming that there is at least one member in the list, we can start with the first as the initial biggest so far:

```
-    exception Max;
>    exception Max
-    (* find biggest in integer list *)
     fun max (h::t) = max1 h t |
         max [] = raise Max;
>    val max = fn : int list -> int
```

We raise an exception if **max** is called with an empty list: an empty list does not have a largest value. For example:

```
-    max [1,3,2,4,7,5,6];
>    7 : int
```

because:

```
max [1,3,2,4,7,5,6] ==>
max1 1 [3,2,4,7,5,6] ==>
max1 3 [2,4,7,5,6] ==>
max1 3 [4,7,5,6] ==>
max1 4 [7,5,6] ==>
max1 7 [5,6] ==>
```

```
max1 7 [6] ==>
max1 7 [] ==>
7
```

Here, **bsf** is called an accumulation variable because it accumulates the inter-mediate information about the biggest so far.

## 6.2 Encapsulation with local declarations

An important principle in programming is that of encapsulation. The idea is that when providing a solution to a problem, only the salient things should be generally accessible. Anything which is part of the overall solution but not used independently of it should only be accessible to the things that use it. This is particularly important where several people are co-operating to build a large system and each requires components from the others. Each individual only needs to know about the overall behaviour of other components in terms of the values they manipulate and the results they return. How those results are found is irrelevant. Thus, lower level details may be hidden from them. Fur-thermore, if all the sub-components of a system are visible other people may be tempted to change them for their own purposes without appreciating the implications of those changes for the original component.

In the problems we are now considering, the final function often calls one or more auxiliary functions that only it needs to know about. These auxiliary functions can be grouped together so that they are accessible within the calling function but not outside it. The function and its grouped auxiliary form a closed unit. Thus, there is no possibility of trying to change an auxiliary func-tion for use elsewhere which might have unexpected or unpredictable effects at the site of its original use. For example, above we only ever access **max1** inside **max**. Thus, the use of **max1** might be restricted to only within **max**.

A local declaration is a way of providing a function with those functions that only it uses so that they are not accessible outside that function. A local declara-tion takes the form:

```
local declaration1
in declaration2
end
```

This says that the declaration *declaration1* is only visible within *declaration2*. For example after:

```
-   local
      fun max1 (bsf:int) [] = bsf |
          max1 bsf (h::t) = if h>bsf
                            then max1 h t
                            else max1 bsf t
    in
      fun max (h::t) = max1 h t |
          max [] = raise Max
    end;
>   val max = fn: int list -> int
```

only **max** can access **max1**.

Note the **end** at the end of the local declaration. It is a common mistake to forget it.


## 6.3 Ascending sequences

Consider building a list of squares in ascending order. We want to generate:

```
[sq 1,sq 2, ... sq n]
```

for some integer **n**. Suppose we are generating squares between **m** and **n**. If **m** is bigger than **n** then return the empty list. Otherwise put the square of **m** onto the list of squares from **m+1** to **n**:

```
-   (* list squares from m to n *)
    fun sqlist1 m n = if m>n
                        then []
                        else sq m::sqlist1 (m+1) n;
>   val sqlist1 = fn : int -> int -> int list
```

We then start the list at **1**:

```
-   (* list squares from 1 to n *)
    val sqlist = sqlist1 1;
>   val sqlist = fn : int -> int list
```

Note that we use a conditional expression to control the generation of a range of values. Pattern matching can detect the presence of a particular value but not a value meeting an arbitrary condition.

Once again, we can hide the declaration of **sqlist1** within **sqlist**:

```
-   local
      fun sqlist1 m n = if m>n
                          then []
                          else sq m::sqlist1 (m+1) n
    in
      val sqlist = sqlist1 1
    end;
>   val sqlist = fn : int -> int list
```

For example:

```
-   sqlist 4;
>   [1,4,9,16] : int list
```

because:

```
sqlist 4 ==>
sqlist1 1 4 ==>
sq 1::sqlist1 2 4 ==>
sq 1::sq 2::sqlist1 3 4 ==>
sq 1::sq 2::sq 3::sqlist1 4 4 ==>
sq 1::sq 2::sq 3::sq 4::sqlist1 5 4 ==>
sq 1::sq 2::sq 3::sq 4::[] ==>
[1,4,9,16]
```

Here, **m** accumulates the starting point for the next range to be generated.

## 6.4 List reversal

Consider reversing a list. We keep track of the reversed list so far. If the list is empty then return the reversed list so far. Otherwise put the head of the list onto the reversed list so far and use it to reverse the tail of the list:

```
-   (* reverse second list onto first list *)
    fun rev1 rlsf [] = rlsf |
        rev1 rlsf (h::t) = rev1 (h::rlsf) t;
>   val rev1 = fn : 'a list -> 'a list -> 'a list
```

To start, set the reversed list so far to the empty list:

```
-   (* reverse list *)
    val rev = rev1 [];
>   val rev = fn : 'a list -> 'a list
```

Here again, **rev1** can be hidden within **reverse**:

```
-   local
      fun rev1 rlsf [] = rlsf |
          rev1 rlsf (h::t) = rev1 (h::rlsf) t
    in
      val rev = rev1 []
    end;
>   val rev = fn : 'a list -> 'a list
```

For example:

```
-   rev ["a","b","c","d"];
>   ["d","c","b","a"] : string list
```

because:

```
rev ["a","b","c","d"] ==>
rev1 [] ["a","b","c","d"] ==>
rev1 "a"::[] ["b","c","d"] ==>
rev1 "b"::"a"::[] ["c","d"] ==>
rev1 "c"::"b"::"a"::[] ["d"] ==>
rev1 "d"::"c"::"b"::"a"::[] [] ==>
"d"::"c"::"b"::"a"::[] ==>
["d","c","b","a"]
```

Here **rlsf** accumulates the reversed list under construction.

**rev** is a predefined SML function.

## 6.5 List mapping

As with numbers, common list processing functions can be generalized through higher order functions. Indeed, list processing in the LISP language was one of the first areas in which higher order functions were used.

Consider squaring every element of an integer list:

```
-   (* square each in integer list *)
    fun sqs [] = [] |
        sqs (h::t) = sq h::sqs t;
>   val sqs = fn : int list -> int list
```

**sq** is of type **int -> int** so **h** must be an integer, and **h::t** and the result must be integer lists.

For example:
```
-    sqs [1,2,3];
>    [1,4,9] : int list
```
because:
```
sqs [1,2,3] ==>
sq 1::sqs [2,3] ==>
sq 1::sq 2::sqs [3] ==>
sq 1::sq 2::sq 3::sqs [] ==>
sq 1::sq 2::sq 3::[] ==>
[1,4,9]
```
Consider, putting **"s"** on the end of every element of a string list:
```
-    (* end string with "s" *)
     fun plural s = s^"s";
>    val plural = fn : string -> string
-    (* end each in string list with "s" *)
     fun plurals [] = [] |
         plurals (h::t) = plural h::plurals t;
>    val plurals = fn : string list -> string list
```
**plural** is of type **string -> string** so h must be a string, and **h::t** and the result must be string lists:
```
-    plurals ["ape","bat","cat"];
>    ["apes","bats","cats"] : string list
```
because:
```
plurals ["ape","bat","cat"] ==>
plural "ape"::plurals ["bat","cat"] ==>
plural "ape"::plural "bat"::plurals ["cat"] ==>
plural "ape"::plural "bat"::plural "cat"::plurals [] ==>
plural "ape"::plural "bat"::plural "cat"::[] ==>
["apes","bats","cats"]
```
**sqs** and **plurals** have similar structure but differ in the action performed on the head. We can generalize by replacing the action with an arbitrary function:
```
-    (* apply function to each in list *)
     fun map _ [] = [] |
         map f (h::t) = f h::map f t;
>    val map = fn : ('a -> 'b) -> 'a list -> 'b list
```
**map** applies function **f** to each element of a list to form a new list. Suppose **f** is an **'a -> 'b** function. Then **h** must be an **'a**, **h::t** must be an **'a list** and the result must be a **'b list**.

Note that when the list is empty, the function **f** is not used so it can be ignored.

**map** may be used to define **sqs**:
```
-    val sqs = map sq;
>    val sqs = fn : int list -> int list
```
**sqs** is like **map** with **f** set to **sq**. **f** is of type **'a -> 'b** and **sq** is of type **int -> int** so **'a** and **'b** are **int** in **sqs**.

For example:

```
-   sqs [4,5,6];
>   [16,25,36] : int list
```

because:

```
sqs [4,5,6] ==>
map sq [4,5,6] ==>
sq 4::map sq [5,6] ==>
sq 4::sq 5::map sq [6] ==>
sq 4::sq 5::sq 6::map sq [] ==>
sq 4::sq 5::sq 6::[] ==>
[16,25,36]
```

Similarly, **plurals** is:

```
-   val plurals = map plural;
>   val plurals = fn : string list -> string list
```

**plurals** is like **map** with **f** set to **plural**. **plural** is of type **string -> string** and **f** is of type **'a -> 'b** so **'a** and **'b** are **string** in **plurals**.

For example:

```
-   plurals ["dog","emu","frog"];
>   ["dogs","emus","frogs"] : string list
```

because:

```
plurals ["dog","emu","frog"] ==>
map plural ["dog","emu","frog"] ==>
plural "dog"::map plural ["emu","frog"] ==>
plural "dog"::plural "emu"::map plural ["frog"] ==>
plural "dog"::plural "emu"::plural "frog"::map plural [] ==>
plural "dog"::plural "emu"::plural "frog"::[] ==>
["dogs","emus","frogs"]
```

Now consider converting a binary digit into the equivalent string:

```
-   (* convert binary digit to string *)
    fun conv 0 = "zero" |
        conv 1 = "one" |
        conv _ = "not binary";
>   val conv = fn : int -> string
```

We can use **map** to define a function to convert a list of digits into strings:

```
-   (* convert binary digit list to string list *)
    val convs = map conv;
>   val convs = fn : int list -> string list
```

**convs** is like **map** with **f** set to **conv**. **conv** is of type **int -> string** and **f** is of type **'a -> 'b** so **'a** is **int** and **'b** is **string** in **convs**.

For example:

```
-   convs [1,0,1];
>   ["one","zero","one"] : string list
```

because:

```
convs [1,0,1] ==>
map conv [1,0,1] ==>
```

```
conv 1::map conv [0,1] ==>
conv 1::conv 0::map conv [1] ==>
conv 1::conv 0::conv 1::map conv [] ==>
conv 1::conv 0::conv 1::[] ==>
["one","zero","one"]
```

**map** is a predefined SML function.

## 6.6 List filtering

**map** applies a function to all elements of a list. Another common operation is to extract all the members of a list satisfying some property.

Consider checking whether or not a word is an article or pronoun:

```
-     (* is word an article or pronoun? *)
      fun isap "a" = true |
          isap "an" = true |
          isap "the" = true |
          isap "his" = true |
          isap "her" = true |
          isap "their" = true |
          isap "our" = true |
          isap "my" = true |
          isap _ = false;
>   val isap = fn : string -> bool
```

Consider extracting all the articles and pronouns from a list of words. Each time, a head element is included only if it is an article or pronoun:

```
-     (* find all articles or pronouns in list *)
      fun getaps [] = [] |
          getaps (h::t) = if isap h
                          then h::getaps t
                          else getaps t;
>   val getaps = fn : string list -> string list
```

For example:

```
-   getaps ["the","cat","ate","my","pie"];
>   ["the","my"] : string list
```

because:

```
getaps ["the","cat","ate","my","pie"] ==>
"the"::getaps ["cat","ate","my","pie"] ==>
"the"::getaps ["ate","my","pie"] ==>
"the"::getaps ["my","pie"] ==>
"the"::"my"::getaps ["pie"] ==>
"the"::"my"::getaps [] ==>
"the"::"my"::[] ==>
["the","my"]
```

Consider checking whether or not a number is even, by dividing by 2 and checking for no remainder:

```
-     (* is integer even? *)
      fun even x = x mod 2=0;
>   val even = fn : int -> bool
```

Consider finding the even elements of an integer list. Each time, the head is only included if it is even:

```
-    (* find even integers in list *)
     fun getevens [] = [] |
         getevens (h::t) = if even h
                           then h::getevens t
                           else getevens t;
>    val getevens = fn : int list -> int list
```

For example:

```
-    getevens [1,2,3,4,5];
>    [2,4] : int list
```

because:

```
getevens [1,2,3,4,5] ==>
getevens [2,3,4,5] ==>
2::getevens [3,4,5] ==>
2::getevens [4,5] ==>
2::4::getevens [5] ==>
2::4::getevens [] ==>
2::4::[] ==>
[2,4]
```

`getaps` and `getevens` have similar structure but use different predicates to test the list head. We can generalize by introducing an arbitrary predicate `p`:

```
-    (* find list elements with property p *)
     fun filter _ [] = [] |
         filter p (h::t) = if p h
                           then h::filter p t
                           else filter p t;
>    val filter = fn : ('a -> bool) -> 'a list -> 'a list
```

`filter` checks each element with `p` and selects those which satisfy it. Suppose `p` is of type `'a -> bool`. `h` must be of type `'a` and `h::t` and the result must be of type `'a list`.

Note that the predicate function `p` is not used in the base case so it can be ignored.

We can use `filter` to define `getaps`:

```
-    val getaps = filter isap;
>    val getaps = fn : string list -> string list
```

`getaps` is like `filter` with `p` set to `isap`. `isap` is a `string -> bool` function and `p` is a `'a -> bool` function so `'a` is `string` in `getaps`. For example:

```
-    getaps ["his","or","her","hat"];
>    ["his","her"] : string list
```

because:

```
getaps ["his","or","her","hat"] ==>
filter isap ["his","or","her","hat"] ==>
"his"::filter isap ["or","her","hat"] ==>
"his"::filter isap ["her","hat"] ==>
"his"::"her"::filter isap ["hat"] ==>
```

```
"his"::"her"::filter isap [] ==>
"his"::"her"::[] ==>
["his","her"]
```

We can use **filter** to define **getevens**:

```
-    val getevens = filter even;
>    val getevens = fn : int list -> int list
```

**getevens** is like **filter** with **p** set to **even**. **even** is of type **int -> bool** and **p** is of type **'a -> bool** so **'a** is **int** in **getevens**. For example:

```
-    getevens [9,8,7,6];
>    [8,6] : int list
```

because:

```
getevens [9,8,7,6] ==>
filter even [9,8,7,6] ==>
filter even [8,7,6] ==>
8::filter even [7,6] ==>
8::filter even [6] ==>
8::6::filter even [] ==>
8::6::[] ==>
[8,6]
```

## 6.7 Ordered lists

A list is said to be ordered if some relationship holds between successive elements. A common relationship is that of increasing or decreasing value where the list is said to be in ascending or descending order.

First of all, consider checking whether or not an integer list is in ascending order. The empty list is ordered. A list with one element is in order. Otherwise the head must come before the head of the tail and the tail must be in order:

```
-    (* is integer list in ascending order? *)
     fun iorder [] = true |
         iorder [(h:int)] = true |
         iorder (h1::h2::t) = h1 <= h2 andalso iorder (h2::t);
>    val iorder = fn : int list -> bool
```

Note that in the second case, the head **h** is nominated as **int**. Thus, the list argument must be an integer list and the system knows that integer comparison is to be used in the third case.

In fact, as **h** is not used in the second case, it can be ignored:

```
-    fun iorder [] = true |
         iorder [(_:int)] = true |
         iorder (h1::h2::t) = h1 <= h2 andalso iorder (h2::t);
>    val iorder = fn : int list -> bool
```

For example:

```
-    iorder [1,3,5,7];
>    true : bool
```

because:

```
   iorder [1,3,5,7] ==>
   true andalso iorder [3,5,7] ==>
   true andalso true andalso iorder [5,7] ==>
   true andalso true andalso true andalso iorder [7] ==>
   true andalso true andalso true andalso true ==>
   true
```

To generalize this to arbitrary lists we need to abstract over the comparison. Now, we check that relationship **p** holds between successive elements:

```
-    (* is list ordered by property p? *)
     fun  order _ [] = true |
          order p [_] = true |
          order p (h1::h2::t) = p h1 h2 andalso order p (h2::t);
>    val order = fn : ('a -> 'a -> bool) -> 'a list -> bool
```

Suppose the list argument is an **'a list**. Then **h1** and **h2** must be of type **'a** so **p** must be of type **'a -> 'a -> bool**. For example, given:

```
-    (* is integer x smaller than y? *)
     fun iless (x:int) y = x<=y;
>    val iless = fn : int -> int -> bool
```

the integer order checker is:

```
-    val iorder = order iless;
>    val iorder = fn : int list -> bool
```

**iorder** is like **order** with **p** set to **iless**. **iless** is of type **int -> int -> bool** and **p** is of type **'a -> 'a -> bool** so **'a** is **int** in **iorder**.

For example:

```
-    iorder [2,4,6];
>    true : bool
```

because:

```
   iorder [2,4,6] ==>
   order iless [2,4,6] ==>
   true andalso order iless [4,6] ==>
   true andalso true andalso order iless [6] ==>
   true andalso true andalso true ==>
   true
```

We can define a string version. Given:

```
-    (* does string s1 precede s2? *)
     fun sless (s1:string) s2 = s1<=s2;
>    val sless = fn : string -> string -> bool
```

then:

```
-    (* is string list in ascending order? *)
     val sorder = order sless;
>    val sorder = fn : string list -> bool
```

**sorder** is like **order** with **p** set to **sless**. **sless** is a **string -> string -> bool** function and **p** is an **'a -> 'a -> bool** function so **'a** is **string** in **sorder**.

For example:

```
-    sorder ["ape","bat","dog","cat"];
>    false : bool
```
because:
```
sorder ["ape","bat","dog","cat"] ==>
order sless ["ape","bat","dog","cat"] ==>
true andalso order sless ["bat","dog","cat"] ==>
true andalso true andalso order sless ["dog","cat"] ==>
true andalso true andalso false andalso order sless ["cat"] ==>
true andalso true andalso false ==>
false
```
Note that **andalso** does not evaluate its second argument if the first argument
is **false**.

## 6.8 Insertion into ordered lists

Consider inserting a new integer into a list of integers in ascending order. If the
list is empty then make a new list for the new value. If the new value comes
before the first in the head then put it on the front of the list. Otherwise, put the
head onto the result of inserting the new value into the list tail:
```
-    (* insert into ascending integer list *)
     fun inserti (v:int) [] = [v] |
         inserti v (h::t) = if v<=h
                            then v::h::t
                            else h::inserti v t;
>    val inserti = fn : int -> int list -> int list
```
Note that **v** is marked as **int** so that integer comparison is used. For example:
```
-    inserti 3 [1,2,4];
>    [1,2,3,4] : int list
```
because:
```
inserti 3 [1,2,4] ==>
1::inserti 3 [2,4] ==>
1::2::inserti 3 [4] ==>
1::2::3::[4] ==>
[1,2,3,4]
```
Once again, we can generalize insertion to an arbitrary relationship between
successive list members. Here **p** is the relation which must hold for the new
value to be positioned:
```
-    (* insert into list with order property p *)
     fun insert _ v [] = [v] |
         insert p v (h::t) = if p v h
                             then v::h::t
                             else h::insert p v t;
>    val insert = fn : ('a -> 'a -> bool) -> 'a -> 'a list -> 'a list
```
Suppose the list is of type **'a list** and the new value are of type **'a**. Then **p**
must be an **'a -> 'a -> bool** function.

For example, the integer insertion function is:

```
-    val inserti = insert iless;
>    val inserti = fn : int -> int list -> int list
```

**inserti** is like **insert** with **p** set to **iless**. **iless** is of type **int -> int ->
bool** and **p** is of type **'a -> 'a -> bool** so **'a** is **int** in **inserti**.

For example:

```
-    inserti 5 [1,3,7];
>    [1,3,5,7] : int list
```

because:

```
inserti 5 [1,3,7] ==>
insert iless 5 [1,3,7] ==>
1::insert iless 5 [3,7] ==>
1::3::insert iless 5 [7] ==>
1::3::5::[7] ==>
[1,3,5,7]
```

Similarly, a string insertion function is:

```
-    (* insert into ascending string list *)
     val inserts = insert sless;
>    val inserts = fn : string -> string list -> string list
```

**inserts** is like **insert** with **p** set to **sless**. **sless** is of type **string -> string
-> bool** and **p** is of type **'a -> 'a -> bool** so **'a** is **string** in **inserts**.

For example:

```
-    inserts "cat" ["ape","bat","dog"];
>    ["ape","bat","cat","dog"] : string list
```

because:

```
inserts "cat" ["ape","bat","dog"] ==>
insert sless "cat" ["ape","bat","dog"] ==>
"ape"::insert sless "cat" ["bat","dog"] ==>
"ape"::"bat"::insert sless "cat" ["dog"] ==>
"ape"::"bat"::"cat"::["dog"] ==>
["ape","bat","cat","dog"]
```

## 6.9 Layered patterns

In **insert**:

```
fun insert _ v [] = [v] |
    insert p v (h::t) = if p v h
                        then v::h::t
                        else h::insert p v t
```

we use the pattern **h::t** so that we can access the head and tail of the list argument independently. However, we then have to use the construct **h::t** in order
to put **v** on the front of the list.

The SML layered pattern provides a means of relating a bound variable to a
pattern so that after matching they both refer to the same thing. It takes the
form:

*name* **as** *pattern*

and may be used anywhere a pattern is valid. *name* and *pattern* may be used interchangeably: they both refer to the same value. Furthermore, the bound variables within *pattern* may be used to access the corresponding elements of that value.

Above, we might use:

```
l as h::t
```

so l and h::t would refer to the same list. We could then use l when we want the whole list and h or t when we want the head or tail:

```
fun insert _ v [] = [v] |
    insert p v (l as h::t) = if p v h
                             then v::l
                             else h::insert p v t
```

## 6.10 Insertion sort

Consider sorting an unordered list of integers into ascending order. If the list is empty then it is sorted. Otherwise, insert the head into the result of sorting the tail:

```
-    (* sort integer list in ascending order *)
     fun sorti [] = [] |
         sorti (h::t) = inserti h (sorti t);
>    val sorti = fn : int list -> int list
```

inserti returns an integer list: so must sorti. inserti has an integer as first argument. Thus, h is an integer and h::t is an integer list.

For example:

```
-    sorti [4,3,2,1];
>    [1,2,3,4] : int list
```

because:

```
sorti [4,3,2,1] ==>
inserti 4 (sorti [3,2,1]) ==>
inserti 4 (inserti 3 (sorti [2,1])) ==>
inserti 4 (inserti 3 (inserti 2 (sorti [1]))) ==>
inserti 4 (inserti 3 (inserti 2  (inserti 1 (sorti [])))) ==>
inserti 4 (inserti 3 (inserti 2  (inserti 1 []))) ==>
inserti 4 (inserti 3 (inserti 2  [1])) ==>
inserti 4 (inserti 3 [1,2]) ==>
inserti 4 [1,2,3] ==>
[1,2,3,4]
```

We can generalize sorting to lists of arbitrary type. First of all, we can abstract over the insertion function:

```
-    (* sort list using specialized insert *)
     fun sort _ [] = [] |
         sort insert (h::t) = insert h (sort insert t);
```

Suppose h::t is an 'a list. Suppose sort returns a 'b list. Then insert is of type 'a -> 'b list -> 'b list so sort is of type:

```
>   val sort =
            fn : ('a -> 'b list -> 'b list) -> 'a list -> 'b list
```

Thus, integer sort is:

```
-   val sorti = sort inserti;
>   val sorti = fn : int list -> int list
```

**sorti** is **sort** with **insert** set to **inserti**. **inserti** is of type **int -> int list -> int list** and **insert** is of type **'a -> 'b list -> 'b list** so **'a** is **int** and **'b** is **int** in **sorti**.

For example:

```
-   sorti [5,3,1];
>   [1,3,5] : int list
```

because:

```
sorti [5,3,1] ==>
sort inserti [5,3,1] ==>
inserti 5 (sort inserti [3,1]) ==>
inserti 5 (inserti 3 (sort inserti [1])) ==>
inserti 5 (inserti 3 (inserti 1 (sort inserti []))) ==>
inserti 5 (inserti 3 (inserti 1 [])) ==>
inserti 5 (inserti 3 [1]) ==>
inserti 5 [1,3] ==>
[1,3,5]
```

However, we have been making insertion functions by specializing **insert** with specific predicates. An alternative generalization for sorting is to use the general **insert** and abstract over the predicate:

```
-   (* sort list on order property p *)
    fun sort _ [] = [] |
        sort p (h::t) = insert p h (sort p t);
```

We know from the previous section that **insert** is of type **('a -> 'a -> bool) -> 'a -> 'a list -> 'a list** so **p** is of type **'a -> 'a -> bool**, **h** is of type **'a** and **h::t** is of type **'a list** so **sort** is of type:

```
>   val sort = fn : ('a -> 'a -> bool) -> 'a list -> 'a list
```

Thus, a string sort is:

```
-   (* sort string list in ascending order *)
    val sorts = sort sless;
>   val sorts = fn : string list -> string list
```

**sorts** is like **sort** with **p** set to **sless**. **sless** is a **string -> string -> bool** function and **p** is an **'a -> 'a -> bool** function so **'a** is **string** in **sorts**.

For example:

```
-   sorts ["cat","bat","ape"];
>   ["ape","bat","cat"] : string list
```

because:

```
sorts ["cat","bat","ape"] ==>
sort sless ["cat","bat","ape"] ==>
insert sless "cat" (sort sless ["bat","ape"])) ==>
```

```
insert sless "cat"
  (insert sless "bat" (sort sless ["ape"])) ==>
insert sless "cat"
  (insert sless "bat" (insert sless "ape" (sort sless []))) ==>
insert sless "cat"
  (insert sless "bat" (insert sless "ape" [])) ==>
insert sless "cat" (insert sless "bat" ["ape"]) ==>
insert sless "cat" ["ape","bat"] ==>
["ape","bat","cat"]
```

## 6.11 Mapping over two lists

Consider forming a new list by adding corresponding elements of two lists together. If both lists are empty then return the empty list. Otherwise put the sum of the heads onto the result of adding corresponding elements in the tails:

```
-   (* add corresponding elements of two integer lists *)
    fun add2 [] [] = [] |
        add2 ((h1:int)::t1) (h2::t2) = h1+h2::add2 t1 t2 |
        add2 _ _ = [];
>   val add2 = fn : int list -> int list -> int list
```

Note that `h1` is tagged as `int`: + is overloaded.

Note that we assume that both lists are the same length. The last case is if one is longer than the other. We only reach this case when one list is empty and the other is not. Here, we return an empty list, discarding all of the rest of the non-empty list.

For example:

```
-   add2 [1,2,3] [4,5,6];
>   [5,7,9] : int list
```

because:

```
add2 [1,2,3] [4,5,6] ==>
1+4::add2 [2,3] [5,6] ==>
1+4::2+5::add2 [3] [6] ==>
1+4::2+5::3+6::add2 [] [] ==>
1+4::2+5::3+6::[] ==>
[5,7,9]
```

Consider ANDing corresponding elements of two lists together. If both are empty then return the empty list. Otherwise, AND the heads and join the result onto the list from ANDing corresponding tail elements:

```
-   (* conjoin corresponding elements of two boolean lists *)
    fun and2 [] [] = [] |
        and2 (h1::t1) (h2::t2) = (h1 andalso h2)::and2 t1 t2 |
        and2 _ _ = [];
>   val and2 = fn : bool list -> bool list -> bool list
```

For example:

```
-   and2 [true,false,true] [false,false,true];
>   [false, false, true] : bool list
```

because:

```
and2 [true,false,true] [false,false,true] ==>
(true andalso false)::and2 [false,true] [false,true] ==>
(true andalso false)::
 (false andalso false)::and2 [true] [true] ==>
(true andalso false)::
 (false andalso false)::(true andalso true)::and2 [] [] ==>
(true andalso false)::
 (false andalso false)::(true andalso true)::[] ==>
[false,false,true]
```

We can generalize by abstracting over the operation applied to the list heads:

```
-   (* apply function to corresponding elements of two lists *)
    fun map2 _ [] [] = [] |
        map2 f (h1::t1) (h2::t2) = f h1 h2::map2 f t1 t2 |
        map2 _ _ _ = [];
>   val map2 = fn : ('a -> 'b -> 'c) -> 'a list -> 'b list -> 'c list
```

Suppose `h1::t1` is an `'a list`, `h2::t2` is a `'b list` and the result is a `'c list`. Then, `f` must be of type `'a -> 'b -> 'c`.

The first and last cases return the same result so they can be folded together into a single case:

```
-   fun map2 f (h1::t1) (h2::t2) = f h1 h2::map2 f t1 t2 |
        map2 _ _ _ = [];
>   val map2 = fn : ('a -> 'b -> 'c) -> 'a list -> 'b list -> 'c list
```

Here, if either or both lists do not have the structure `h::t`, i.e. one or both are empty, then the empty list is returned.

For example, `add2` is like `map2` with `f` set to `add`:

```
-   fun add (x:int) y = x+y;
>   val add = fn : int -> int -> int
-   val add2 = map2 add;
>   val add2 = fn : int list -> int list -> int list
```

`f` is an `'a -> 'b -> 'c` function and `add` is an `int -> int -> int` function so `'a`, `'b` and `'c` are all `int`.

For example:

```
-   add2 [7,8,9] [10,11,12];
>   [17,19,21] int list
```

because:

```
add2 [7,8,9] [10,11,12] ==>
map2 add [7,8,9] [10,11,12] ==>
add 7 10::map2 add [8,9] [11,12] ==>
add 7 10::add 8 11::map2 add [9] [12] ==>
add 7 10::add 8 11::add 9 12::map2 add [] [] ==>
add 7 10::add 8 11::add 9 12::[] ==>
[17,19,21]
```

## 6.12 Merge sort

Consider merging two integer lists which are both in ascending order:

```
-   merge [1,3,4,7] [2,5,6];
>   [1,2,3,4,5,6,7] : int list
```

If the head of the first is bigger than the head of the second then put it onto merging the tail of the first and the second. If the head of the second is bigger than the head of the first then put it onto merging the first and the tail of the second. If one is empty then return the other:

```
-   (* merge two ascending ordered integer lists *)
    fun merge (l1 as (h1:int)::t1) (l2 as h2::t2) =
        if h1<h2
        then h1::merge t1 l2
        else h2::merge l1 t2 |
    merge l1 [] = l1 |
    merge [] l2 = l2;
>   val merge = fn : int list -> int list -> int list
```

For example:

```
merge [1,3,4,7] [2,5,6] ==>
1::merge [3,4,7] [2,5,6] ==>
1::2::merge [3,4,7] [5,6] ==>
1::2::3::merge [4,7] [5,6] ==>
1::2::3::4::merge [7] [5,6] ==>
1::2::3::4::5::merge [7] [6] ==>
1::2::3::4::5::6::merge [7] [] ==>
1::2::3::4::5::6::[7] ==>
[1,2,3,4,5,6,7]
```

## 6.13 Folding lists of lists

Consider appending a list of lists end to end:

```
-   appendall [[1,2,3],[4,5,6],[7,8,9]];
>   [1,2,3,4,5,6,7,8,9] : int list
```

If the list is empty then return the empty list. Otherwise, append the head list onto appending all the lists in the tail:

```
-   (* append a list of lists end to end *)
    fun appendall [] = [] |
        appendall (h::t) = append h (appendall t);
>   val appendall = fn : ('a list) list -> 'a list
```

append is an 'a list -> 'a list -> 'a list function so h must be an 'a list and h::t must be an 'a list list.

For example:

```
appendall [[1,2,3],[4,5,6],[7,8,9]] ==>
append [1,2,3] (appendall [[4,5,6],[7,8,9]]) ==>
append [1,2,3] (append [4,5,6] (appendall [[7,8,9]])) ==>
append [1,2,3]
  (append [4,5,6] (append [7,8,9] (appendall []))) ==>
append [1,2,3] (append [4,5,6] (append [7,8,9] [])) ==>
```

```
append [1,2,3] (append [4,5,6] [7,8,9]) ==>
append [1,2,3] [4,5,6,7,8,9] ==>
[1,2,3,4,5,6,7,8,9]
```

Consider merging a list of ordered integer lists:

```
-    mergeall [[1,4,7,10],[2,5,8,11],[3,6,9]];
>    [1,2,3,4,5,6,7,8,9,10,11] : int list
```

If the list is empty then return the empty list. Otherwise merge the list in the head into the result of merging the lists in the tail:

```
-    (* merge a list of ascending order integer lists together *)
     fun mergeall [] = [] |
         mergeall (h::t) = merge h (mergeall t);
>    val mergeall = fn : int list list -> int list
```

For example:

```
mergeall [[1,4,7,10],[2,5,8,11],[3,6,9]] ==>
merge [1,4,7,10] (mergeall [[2,5,8,11],[3,6,9]]) ==>
merge [1,4,7,10] (merge [2,5,8,11] (mergeall [[3,6,9]])) ==>
merge [1,4,7,10]
  (merge [2,5,8,11] (merge [3,6,9] (mergeall []))) ==>
merge [1,4,7,10] (merge [2,5,8,11] (merge [3,6,9] [])) ==>
merge [1,4,7,10] (merge [2,5,8,11] [3,6,9]) ==>
merge [1,4,7,10] [2,3,5,6,8,9,11] ==>
[1,2,3,4,5,6,7,8,9,10,11]
```

We can generalize these examples by abstracting over the operation applied to the head and the result of processing the tail of the list:

```
-    (* fold function across list of lists from right *)
     fun listfoldr _ [] = [] |
         listfoldr f (h::t) = f h (listfoldr f t);
>    val listfoldr =
         fn : ('a -> 'b list -> 'b list) -> 'a list -> 'b list
```

Suppose h::t is a list of 'a. Suppose listfoldr returns a 'b list. Then f must be applied to an 'a from the head of h::t and the 'b list returned by listfoldr. Thus f must also return a 'b list.

For example, mergeall is like listfoldr with f set to merge:

```
-    val mergeall = listfoldr merge;
>    val mergeall = int list list -> int list
```

In listfoldr, f is an 'a -> 'b list -> 'b list function and merge is an int list -> int list -> int list function so 'a must be int list and 'b must be int. For example:

```
-    mergeall [[2,5,9],[1,3,4],[6,7,8]];
>    [1,2,3,4,5,6,7,8,9] : int list
```

because:

```
mergeall [[2,5,9],[1,3,4],[6,7,8]] ==>
listfoldr merge [[2,5,9],[1,3,4],[6,7,8]] ==>
merge [2,5,9] (listfoldr merge [[1,3,4],[6,7,8]]) ==>
merge [2,5,9]
       (merge [1,3,4] (listfoldr merge [[6,7,8]])) ==>
```

```
merge [2,5,9]
        (merge [1,3,4]
                (merge [6,7,8] (listfoldr merge []))) ==>
merge [2,5,9]
        (merge [1,3,4]
                (merge [6,7,8] [])) ==>
merge [2,5,9]
        (merge [1,3,4] [6,7,8]) ==>
merge [2,5,9] [1,3,4,6,7,8] ==>
[1,2,3,4,5,6,7,8,9]
```

Similarly, **appendall** is like **listfoldr** with **f** set to **append**:

```
-   val appendall = listfoldr append;
>   val appendall = fn : 'a list list -> 'a list
```

**f** is of type **'a -> 'b list -> 'b list** and **append** is of type **'a list -> 'a list -> 'a list** so in **appendall 'a** must be **'a list** and **'b** must be **'a**.
   For example:

```
-   appendall [["a","b","c"],["d","e"],["f","g","h"]];
>   ["a","b","c","d","e","f","g","h"] : string list
```

because:

```
appendall [["a","b","c"],["d","e"],["f","g","h"]] ==>
listfoldr append [["a","b","c"],["d","e"],["f","g","h"]] ==>
append ["a","b","c"]
        (listfoldr append [["d","e"],["f","g","h"]]) ==>
append ["a","b","c"]
        (append ["d","e"]
                (listfoldr append [["f","g","h"]])) ==>
append ["a","b","c"]
        (append ["d","e"]
                (append ["f","g","h"]
                        (listfoldr append []))) ==>
append ["a","b","c"]
        (append ["d","e"]
                (append ["f","g","h"] [])) ==>
["a","b","c","d","e","f","g","h"]
```

Note that **listfoldr** is the same as the first generalization of sorting:

```
-   fun sort _ [] = [] |
        sort insert (h::t) = insert h (sort insert t);
> val sort = fn : ('a -> 'b list -> 'b list) -> 'a list -> 'b list
```

## 6.14 Generalized folding

The function **listfoldr** folds a function across a list of lists to form a new list.
We can abstract again to fold a function across a list to form a value:

```
-   (* fold function across list from right *)
    fun foldr _ b [] = b |
        foldr f b (h::t) = f h (foldr f b t);
>   val foldr = fn : ('a -> 'b -> 'b) -> 'b -> 'a list -> 'b
```

Here, when the list is empty we return a base value **b**. Otherwise we apply **f** to the list head and the result of folding **f** with **b** over the list tail.

Consider the list:

[ *e1* , *e2* , ... , *eN* ]

If we fold some arbitrary function *f* over this list then the effect is:

**foldr** *fb* [ *e1* , *e2* , ... , *eN* ] **==>**
*fe1* ( **foldr** *fb* [ *e2* , ... , *eN* ]) **==>**
*fe1* ( *f e2* (**foldr** *fb* [ ... , *eN* ])) **==>**
*fe1* ( *f e2* ( ... ( *feN b* ) ... ))

i.e. to apply the function to each element and the result of folding the function across the rest of the elements.

For example, we can sum an integer list:

```
-    fun add (i1:int) i2 = i1+i2;
>    val add = fn : int -> int -> int

-    val sum = foldr add 0;
>    val sum = fn : int list -> int
```

Here, we fold **add** over the list using the base value **0** at the end.

For example:

```
-    sum [1,2,3,4];
>  10 : int
```

because:

```
sum [1,2,3,4] ==>
foldr add 0 [1,2,3,4] ==>
add 1 (foldr add 0 [2,3,4])  ==>
add 1 (add 2 (foldr add 0 [3,4])) ==>
add 1 (add 2 (add 3 (foldr add 0 [4]))) ==>
add 1 (add 2 (add 3 (add 4 (foldr add 0 [])))) ==>
add 1 (add 2 (add 3 (add 4 0)))) ==>
10
```

Our list of lists fold function **listfoldr** is like **foldr** but with an empty list as the base value:

```
-    fun listfoldr f = foldr f [];
>    val listfoldr =
        fn : ('a -> 'b list -> 'b list) -> 'a list -> 'b list
```

## 6.15 Testing groups of functions

Our functions are now somewhat more complicated and often call other functions. It is important to test out functions individually before using them in other functions, to reassure ourselves that each stage works.

For example, suppose we want to sort a list of real numbers in descending order. We need a real comparison function:

```
-    (* is one real greater than another? *)
     fun rmore (r1:real) r2 = r1>=r2;
>    val rmore = fn : real -> real -> bool
```

which we should test first with values to make the boolean expression both true and false:

```
-   rmore 6.1 6.2;
>   false : bool

-   rmore 8.9 7.6;
>   true : bool
```

Suppose we are using the insertion function:

```
-   fun insert _ v [] = [v] |
        insert p v (l as h::t) = if p v h
                                 then v::l
                                 else h::insert p v t;
>   val insert = fn : ('a -> 'a -> bool) -> 'a -> 'a list -> 'a list
```

We next define a real insertion function:

```
-   (* insert into descending order real list *)
    val rinsert = insert rmore;
>   val rinsert = fn : real -> real list -> real list
```

and test the base case:

```
-   rinsert 3.4 [];
>   [3.4] : real list
```

and the recursion case:

```
-   rinsert 3.4 [5.6,4.5,2.3,1.2];
>   [5.6,4.5,3.4,2.3,1.2] : real list
```

We will use the first version of sort:

```
-   fun sort _ [] = [] |
        sort insert (h::t) = insert h (sort insert t);
>   val sort = fn : ('a -> 'b list -> 'b list) -> 'a list -> 'b list
```

so we define a real sorting function:

```
-   (* sort real list in descending order *)
    val rsort = sort rinsert;
>   val rsort = fn : real list -> real list
```

Finally, we test the sort function base case:

```
-   rsort [];
>   [] : real list
```

and recursion case:

```
-   rsort [1.2,2.3,3.4,4.5,5.6];
>   [5.6,4.5,3.4,2.3,1.2] : real list
```

Similarly, when using a local declaration to hide auxiliary functions, it is important to test each auxiliary function before combining them to test calling functions.

Testing alone cannot guarantee that a program is correct for all possible argument values. For that, mathematical proof techniques are needed. Nonetheless, thorough testing can give us confidence that our programs do indeed do what they are supposed to do.

## 6.16 Summary

In this chapter we started by looking at the use of accumulation variables to pass intermediate values between recursive function calls. We then considered the use of local declarations to encapsulate functions and the auxiliaries that they call. We next discussed the **map** higher order function for applying a function to each element in a list and the **filter** higher order function for selecting list elements with particular properties. Then we looked at generalizing insertion into ordered lists to form a general purpose higher order sorting function. Finally, we looked mapping over two lists and at folding functions over lists of lists. We are now in a position to start considering the representation of collections of multi-property things as tuples. In the next chapter we will use directly or modify the functions from the previous and this chapter to manipulate tuple lists.

## 6.17 Exercises

1) Identify the types of the following functions:

a) ```
fun a _ [] = [] |
    a f (h::t) = 2*(f h)::a f t
```

b) ```
fun b _ [] = 0 |
    b f (h::t) = f h+b f t
```

c) ```
fun c _ [] = [] |
    c f (h::t) = if f h
                    then f h::c f t
                    else c f t
```

d) ```
fun d _ _ [] = [] |
    d p f (h::t) = if p h
                      then f h::d p f t
                      else d p f t
```

e) ```
fun e _ _ [] = [] |
    e f1 f2 (h::t) = f1 (f2 h)::e f1 f2 t
```

f) ```
fun f _ _ [] = [] |
    f p1 p2 (h::t) = if p1 (p2 h)
                        then h::f p1 p2 t
                        else f p1 p2 t
```

g) ```
fun g _ [] [] = [] |
    g f (h1::t1) (h2::t2) = if f h1
                              then h2::g f t1 t2
                              else g f t1 t2
```

h) ```
fun h _ _ [] [] = [] |
    h f1 f2 (h1::t1) (h2::t2) =
     if f1 h1
     then f2 h2::(f f1 f2 t1 t2)
     else f f1 f2 t1 t2
```

2) Write and test the following functions. Identify the type of each function:

a) find the shortest element in a string list
b) generate a list of cubes of integers between **m** and **n** in ascending order
c) generate a list by applying function **f** to each integer value between **m** and **n** in ascending order

d) define function b) using the function from c)

e) generate a list of halves of integers between **m** and **n** in steps of **s**:

```
-   halves 1 10 2;
>   [0,1,2,3,4] : int list
```

f) generate a list by applying function **f** to each integer value between **m** and **n** in steps of **s**

g) define
   i) function e)
   ii) function b)
   iii) a function to return a list of integers from **m** to **n** in steps of **s** using the function from f).

3) Write and test a function to check if a list is a palindrome i.e. is the same when reversed:

```
-   palin ["m","a","d","a","m","i","m","a","d","a","m"];
>   true : bool
```

What is the type of this function?

4) Write and test the following functions. Identify the type of each function:

a) use **map** to generate a list of tuples of numbers and squares from a list of numbers:

```
-   numsq [1,2,3,4];
>   [(1,1),(2,4),(3,9),(4,16)] : int list
```

b) use **map** to generate a list of booleans indicating whether or not each of a list of integers is odd:

```
-   odds [1,2,3,4,5];
>   [true,false,true,false,true] : bool list
```

c) use **map** to generate a list of tuples of strings and integer sizes from a list of strings:

```
-   sizes ["time","for","a","cup","of","tea"];
>   [("time",4),("for",3),("a",1),("cup",3),("of",2),("tea",3)]:
    (string * int) list
```

5) Write and test the following functions. Identify the type of each function:

a) use filter to select all the strings in a list which have at least 3 letters:

```
-   more3 ["time","to","wake","up"];
>   ["time","wake"] : string list
```

b) use **filter** to select all the negative numbers from a list of integers:

```
-   getnegs [1,~1,2,~2,3,~3];
>   [~1,~2,~3] : int list
```

c) use **map, filter** and 2)g)iii) above to find all the even squares of integers between **m** and **n** which divide by 7. Test the function on the range 1 to 1000.

6) Write and test the following functions. Identify the type of each function:

a) use **sort** to sort a list of integers in descending order:

```
-   sortdi [1,2,3,4,5];
>   [5,4,3,2,1] : int list
```

b) use **sort** to sort a list of strings in ascending order of their lengths:

```
     -   sortas ["how","long","is","the","longest","word"];
     >   ["is","how","the","long","word","longest"] : string list
```

7) Write and test the following functions. Identify the type of each function:

a) use **map2** to join corresponding elements of two string lists together:

```
     -   join2 ["a","b","c"] ["1","2","3"];
     >   ["a1","b2","c3"] : string list
```

b) use **map2** to form a list of tuples of corresponding list elements from two lists:

```
     -   zip [1,2,3,4] ["one","two","three","four"];
     >   [(1,"one"),(2,"two"),(3,"three"),(4,"four")] : (int * string) list
```

8) Write and test the following functions. Identify the type of each function:

a) use **listfoldr** to add together corresponding elements of a list of integer lists:

```
     -   addall [[1,2,3],[4,5,6],[7,8,9]];
     >   [12,15,18] : int list
```

(Hint: write a function that adds together corresponding elements of two integer lists but if either list is empty then return the other.)

b) use **listfoldr** to find the longest list in a list of lists:

```
     -   longest [[1,2,3],[4,5,6,7],[8,9]];
     >   [4,5,6,7] : int list
```

(Hint: write a function that returns the longer of two lists.)

9) A botanist is experimenting with a new fertilizer. Every week the lengths of plants are measured in cm and maintained in individual lists. For example:

```
     [1.2,1.7,1.9,2.3,2.5,2.6]
```

a) Write a function to return a list of how much a plant has grown week by week from a list of lengths. For an empty list or a list with one element return the empty list. Otherwise, subtract the head from the head of the tail and put the result in front of the growth list from the tail:

```
     -   growth [1.2,1.7,1.9,2.3,2.5,2.6];
     >   [0.5,0.2,0.4,0.2,0.1] : real list
```

What is the type of this function?

b) Write a function to find the average weekly growth from a growth list. What is the type of this function?

c) Write a function which, given a list of growth lists, uses **map** and the function from b) to return a list of average weekly growths. What is the type of this function?

d) Write a function which given a list of growth lists, uses **filter** and the function from b) to return a list of growth lists whose average weekly growth is at least 0.3 cm. What is the type of this function?

e) Write a function which, given a list of average weekly growths, counts how many average weekly growths are less than 0.4 cm. What is the type of this function?

f) Write a function which, given a growth list, returns a string list to indicate whether or not each element represents high, medium or low growth:

```
"high"     ==   growth > 2*average
"medium"   ==   growth <= 2* average and growth >= average/2
"low"      ==   growth < average/2
```

Use **map** and the function from b). What is the type of this function?

10) Write and test the following functions. Identify the type of each function:
  a) given a list of integers, return a list of sums of each element and the next:

  ```
  -   sum2 [1,2,3,4,5,6];
  >   [3,5,7,9,11] : int list
  ```

  For an empty or one-element list, an empty list should be returned.

  b) given a list of strings, return a list formed by joining each element to the next:

  ```
  -   join2 ["happy","birthday","party","time"];
  >   ["happybirthday","birthdayparty","partytime"] : string list
  ```

  For an empty or one-element list, an empty list should be returned.

  c) given a list, return a list formed by applying function **f** to each element and the next. For an empty or one-element list, an empty list should be returned.

  d) define the functions from a) and b) using the function from c).

11) Write and test the following functions. Identify the type of each function:
  a) return a list consisting of twice every non-zero element in an integer list:

  ```
  -   twicenot0 [1,0,2,0,3];
  >   [2,4,6] : int list
  ```

  b) return a list consisting of the string **"s"** joined to the end of every element in a list of strings with more than 4 letters:

  ```
  -   pluralmore4 ["ape","beaver","cow","dragon"];
  >   ["beavers","dragons"] : string list
  ```

  c) return a list resulting from applying function **f** to every element of a list satisfying predicate **p**.

  d) define the functions from a) and b) using the function from c).

12) Write and test the following functions. Identify the type of each function:
  a) return the sum of all odd elements in a list of integers.
  b) return the sum of all elements greater than 10 in a list of integers.
  c) return the sum of all elements satisfying predicate **p** in a list of integers.
  d) define the functions from a) and b) using the function from c).
  e) return a string formed by joining together all the elements of a string list satisfying predicate **p**.
  f) return the result of applying function **f** cumulatively to all the elements of a list satisfying predicate **p**. For an empty list the function should return value **v**.
  g) define the functions from a), b), c) and e) using the function from f).

13) Write and test the following functions. Identify the type of each function:
  a) count how often a **1** is followed by a **2** in a list of integers.
  b) count how often value **v1** is followed by value **v2** in a list of appropriate type.

c)  define the function from a) using the function from b).
d)  count how often an odd integer is followed by an even integer in a list of integers.
e)  count how often an element satisfying predicate **p1** is followed by an element satisfying predicate **p2** in a list of appropriate type.
f)  define the functions from a), b) and d) using the function from e).

# CHAPTER 7
# Tuple lists

## 7.1 Introduction

We can now complete the odyssey that we started in Chapter 1. We said that model making is based on collections of things and things are groups of properties. We have seen that properties may be represented as values of types and that fixed size groups of properties may be represented by tuples. We have also seen that lists may be used to represent collections as variable length sequences of values. We will now look at the use of list processing techniques to manipulate collections of things represented as lists of tuples.

## 7.2 Pattern matching with tuples

Until now we have been rather coy about tuples. We have seen how tuples may be formed and typed but have not yet seen how to extract their values. As with lists, functions may be defined with tuples of patterns. When such a function is applied to a tuple value, it is matched against the tuple of patterns. If they have the same structure, that is the same number of elements with elements of corresponding type in the same positions, then each bound variable in the tuple pattern is set to the corresponding element of the tuple value.

Thus, tuple pattern matching may be used to extract elements from tuples. For example, suppose we wish to extract the first element from a tuple with 3 elements:

```
-    (* select first element from three-element tuple *)
     fun first (x,y,z) = x;
>    val first = fn : 'a * 'b * 'c -> 'a
```

This function is defined with a tuple of bound variables **x**, **y** and **z**. In the body of the function, no operations are performed on **x**, **y** or **z**. Thus, they may be of any types, say:

```
x : 'a
y : 'b
z : 'c
```

The function returns the value of **x** which is an **'a**. Thus, the function type is:

```
'a * 'b * 'c -> 'a
```

Consider:

```
-    first (1,1.0,"one");
>    1 : int
```

Here, **x** is set to **1**, **y** is set to **1.0**, **z** is set to **"one"** and **1** is returned from **x**. Consider:

```
-    first (("one",1),("two",2),("three",3));
>    ("one",1) : string * int
```

Here, **x** is set to **("one",1)**, **y** is set to **("two",2)**, **z** is set to **("three",3)** and **("one",1)** is returned from **x**.

Note that **y** and **z** are not used so they can be ignored:

```
-    fun first (x,_,_) = x;
>    val first = fn : 'a * 'b * 'c -> 'a
```

Similarly, we could select the second in a 3-element tuple with:

```
-    (* select second element from three-element tuple *)
     fun second (_,y,_) = y;
>    val second = fn : 'a * 'b * 'c -> 'b
```

For example, in:

```
-    second ("Dennis","Menace",8);
>    "Menace" : string
```

**"Dennis"** and **8** are ignored, **y** is set to **"Menace"** and **"Menace"** is returned. Similarly, we could select the third in a 3-element tuple with:

```
-    (* select third element from three-element tuple *)
     fun third (_,_,z) = z;
>    val third = fn : 'a * 'b * 'c -> 'c
```

For example, in:

```
-    third (2,2.0,[2,4,8,16]);
>    [2,4,8,16] : int list
```

**2**, and **2.0** are ignored. **z** is set to **[2,4,8,16]** which is returned.

Elements may be selected from nested tuple values by pattern matching with nested tuples of patterns. At each level of matching, the bound variable structure is matched against the element structure. For example, a telephone book entry might be represented by:

( ( *forename* , *surname* ), *department* , *extension* )

such as:

```
-    (("Alice","Apple"),"Accounts",2222);
>    (("Alice","Apple"),"Accounts",2222) : (string * string) * string * int
```

Suppose we want to find someone's surname from their entry:

```
-    (* select surname *)
     fun surname ((f,s),d,e) = s;
>    val surname = fn : ('a * 'b) * 'c * 'd -> 'b
```

Here no operations are performed on **f**, **s**, **d** or **e** so they can be any types, say:

```
f : 'a
s : 'b
d : 'c
e : 'd
```

Consider:

```
-   surname (("Bill","Banana"),"Bakery",3210);
>   "Banana" : string
```

Here (**f,s**) matches (**"Bill","Banana"**), d matches **"Bakery"** and e matches **3210**. Furthermore, **f** matches **"Bill"** and **s** matches **"Banana"** so **"Banana"** is returned from **s**. Once again, as **f**, **d**, and **e** are not used they may be ignored:

```
-   fun surname ((_,s),_,_) = s;
>   val surname = fn : ('a * 'b) * 'c * 'd -> 'b
```

For pattern matching with tuples, constants may appear in the bound variable structure. Then, the tuple value to which the function is applied must have the same constants in the same position. For example, to return the name of someone if they are in the **"Cookery"** department:

```
-   (* select name from tuple with "Cookery" department *)
    fun cookname (n,"Cookery",_) = n;
>   val cookname = fn : 'a*string*'b -> 'a
```

Here, no operations are performed on **n** or _ so they can be any types, say:

```
n : 'a
_ : 'b
```

but the second element must be a string. Furthermore, for the match to succeed it must have the value **"Cookery"**. For example:

```
-   cookname (("Clare","Cherry"),"Cookery",2345);
>   ("Clare","Cherry") : string*string
```

Here **n** is set to (**"Clare","Cherry"**), **"Cookery"** matches **"Cookery"**, **2345** is ignored and (**"Clare","Cherry"**) is returned from **n**.

If the second element was not **"Cookery"** then the match would fail and a system exception would be raised. This function has only one case so a warning will be issued when the function is first defined that not all values have been catered for.

## 7.3 Tuples for accumulation variables

Tuples are useful when we want to accumulate a variety of information about a sequence of values. Here, a function might be defined with a tuple of accumulation variables. The tuple is initialized to appropriate values, updated as each element of the sequence is considered and passed on to the next stage. At the end of the sequence, the whole tuple is returned.

For example, suppose we want to find how many integers in a list are equal to, less than or greater than **0**. We can record the counts for each possibility in a tuple and return it when the end of the list is reached:

```
-   fun count1 (less,equal,greater) [] = (less,equal,greater) |
```

If the list starts with a 0 then we add 1 to **equal** and check the tail:

```
-   fun count1 (less,equal,greater) [] = (less,equal,greater) |
        count1 (less,equal,greater) (0::t) =
        count1 (less,equal+1,greater) t |
```

Similarly, if the list head is positive then **greater** is incremented. Otherwise **less** is incremented:

```
-   (* count integers less than, equal to or greater than zero
       in a list with accumulation tuple *)
    fun count1 (less,equal,greater) [] = (less,equal,greater) |
        count1 (less,equal,greater) (0::t) =
         count1 (less,equal+1,greater) t |
        count1 (less,equal,greater) (h::t) =
         if h>0
         then count1 (less,equal,greater+1) t
         else count1 (less+1,equal,greater) t;
>   val count1 = fn : int * int * int -> int list -> int * int * int
```

Initially, all counts are set to 0:

```
-   local
      fun count1 ... = ...
    in
     (* count integers less than, equal to or
        greater than zero in a list *)
     val count = count1 (0,0,0)
    end;
>   val count = fn : int list -> int * int * int
```

For example:

```
-   count [1,0,~2,0,3,0,~4,0,5];
>   (2,4,3) : int * int * int
```

because:

```
count [1,0,~2,0,3,0,~4,0,5] ==>
count1 (0,0,0) [1,0,~2,0,3,0,~4,0,5] ==>
count1 (0,0,1) [0,~2,0,3,0,~4,0,5] ==>
count1 (0,1,1) [~2,0,3,0,~4,0,5] ==>
count1 (1,1,1) [0,3,0,~4,0,5] ==>
count1 (1,2,1) [3,0,~4,0,5] ==>
count1 (1,2,2) [0,~4,0,5] ==>
count1 (1,3,2) [~4,0,5] ==>
count1 (2,3,2) [0,5] ==>
count1 (2,4,2) [5] ==>
count1 (2,4,3) [] ==>
(2,4,3)
```

## 7.4 Pattern matching with lists of tuples

A tuple of patterns is itself a pattern and so can appear in any other pattern. As well as list patterns with constants, variables and lists, we can use tuple patterns as parts of list patterns. We will now use tuples to represent things and lists of tuples to represent collections of things. When we are writing recursive functions to process a list of tuples it is typical to have a recursion case with a tuple pattern as the head of a list pattern. Many of the functions from the last two chapters can be used directly with tuple lists or with a little modification to reflect particular sorts of tuples.

For example, suppose we have a list of tuples of pairs and we want to swap the order of the elements in the tuple:

```
-   swap [("Anna","Ant"),("Bill","Bee"),("Clea","Cicada")];
>   [("Ant","Anna"),("Bee","Bill"),("Cicada","Clea")] : (string * string) list
```

**swap** is like **map** applied to a function that inverts the element of one pair:

```
-    (* reverse elements of two-element tuple *)
     fun inv (x,y) = (y,x);
>    val inv = 'a*'b -> 'b*'a

-    (* reverse all tuple elements in two-element tuple list *)
     val swap = map inv;
>    val swap = fn : ('a * 'b) list -> ('b * 'a) list
```

For the above example:

```
swap [("Anna","Ant"),("Bill","Bee"),("Clea","Cicada")] ==>
map inv [("Anna","Ant"),("Bill","Bee"),("Clea","Cicada")] ==>
inv ("Anna","Ant")::map inv [("Bill","Bee"),
    ("Clea","Cicada")] ==>
inv ("Anna","Ant")::
    inv ("Bill","Bee")::map inv [("Clea","Cicada")] ==>
inv ("Anna","Ant")::
    inv ("Bill","Bee")::inv ("Clea","Cicada")::map inv []
==>
("Ant","Anna")::("Bee","Bill")::("Cicada","Clea")::[] ==>
[("Ant","Anna"),("Bee","Bill"),("Cicada","Clea")]
```

For example, suppose we have a list of two element tuples and we want a list of the first elements only:

```
-    getfirsts [(1,1),(2,4),(3,9),(4,16)];
>    [1,2,3,4] : int list
```

Once again, **getfirsts** is like **map** applied to a function to get the first from a tuple:

```
-    (* select first element from two-element list *)
     fun first (x,_) = x;
>    val first = fn : 'a * 'b -> 'a

-    (* select first elements from list of two-element tuples *)
     val getfirsts = map first;
>    val getfirsts = fn : ('a * 'b) list -> 'a list
```

Thus:

```
getfirsts [(1,1),(2,4),(3,9),(4,16)] ==>
map first [(1,1),(2,4),(3,9),(4,16)] ==>
first (1,1)::map first [(2,4),(3,9),(4,16)] ==>
first (1,1)::first (2,4)::map first [(3,9),(4,16)] ==>
first (1,1)::first (2,4)::first (3,9)::map first [(4,16)] ==>
first (1,1)::
  first (2,4)::first (3,9)::first (4,16)::map first [] ==>
1::2::3::4::[] ==> [1,2,3,4]
```

All our polymorphic and higher order list functions apply to tuple lists.

## 7.5 Accumulation with lists

Consider separating a list of 2 element tuples into two lists, one for the first elements and one for the second elements:

```
-    unzip [("a",1),("b",2),("c",3)];
>    (["c","b","a"],[3,2,1]) : string list*int list
```

The two lists are accumulated in a tuple which is returned when the end of the original list is found:

```
-   fun unzip1 (f,s) [] = (f,s) |
```

If the list is not empty then the first element is added to the first list, the second element is added to the second list and the tuple is passed to the next stage:

```
-   (* split two-element tuple list into two
       singleton lists using accumulation lists *)
    fun unzip1 (f,s) [] = (f,s) |
        unzip1 (f,s) ((e1,e2)::t) = unzip1 (e1::f,e2::s) t;
>   val unzip1 = fn : 'a list * 'b list -> ('a * 'b) list -> 'a list * 'b list
```

No operations are performed on **e1** or **e2** so they may be any types, say:

```
e1 : 'a
e2 : 'b
```

Thus, **(e1,e2)::t** is an **('a*'b) list**. **e1** is joined to **f** so **f** must be an **'a list**. **e2** is joined to **s** so **s** must be a **'b list**. Thus, the result must be an:

```
'a list * 'b list
```

Initially, the accumulation lists are empty:

```
-   local
      fun unzip1 ... = ...
    in
      (* split two-element list into two singleton lists *)
      val unzip = unzip1 ([],[])
    end;
>   val unzip = fn : ('a * 'b) list -> 'a list * 'b list
```

For example:

```
-   unzip [(1.0,1),(2.0,2),(3.0,3)];
>   ([3.0,2.0,1.0],[3,2,1]) : real list * int list
```

because:

```
unzip [(1.0,1),(2.0,2),(3.0,3)] ==>
unzip1 ([],[]) [(1.0,1),(2.0,2),(3.0,3)] ==>
  (f,s) == ([],[])
  (e1,e2) == (1.0,1)
  t == [(2.0,2),(3.0,3)]
unzip1 ([1.0],[1]) [(2.0,2),(3.0,3)] ==>
  (f,s) == ([1.0],[1])
  (e1,e2) == (2.0,2)
  t == [(3.0,3)]
unzip1 ([2.0,1.0],[2,1]) [(3.0,3)] ==>
  (f,s) == ([2.0,1.0],[2,1])
  (e1,e2) == (3.0,3)
  t == []
unzip1 ([3.0,2.0,1.0],[3,2,1]) [] ==>
([3.0,2.0,1.0],[3,2,1])
```

Note that the element lists are in reverse order. We will see how to assemble them in the correct order later.

## 7.6 Generalized list find, delete and replace

In Chapter 5 we met functions to see if a list contained a value, to delete a value from a list and to replace a value in a list. We will now generalize these functions so that rather than looking for a specific value we look for a value satisfying some predicate **p**.

Consider finding the first element of a list satisfying predicate **p**:

```
-   (* find list element with property p *)
    fun findp _ b [] = b |
        findp p b (h::t) = if p h
                           then h
                           else findp b p t;
>   val findp = fn : ('a -> bool) -> 'a -> 'a list -> 'a
```

If the list does not contain the value then return the base value **b**. Otherwise, if the first element satisfies **p** then return it. Otherwise look in the rest of the list.

For example, to find the first record in a list of names and ages, represented as **string * int** tuples, with name set to **"jo"**:

```
-   fun isjo (name,_) = name="jo";
>   val isjo = fn : string * 'a -> bool
-   findp isjo [("pat",1),("chris",2),("jo",3),("les",4)];
>   ("jo",3) : string*int
```

because:

```
findp isjo ("fail",0)
           [("pat",1),("chris",2),("jo",3),("les",4)] ==>
findp isjo ("fail",0) [("chris",2),("jo",3),("les",4)] ==>
findp isjo ("fail",0) [("jo",3),("les",4)] ==>
("jo",3)
```

Consider deleting the first element of a list satisfying predicate **p**:

```
-   (* delete list element with property p *)
    fun deletep _ [] = [] |
        deletep p (h::t) = if p h
                           then t
                           else h::deletep p t;
>   val deletep = fn : ('a -> bool) -> 'a list -> 'a list
```

If **p** is true for the list head then return the list tail. Otherwise, put the head back onto deleting the first satisfying **p** in the tail.

For example, to delete the record with name **"jo"** in a list of name/age records:

```
-   deletep isjo [("pat",1),("chris",2),("jo",3),("les",4)];
>   [("pat",1),("chris",2),("les",4)] : (string * int) list
```

because:

```
deletep isjo [("pat",1),("chris",2),("jo",3),("les",4)] ==>
("pat",1)::deletep isjo [("chris",2),("jo",3),("les",4)] ==>
("pat",1)::("chris",2)::deletep isjo [("jo",3),("les",4)] ==>
("pat",1)::("chris",2)::[("les",4)] ==>
[("pat",1),("chris",2),("les",4)]
```

Similarly, consider replacing the first value satisfying predicate **p** in a list:

```
-   (* replace list element with property p *)
    fun replacep _ _ [] = [] |
        replacep p v (h::t) = if p h
                              then v::t
                              else h::replacep p v t;
>   val replacep = fn : ('a -> bool) -> 'a -> 'a list -> 'a list
```

If **p** is true for the list head then it is replaced with the new value. Otherwise the list head is joined to the result of making the replacement in the tail.

For example, to replace the record with name **"jo"** with a new record **("jo",4)**:

```
-   replacep isjo ("jo",4) [("pat",1),("chris",2),("jo",3),
    ("les",4)];
>   [("pat",1),("chris",2),("jo",4),("les",4)] : (string * int) list
```

because:

```
replacep isjo ("jo",4)
         [("pat",1),("chris",2),("jo",3),("les",4)] ==>
("pat",1)::
  replacep isjo ("jo",4) [("chris",2),("jo",3),("les",4)] ==>
("pat",1)::
("chris",2)::replacep isjo ("jo",4) [("jo",3),("les",4)] ==>
("pat",1)::("chris",2)::("jo",4)::[("les",4)] ==>
[("pat",1),("chris",2),("jo",4),("les",4)]
```

## 7.7 Example – telephone directory

We might represent someone's departmental telephone number as a tuple consisting of:

| name | – | string |
|------|---|--------|
| department | – | string |
| extension | – | integer |

For example:

| name | department | extension |
|------|-----------|-----------|
| Anna | Anatomy | 123 |

can be represented as:

```
-   ("Anna","Anatomy",123);
>   ("Anna","Anatomy",123) : string * string * int
```

A telephone directory might then be represented as a list of phone number tuples. For example the table:

| name | department | extension |
|------|-----------|-----------|
| Anna | Anatomy | 123 |
| Bill | Biology | 234 |
| Clea | Chemistry | 345 |
| Doug | Dentistry | 456 |
| Ellen | Biology | 567 |

can be represented by the tuple list:

```
-   val dir = [("Anna","Anatomy",123),
               ("Bill","Biology",234),
               ("Clea","Chemistry",345),
               ("Doug","Dentistry",456),
               ("Ellen","Biology",567)];
>   val dir =    [("Anna","Anatomy",123),
                ("Bill","Biology",234),
                ("Clea","Chemistry",345),
                ("Doug","Dentistry",456),
                ("Ellen","Biology",567)] : (string * string * int) list
```

To find the number for a given name we can use **findp** again:

```
-    (* find record for given name in directory *)
     fun findn n = findp (fn (n1,_,_) => n1=n)
                         ("fail","fail",0);
>    val findn = fn : string -> (string * string * int) list -> string * string * int
```

Note that we cannot use **findp** directly. Instead we define a predicate:

```
fn (n1,_,_) => n1=n
```

that refers to the bound variable **n** for the required name.

Note that **n1** and **n** are compared so they must have the same equality type, say ''**a**. No operations are performed on the other anonymous tuple elements so they can be any types. For example:

```
-    findn "Clea" [("Anna","Anatomy",123),
                   ("Bill","Biology",234),
                   ("Clea","Chemistry",345)];
>    ("Clea","Chemistry",345) : string * string * int
```

We can insert a new entry into a directory in name alphabetic order using the general purpose insertion function from Chapter 6:

```
fun insert _ v [] = [v] |
    insert p v (l as h::t) = if p v h
                             then v::l
                             else h::insert p v t
```

We need to define a comparison function for directory records which checks if one record's name comes before another record's name:

```
-    (* does one record come before another in name order? *)
     fun nless (n1:string,_,_) (n2,_,_) = n1<n2;
>    val nless = fn : string*'a*'b -> string *'c*'d -> bool
```

Now we can define the directory insertion function:

```
-    (* insert record into directory in name order *)
     val dinsert = insert nless;
>    val dinsert = fn : string*'a*'b -> (string*' a *'b) list (string*' a *'b) list
```

For example:

```
-    dinsert ("Dora","Debts",777) [("Anna","Anatomy",123)
                                   ("Bil"    Biology",234),
                                   ("Clea", "Chemistry",345)];
>    [("Anna","Anatomy",123),
     ("Bill","Biology",234),
     ("Clea","Chemistry",345),
     ("Dora","Debts",777)] : (string * string*int) list
```

Suppose we want to find all the people in the same department. We can use **filter** with a new predicate to match the department in a tuple with a required department:

```
-    (* find all records in directory with given department *)
     fun samedept d = filter (fn (_,d1,_) => d=d1);
>    val samedept = fn : ''a -> ('b*''a * 'c) list -> ('b * ''a * 'c) list
```

For example:

```
-    samedept "Biology" dir;
>    [("Bill","Biology",234),
     ("Ellen","Biology",567)] : (string * string * int) list
```

Suppose we want to change someone's record with **replacep**:

```
-   (* replace record with given name in directory *)
    fun changer (n,d,e) =
        replacep (fn (n1,_,_) => n1=n)(n,d,e);
>   val changer = fn : ''a * 'b * 'c ->
                        (''a * 'b * 'c) list ->
                        (''a * 'b * 'c) list
```

For example:

```
-   val newdir = changer ("Clea","Computing",987) dir;
>   val newdir = [("Anna","Anatomy",123),
                  ("Bill","Biology",234),
                  ("Clea","Computing",987),
                  ("Doug","Dentistry",456),
                  ("Ellen","Biology",567)] : (string * string * int) list
```

## 7.8 Example – stock control

Consider a stock record:

( *item* , *stock level* , *reorder level* )

The *item* is the name of an item held in stock. The *stock level* is the number of *item* currently in stock. When the *stock level* falls below the *reorder level* the item should be reordered. For example:

| item | level | reorder |
|------|-------|---------|
| bath | 200   | 150     |

which could be represented as a tuple:

```
-   ("bath",200,150);
>   ("bath",200,150) : string * int * int
```

An example table of stock records is:

| item | level | reorder |
|------|-------|---------|
| bath | 200   | 150     |
| tap  | 200   | 300     |
| sink | 75    | 200     |
| tile | 3000  | 1500    |

which can be represented as a list of tuples:

```
-   [("bath",200,150),("tap",200,300),
     ("sink",75,200),("tile",3000,1500)];
>   [("bath",200,150),("tap",200,300),
     ("sink",75,200),("tile",3000,1500)] : (string * int * int) list
```

Consider deleting the record for item i using **deletep**:

```
-   (* delete record with name i from stock list *)
    fun deleter i = deletep (fn (i1,_,_) => i1=i);
>   val deleter = fn : ''a -> (''a * 'b * 'c) list -> (''a * 'b * 'c) list
```

**deleter** is polymorphic and will delete the tuple with a given first element from a list of arbitrary three-element tuples. For example:

```
-   deleter "sink" [("bath",200,150),("tap",200,300),
                    ("sink",75,200),("tile",3000,1500)];
>   [("bath",200,150),("tap",200,300), ("tile",3000,1500)] :
    (string * int * int) list
```

Consider finding all the records for items whose *stock levels* are less than the *reorder levels.* Here we can use **filter** applied to a function to check if the stock level is less than the reorder level:

```
-    (* is stock level less than reorder level? *)
     fun less_stock (_,s:int,r) = s<r;
>    val less_stock = fn : 'a * int * int -> bool

- (* find all stock with stock level less
      than reorder level in stock list *)
     val reorder = filter less_stock;
>    val reorder = fn : ('a * int * int) list -> ('a * int * int) list
```

For example:

```
-    reorder [("bath",200,150),("tap",200,300),
                ("sink",75,200),("tile",3000,1500)];
>    [("tap",200,300),("sink",75,200)] : (string * int * int) list
```

Consider finding out how many of each item need to be reordered to bring the stock level back to the reorder level. If the list is empty then return the empty list. If the first item needs to be reordered then put a tuple for the item and the difference between the reorder and stock levels onto the result of checking the rest of the list. Otherwise check the rest of the list:

```
-    (* for each record with stock level less than reorder
         level in a stock list, find quantity needed to bring
         stock level up to reorder level *)
     fun needed [] = [] |
         needed ((i,(l:int),r)::t) =
     if l<r
     then (i,r-1)::needed t
     else needed t;
>    val needed = fn : ('a * int * int) list -> ('a * int) list
```

One of l and r must be typed as they are compared with the overloaded <. i may be any type. For example:

```
-    needed [("bath",200,150),("tap",200,300),
                ("sink",75,200),("tile",3000,1500)];
>    [("tap",100),("sink",125)] : (string * int) list
```

because:

```
needed [("bath",200,150),("tap",200,300),
        ("sink",75,200),("tile",3000,1500)] ==>
needed
  [("tap",200,300),("sink",75,200),("tile",3000,1500)] ==>
("tap",100)::
  (needed [("sink",75,200),("tile",3000,1500)]) ==>
("tap",100)::
 ("sink",125)::
  (needed [("tile",3000,1500)]) ==>
("tap",100)::
 ("sink",125)::
  (needed []) ==>
("tap",100)::
 ("sink",125)::
  [] ==>
[("tap",100),("sink",125)]
```

Consider updating the stock level for a given item i by a given amount a. If the list is empty then return the empty list. If the first record is for the required item then add the amount to the stock level making a new tuple and put it in front of the rest of the records. Otherwise put the first tuple onto the result of performing the update in the rest of the records:

```
-    (* increment stock level in record for given item in stock
        list *)
     fun update _ [] = [] |
         update (i,a:int) ((i1,l1,r1)::t) =
      if i=i1 then (i1,l1+a,r1)::t
      else (i1,l1,r1)::update (i,a) t;
>    val update = fn : ''a*int -> (''a * int * 'b) list -> (''a * int * 'b) list
```

i1 and i are only compared with the polymorphic = so they may have the same equality type ''a. r1 is not used so it may have any type, say 'b. a or l1 must be typed explicitly for the addition. They have the same int type. For example:

```
-    update ("sink",200) [("bath",200,150),("tap",200,300),
                              ("sink",75,200),("tile",3000,1500)];
>    [("bath",200,150),("tap",200,300),
      ("sink",275,200),("tile",3000,1500)] : (string * int * int) list
```

because:

```
update ("sink",200) [("bath",200,150),("tap",200,300),
                        ("sink",75,200),("tile",3000,1500)] ==>
("bath",200,150)::
 update ("sink",200) [("tap",200,300),
                        ("sink",75,200),("tile",3000,1500)] ==>
("bath",200,150)::
 ("tap",200,300)::
  update ("sink",200)
          [("sink",75,200),("tile",3000,1500)] ==>
("bath",200,150)::
 ("tap",200,300)::
  ("sink",275,200)::[("tile",3000,1500)] ==>
[("bath",200,150),("tap",200,300),
 ("sink",275,200),("tile",3000,1500)]
```

A list of updates might be represented by a list of tuples of items and amounts, for example:

```
-    [("tap",150),("tile",200),("bath",50)];
>    [("tap",150),("tile",200),("bath",50)] : (string * int) list
```

Consider updating a list of stock records from a list of updates. If the update list is empty then return the record list. Otherwise, use the first update record to update the new record list from using the rest of the update records to process the original record list. Here we can use foldr to apply update with each of the update records in turn. We use the original record list as the base case to be returned by foldr when there are no update records left:

```
-    (* update stock list from reorder list *)
     val updateall = foldr update;
>    val updateall = fn : (''a * int * 'b) list ->
                           (''a * int) list ->
                           (''a * int * 'b) list
```

For example:

```
-   updateall [("bath",200,150),("tap",200,300),
               ("sink",75,200),("tile",3000,1500)]
              [("tap",150),("tile",200),("bath",50)];
>   [("bath",250,150),("tap",350,300),
      ("sink",75,200),("tile",3200,1500)] : (string * int * int) list
```

because:

```
updateall [("bath",200,150),("tap",200,300),
           ("sink",75,200),("tile",3000,1500)]
          [("tap",150),("tile",200),("bath",50)] ==>

foldr update [("bath",200,150),("tap",200,300),
              ("sink",75,200),("tile",3000,1500)]
             [("tap",150),("tile",200),("bath",50)] ==>

update ("tap",150)
 (foldr update [("bath",200,150),("tap",200,300),
                ("sink",75,200),("tile",3000,1500)]
               [("tile",200),("bath",50)]) ==>

update ("tap",150)
 (update ("tile",200)
  (foldr update [("bath",200,150),("tap",200,300),
                 ("sink",75,200),("tile",3000,1500)]
                [("bath",50)])) ==>

update ("tap",150)
 (update ("tile",200)
  (update ("bath",50)
   (foldr update [("bath",200,150),("tap",200,300),
                  ("sink",75,200),("tile",3000,1500)]
                 [])) ==>

update ("tap",150)
 (update ("tile",200)
  (update ("bath",50)
   [("bath",200,150),("tap",200,300),
    ("sink",75,200),("tile",3000,1500)])) ==>

update ("tap",150)
 (update ("tile",200)
   [("bath",250,150),("tap",200,300),
    ("sink",75,200),("tile",3000,1500)]) ==>

update ("tap",150)
 [("bath",250,150),("tap",200,300),
  ("sink",75,200),("tile",3200,1500)] ==>

[("bath",250,150),("tap",350,300),
 ("sink",75,200),("tile",3200,1500)]
```

## 7.9 Type expressions and type abbreviations

We have seen that we can specify a variable's type with a type expression built
from type constructors like **int**, **real**, **string**, **bool** and **list**. So far, a type
expression may be a single type constructor or a type variable or a function
type or a tuple type or a bracketed type expression or a type expression or the
**list** type constructor.

SML enables the use of abbreviated types as a shorthand for type expressions. A name may be associated with a type expression using a type binding of the form:

**type** *name* = *type expression*

The *name* is an identifier which may be used in subsequent type expressions. For example, in the telephone directory example we are using entries of type:

**string \* string \* int**

and entry lists of type

**(string \* string \* int) list**

These do not tell us much about what they represent. We might rename the directory entry type by:

```
-   type person = string;
>   type person = string

-   type department = string;
>   type department = string

-   type extension = int;
>   type extension = int

-   type entry = person * department * extension;
>   type entry = person * department * extension
```

and the directory type by:

```
-   type directory = entry list;
>   type directory = entry list
```

We could now write a function to find everyone on the same extension using the new types:

```
-   (* find all records in directory with given extension *)
    fun findext e [] = [] |
        findext (e:extension) (((n1,d1,e1)::t):directory) =
     if e = e1
     then (n1,d1,e1)::findext e t
     else findext e t;
>   val findext = fn : extension ->
                        (person * department * extension) list ->
                        (person * department * extension) list
```

Here, we have been explicit about **e** being an **extension** and the list **(n1, d1,e1)::t** being a **directory**. This is a bit more long-winded than the lack of explicit types in the previous section but it makes it easier to read the function. Here, the type definitions help us rather than the computer: they make us focus on the intended meaning of the data values rather than the way in which they are represented.

Note that a new type constructor is syntactically equivalent to its defining expression. Thus, if we define:

```
-   type whole_numb = int;
>   type whole_numb = int

-   type integer = int;
>   type integer = int
```

then values of type **whole_numb, integer** and **int** may be used in the same places without causing type errors. This form of type binding just disguises a longer type expression.

## 7.10 Curried and uncurried functions

You may have noticed that a function with a tuple argument is apparently similar to nested functions of single arguments. For example, suppose we want to calculate:

**a\*x\*x+b\*x+c**

We could write:

```
-   fun quad1 a b c (x:int) = a*x*x+b*x+c;
>   val quad1 = fn : int -> int -> int -> int -> int
```

So that:

```
-   quad1 1 2 1 3;
>   16 : int
```

Alternatively, we could put **a, b, c** and **x** together into a tuple:

```
-   fun quad2 (a,b,c,x:int) = a*x*x+b*x*c;
>   val quad2 = fn : int * int * int * int -> int
```

and pass the values in all together:

```
-   quad2 (1,2,1,3);
>   16 : int
```

The first form, where functions of single bound variables are nested, is known as a curried function, after Haskell Curry, the American mathematical logician. The second form, using a single function with a tuple of bound variables, is known as an uncurried function.

Curried functions may be converted to uncurried by running all the nested bound variables into a single tuple. We can generalize for a specific depth of nesting with a higher order function. For example, consider a function of an arbitrary bound variable whose body is another function of an arbitrary bound variable:

```
-   fun F X Y = ...
>   val F = fn : 'a -> 'b -> 'c
```

This may be converted to an uncurried function, that is a function which is called with a tuple of arguments for **x** and **y**:

```
-   (* convert curried to uncurried *)
    fun uncurry f (x,y) = f x y;
>   val uncurry = fn : ('a -> 'b -> 'c) -> 'a * 'b -> 'c
```

We can use this to uncurry **F** above:

```
-   val uncurry_F = uncurry F;
>   val uncurry_F = fn : 'a * 'b -> 'c
```

Thus, calling **uncurry _F** with a tuple of two values, say *value1* and *value2*, is equivalent to calling **F** with the first value and calling the result with the second value:

```
    uncurry_F ( value1 , value2 ) ==>
    uncurry F ( value1 , value2 ) ==>
    F value1 value2
```

Here, the uncurried function **uncurry _F** was called with a tuple of two values which were unpacked through pattern matching and passed to the curried function **F**.

Similarly, an arbitrary two-variable uncurried function:

```
    -    fun G (X,Y) = ...
    >    val G = fn : 'a * 'b -> 'c
```

may be converted to curried form with a higher order function which parcels up the nested arguments into a tuple:

```
    -    (* convert uncurried to curried *)
         fun curry f x y = f (x,y);
    >    val curry = fn : ('a * 'b -> 'c) -> 'a -> 'b -> 'c
```

For example, we can curry **G**:

```
    -    val curry_G = curry G;
    >    val curry_G = fn : 'a -> 'b -> 'c
```

Calling **curry _G** with two nested values is equivalent to calling **G** with a tuple of those variables:

```
    curry_G value1 value2 ==>
    curry G value1 value2 ==>
    G ( value1 , value2 )
```

Here, the curried function **curry_G** was called with two values which were packed up into a tuple and passed to the uncurried function **G**.

In general, curried functions have equivalent uncurried versions and vice versa. The advantage of the curried form is that the outer bound variables can be frozen to make a specialized function. For example, for:

```
    x*x+2*x+3
```

we can write:

```
    -    val quad1_123 = quad1 1 2 3;
    >    val quad1_123 = fn: int -> int
```

with the curried version. The same effect with the uncurried version is much more long-winded:

```
    -    fun quad2_123 x = quad2 (1,2,3,x);
    >    val quad2_123 = fn : int -> int
```

as we have to make the bound variable **x** explicit to place it in the tuple. However, uncurried functions may be implemented more efficiently as the system does not need to keep track of the function nesting.

## 7.11 Summary

In this chapter we have looked at list processing with tuples. We have seen how we can use tuples to represent things as fixed groups of different types of property values and lists to represent variable length collections of the same type of thing. We have used or modified our list processing functions from the previous chapters to manipulate tuple lists. We also looked at type abbreviations as a way of specifying types with names that are meaningful to us. Finally, we looked at the relationship between curried and uncurried functions.

In the next chapter, we will consider the use of list processing techniques for elementary text processing.

## 7.12 Exercises

1) Identify the types of the following functions:

a) ```
fun a [] = [] |
    a ((x,y)::t) = x::a t
```

b) ```
fun b [] = [] |
    b ((x,y,z)::t) = x+y/z::b t
```

c) ```
fun c _ [] = [] |
    c f ((x,y)::t) = f x y::c f t
```

d) ```
fun d [] = [] |
    d ((p,q)::t) = p q::d t
```

e) ```
fun e _ [] = [] |
    e f ((x,y)::t) = (f x,f y)::e f t
```

f) ```
fun f ((x1,y1)::t1) ((x2,y2)::t2) =
      (x1,x2,y1,y2)::f t1 t2 |
    f _ _ = []
```

g) ```
fun g f ((x1,y1)::t1) ((x2,y2)::t2) =
      if f x1 x2
      then (y1,y2)::g f t1 t2
      else g f t1 t2 |
    g _ _ _ = []
```

h) ```
fun h ((x1,y1)::t1) ((x2,y2)::t2) =
      (x1 x2,y1 y2)::h t1 t2 |
    h _ _ _ = []
```

2) Write functions to solve the following problems.

   a) Given a list of pairs of integers, write a function to form a new list by adding the elements from each pair together:
   ```
   -  addpair [(1,1),(2,2),(3,3)];
   >  [2,4,6] : int list
   ```
   without using **map**. What is the type of this function?

   b) Given a list of pairs of strings, form a new list by joining the elements from each pair together:
   ```
   -  joinpair [("Happy","Birthday"),
                ("Good","Morning"),
                ("Hot","Dog")];
   >  ["HappyBirthday","GoodMorning","HotDog"] : string list
   ```
   without using **map**. What is the type of this function?

   c) Given a list of pairs of strings and integers, form a list of booleans which indicates whether or not each string has the associated integer as its length:
   ```
   -  checksize [("cat",4),("dog",3),("ant",2)];
   >  [false,true,false] : bool list
   ```

without using **map**. What is the type of this function?

   d) Use **map** to define the functions from a), b) and c) above.

3) A name may be represented as a tuple of a given name and a family name.

   a) Write a function which inserts a name into a list of names in ascending alphabetical order of family name. For two names with the same family name, the given name is used to determine the order:

```
-  ninsert ("Pat","Penguin")
   [("Chris","Cat"),("Zoe","Zebra")];
>  [("Chris","Cat"),("Pat","Penguin"),("Zoe","Zebra")] :
   (string * string) list

-  ninsert ("Ziggy","Zebra")
   [("Chris","Cat"),("Zoe","Zebra")];
>  [("Chris","Cat"),("Ziggy","Zebra"),("Zoe","Zebra")] :
   (string * string) list
```

What is the type of this function?

   b) Write a function to sort a list of names in order of the length of the family name:

```
-  nsort
   [("Chris","Cat"),("Pat","Penguin"),("Zoe","Zebra")];
>  [("Chris","Cat"),("Zoe","Zebra"),("Pat","Penguin")] :
   (string * string) list
```

What is the type of this function?

   c) Use **map** to define a function which given a list of names returns a list of tuples of given name and family name lengths:

```
-  name_lengths
   [("Chris","Cat"),("Pat","Penguin"),("Zoe","Zebra")];
>  [(5,3),(3,7),(3,5)] : (int*int) list
```

What is the type of this function?

4) Exam marks for one person may be held as a tuple of their name, as in 3) above, and a list of integer marks. For example, the following table:

| given | family | mark1 | mark2 | mark3 ... |
|-------|--------|-------|-------|-----------|
| Allan | Anchor | 45 | 56 | 78 |
| Betty | Boat | 75 | 80 | |
| Colin | Compass | 33 | 39 | 41 |

would be represented as:

```
-  [(("Allan","Anchor"),[45,56,78]),
    (("Betty","Boat"),[75,80]),
    (("Colin","Compass"),[33,39,41])];
>  [(("Allan","Anchor"),[45,56,78]),
    (("Betty","Boat"),[75,80]),
    (("Colin","Compass"),[33,39,41])] : (string * string) * int list
```

   a) Write a function which given a name, a mark and a list of exam marks adds the mark to the integer mark list for the name. If the name is not in the list then add a new pair for that name with a list containing that mark:

```
-  addmark ("Betty","Boat") 55
          [(("Allan","Anchor"),[45,56,78]),
           (("Betty","Boat"),[75,80]),
           (("Colin","Compass"),[33,39,41])];
```

```
>   [(("Allan","Anchor"),[45,56,78]),
     (("Betty","Boat"),[55,75,80]),
     (("Colin","Compass"),[33,39,41])] : (string * int list) list

-   addmark ("Betty","Boat") 55
            [(("Allan","Anchor"),[45,56,78]),
             (("Colin","Compass"),[33,39,41])];
>   [(("Allan","Anchor"),[45,56,78]),
     (("Colin","Compass"),[33,39,41]),
     (("Betty","Boat"),[55])] : (string * int list) list
```

What is the type of this function?

b) Write a function which given a name and a list of exam marks returns the list of individual marks for the name:

```
-   getmarks ("Colin","Compass")
            [(("Allan","Anchor"),[45,56,78]),
             (("Betty","Boat"),[55,75,80]),
             (("Colin","Compass"),[33,39,41])];
>   [33,39,41] : int list
```

What is the type of this function?

c) Write a function which given a list of exam marks finds the average mark for each person, using **map**:

```
-   avmark [(("Allan","Anchor"),[45,56,78]),
             (("Betty","Boat"),[55,75,80]),
             (("Colin","Compass"),[33,39,41])];
>   [(("Allan","Anchor"),59),
     (("Betty","Boat"),70),
     (("Colin","Compass"),37)] : ((string * string) * int) list
```

What is the type of this function?

5) In a simple graphics system, lines are represented by tuples of start and finish $x/y$ coordinates. For example:

```
from 4,5 to 8,9 ==
```

```
x1 y1 x2 y2
4  5  8  9
```

is represented by:

```
(4,5,8,9)
```

Similarly, a table of lines, for example:

```
x1 y1 x2 y2
4  5  8  9
1  1  1  7
2  3  6  3
3  6  6  3
```

is represented as a list of tuples:

```
-   [(4,5,8,9),(1,1,1,7),(2,3,6,3),(3,6,6,3)];
>   [(4,5,8,9),(1,1,1,7),(2,3,6,3),(3,6,6,3)] :
     (int * int * int * int) list
```

Lines may be horizontal from left to right, vertical from top to bottom, or diagonal from top or bottom left to bottom or top right. For horizontal lines the $x$ coordinates must be the same. For vertical lines the $y$ coordinates must be the same. For diagonal lines, the difference between the $x$

coordinates must be the same as the difference betweeen the $y$ coordinates.

a)   Write a function to return a tuple to indicate the class of a line:

```
-    lclass (4,3,7,3);
>    ("horiz",(4,3,7,3)) : string * (int * int * int * int)
-    lclass (3,4,3,7);
>    ("vert",(3,4,3,7)) : string * (int * int * int * int)
-    lclass (7,9,11,13);
>    ("diag",(7,9,11,13) : string * (int * int * int * int)
```

What is the type of this function?

b)   Write a function which given a list of lines returns a list of line class tuples, using **map** and the function from a). What is the type of this function?

c)   Write a function which given a horizonal line tuple returns all the points on the line as $x/y$ coordinate tuples:

```
-    hpoints (4,3,7,3);
>    [(4,3),(5,3),(6,3),(7,3)] : (int * int) list
```

If the start $x$ coordinate is bigger than the finish $x$ coordinate then return the empty list. Otherwise put a tuple for the start point onto the list for the line from the start point with incremented $x$ coordinate. What is the type of this function?

d)   Write a function which given a vertical line tuple returns all the points on the line as a list of $x/y$ coordinate tuples:

```
-    vpoints (3,4,3,7);
>    [(3,4),(3,5),(3,6),(3,7)] : (int * int) list
```

What is the type of this function?

e)   Write a function which given a predicate **final** and a function **next** and a line tuple, returns the empty list if **final** is true for the line tuple. Otherwise, it joins the start point from the tuple onto the result of applying the function itself to the line tuple after **next** is applied to it. What is the type of this function?

f)   define the functions from c) and d) using the function from e).

g)   Write a function which given a list of line classes returns a list of lists of points for all the horizontal lines. What is the type of this function?

6)  A car park computer holds records of when cars enter as integer hours, minutes and seconds. A time:

```
hour minute second
12    35      16
```

may be represented as a tuple:

```
-    (12,35,16);
>    (12,35,16) : int * int * int
```

a)   Write a function to convert a time tuple into seconds. What is the type of this function?

b)   Write a function to convert a time in seconds into a time tuple. What is the type of this function?

When a car enters the car park, a record is kept of the registration number as a string and the entry time. A record, for example

```
number   hour  minute second
ABC 123  15     9        27
```

may be represented by tuple of the registration number and time:

```
-   ("ABC 123",(15,9,27));
>   ("ABC 123",(15,9,27)) : string * (int * int * int)
```

and a table of car entry records:

```
number      hour      minute    second
ABC 123     15        9         27
XSG 309     17        15        40
OSX 786     21        37        17
```

may be represented by a tuple list:

```
-   [("ABC 123",(15,9,27)),
     ("XSG 309",(17,15,40)),
     ("OSX 786",(21,37,17))];
>   [("ABC 123",(15,9,27)),
     ("XSG 309",(17,15,40)),
     ("OSX 786",(21,37,17))] : (string * (int * int * int)) list
```

c)  Write a function which adds an entry record to a list of entry records in ascending order of registration number. What is the type of this function?

d)  Write a function which given a registration number, an exit time and an entry list, returns the time spent by the car in the car park in seconds. What is the type of this function?

A long-term list is kept of how long each car spends in the car park. Each record consists of a tuple of a registration number and a cumulative time in seconds.

e)  Write a function which, given a car's registration number, a time in seconds and a long-term list, updates the cumulative time for that car by adding the new time to the cumulative time in its record. If there is no record in the list for that registration number then a new one should be created with the time as the initial cumulative time. What is the type of this function?

f)  Write a function which returns the record in the long-term list with the longest cumulative time. What is the type of this function?

7)  Dates consisting of integer day, month and year, for example:

```
day     month    year
15      2        1997
```

may be represented as tuples:

```
-   (15,2,1997);
>   (15,2,1997) : int * int * int
```

a)  Write a function to convert an integer month to the equivalent string, for example:

```
-   month 5;
>   "May" : string
```

What is the type of this function?

A table of dates, for example:

```
day    month   year
17     3       1997
24     9       2001
5      11      1995
```

may be represented as a list of tuples:

- `[(17,3,1997),(24,9,2001),(5,11,1995)];`
> `[(17,3,1997),(24,9,2001),(5,11,1995)] : (int * int * int) list`

b) Write a function which given a list of dates converts it to a list of dates with string months using **map**:

- `mconv [(17,3,1997),(24,9,2001),(5,11,1995)];`
> `[(17,"March",1997),(24,"September",2001),(5,"November",1995)] : (int * string * int) list`

What is the type of this function?

c) Write a function which given a list of dates returns all those in a given year. The result list should have string months. What is the type of this function?

d) Write a function which adds a value to a list provided that value is not in the list already. What is the type of this function?

e) Use the function from d) to write a function which, given one date and a list of years, adds the year from that date to the list of years if it is not already in the list. What is the type of this function?

f) Use the function from e) to write a function to find all the unique years in a list of dates. It will be applied to a list of unique years, initially empty, and a list of dates. What is the type of this function?

g) Write a function which adds a date to a list of dates in ascending date order. What is the type of this function?

h) Write a function that counts how many dates in a list have a specific year. What is the type of this function?

8) A road monitor notes the vehicles that pass it. When a sequence of the same vehicle passes the monitor they are counted. At the end of the day all the vehicle sequence records are returned with the records in the order in which the corresponding sequences passed the monitor. A record is a string vehicle name and an integer count of the number of vehicles in that sequence. For example, the table of records:

```
vehicle number
car       3
bus       1
car       5
lorry     2
bus       1
```

may be represented by the list of tuples:

- `[("car",3),("bus",1),("car",5),("lorry",2),("bus",1)];`
> `[("car",3),("bus",1),("car",5),("lorry",2),("bus",1)] : (string * int) list`

a) Write a function to find all the sequence records with a given name using **filter**. What is the type of this function?

b) Write a function to count how many vehicles with a given name passed the monitor in total. What is the type of this function?

c) Write a function to insert a sequence record into a list of sequence records in ascending vehicle name order. Where two records have the same name they should be inserted in ascending vehicle number order. What is the type of this function?

d) Write a function to delete the first sequence record with a given vehicle name from a list of records. What is the type of this function?

e) Write a function to delete the ith sequence record with a given vehicle name from a list of records. What is the type of this function?

f) Write a function to find the name of the vehicle with the highest sequence number from a list of records. What is the type of this function?

9) In a bank, exchange rate records are held for each currency. For example, if 1 pound is worth 9.8 francs, 2161.1 lire or 1.4 ecu then the record is:

```
currency   rate1   to1     rate2   to2      rate3 to3 ...
pound      9.8     franc   2161.1 lire      1.4   ecu
```

which may be represented as a tuple of a string and a list of tuples:

```
-   ("pound",[(9.8,"franc"),(2161.1,"lire"),(1.4,"ecu")]);
>   ("pound",[(9.8,"franc"),(2161.1,"lire"),(1.4,"ecu")]) :
    string*(real*string) list
```

a) Write a function which, given a record for a currency and the string name of another currency, finds the exchange rate for converting from the first to the second currency. What is the type of this function?

b) Write a function which, given a currency and a list of exchange rate records, finds the record for that currency. What is the type of this function?

Exchange rate request records are held as tuples. For example, if 5 pounds is to be converted to ecu then the request record is:

```
-   ("pound",5.0,"ecu");
>   ("pound",5.0,"ecu") : string * real * string
```

c) Write a function which, given an exchange request record and a list of exchange rate records, finds the result of converting the specified amount of the first currency in the request record to the second currency in the request record. The result should be returned as a tuple of a currency name and an amount. What is the type of this function?

d) Write a function using that from c) which, given a list of exchange rate records and a list of exchange request records, returns a list of results for those requests. What is the type of this function?

# CHAPTER 8
# Text processing

## 8.1 Introduction
In this chapter we are going to apply the list processing techniques from Chapters 5 and 6 to text processing. We will treat a text as a list of single letter strings and develop general list processing functions for locating and manipulating one list within another list.

## 8.2 String to list conversion
SML provides built in functions for converting between strings and lists of strings. The function:

```
explode
```

turns a string into a list of single letter strings:

```
-   explode "banana";
>   ["b","a","n","a","n","a"] : string list
-   explode;
>   fn : string - > string list
```

The function:

```
implode
```

turns a list of strings into a single string by joining the strings end to end:

```
-   implode ["p","o","t","a","t","o"];
>   "potato" : string
-   implode;
>   fn : string list - > string
```

For text processing based on strings, it is most efficient to have an outer level function which **explode**s the strings, calls other functions to process them and then **implode**s the result. Text processing then reduces to list processing.

## 8.3 Text editing
Editors usually provide facilities to find, add, delete and replace text. We will now look at how to implement equivalent low level editing functions based on string processing.

### 8.3.1 Does one string start another?

Consider checking whether a string starts with another string:

```
-   starts "the" "the cat sat on the dog";
>   true : bool
```

We **explode** the strings and call an auxiliary function to check if the first list starts the second list:

```
-   local
      fun starts1 ... = ...
    in
    (* does one string start another? *)
    fun starts s1 s2 = starts1 (explode s1) (explode s2)
    end;
>   val starts = fn : string -> string -> bool
```

We assume that **starts1** returns a **bool**. **s1** and **s2** must be of type **string** because they are arguments to **explode**.

The problem now reduces to checking if one list starts another list. If the first list is empty then checking has succeeded: it has been found completely in the second list. If the second list is empty then checking has failed: there is no more second list to check. If the first element of the first list is the first element of the second list then check if the tail of the first list starts the tail of the second list. Otherwise, the check fails:

```
-   (* does one list start another? *)
    fun starts1 [] _ = true |
        starts1 _ [] = false |
        starts1 (h1::t1) (h2::t2) =
          if h1=h2
          then starts1 t1 t2
          else false;
>   val starts1 = fn : ''a list -> ''a list -> bool
```

**h1** and **h2** are compared with polymorphic = but no other operations are applied to them. Thus, they can both have the same equality type **''a**. For example:

```
-   starts "the" "the cat";
>   true: bool
```

because:

```
starts "the" "the cat" ==>
starts1 ["t","h","e"] ["t","h","e"," ","c","a","t"] ==>
starts1 ["h","e"] ["h","e"," ","c","a","t"] ==>
starts1 ["e"] ["e"," ","c","a","t"] ==>
starts1 [] [" ","c","a","t"] ==>
true
```

Note that:

```
h1=h2 andalso starts1 t1 t2
```

could be used instead of:

```
if h1=h2
then starts1 t1 t2
else false
```

**andalso** is a sequential operator which returns **false** if the first operand is **false**, without evaluating the second operand.

### 8.3.2. Does one string contain another?

Consider checking if one string is contained in another string:

```
-    contains "beans" "eat beans";
>    true : bool
```

Once again, the strings are **explode**d and an auxiliary function is called:

```
-    local
       fun contains1 ... = ...
     in
       (* does one string contain another? *)
       fun contains s1 s2 = contains1 (explode s1) (explode s2)
     end;
>    val contains = fn : string -> string -> bool
```

We assume that **contains1** returns a value of type **bool**.

**contains1** checks if an arbitrary typed list is contained in another list of the same type. If the second list is empty then the check fails. If the first list starts the second list then the check succeeds. Otherwise check if the first list is contained in the tail of the second list:

```
-    (* does one list contain another? *)
     fun contains1 _ [] = false |
         contains1 l1 (l2 as _::t2) =
           if starts1 l1 l2
           then true
           else contains1 l1 t2;
>    val contains1 = fn : ''a list -> ''a list -> bool
```

As before, **l1** and **l2** may be arbitrary equality typed lists but of the same type. For example:

```
-    contains "and" "stand up";
>    true : bool
```

because:

```
contains "and" "stand up" ==>
contains1 ["a","n","d"] ["s","t","a","n","d"," ","u","p"] ==>
  starts1 ["a","n","d"] ["s","t","a","n","d"," ","u","p"] ==>
     false
contains1 ["a","n","d"] ["t","a","n","d"," ","u","p"] ==>
  starts1 ["a","n","d"] ["t","a","n","d"," ","u","p"] ==>
     false
contains1 ["a","n","d"] ["a","n","d"," ","u","p"] ==>
  starts1 ["a","n","d"] ["a","n","d"," ","u","p"] ==>
     true
```

Note that:

```
starts1 l1 (h2::t2) orelse contains l1 t2
```

could be used instead of:

```
if starts1 l1 (h2::t2)
then true
else contains l1 t2
```

**orelse** is a sequential operator which returns **true** if its first operand is **true**, without evaluating the second operand.

### 8.3.3 Delete one string from another

Consider deleting a string from another string:

```
-   delete "cat" "the cat sat";
>   "the  sat" : string
```

First of all, both strings are **explode**d and an auxiliary function is called to delete one list from another. The resultant list is then **implode**d

```
-   local
      fun delete1 ... = ...
    in
      (* delete one string from another *)
      fun delete s1 s2 = implode (delete1
      (explode s1)(explode s2)) end;
>   val delete = fn : string -> string -> string
```

We assume that **delete1** returns a **string list**.

To delete one list from another list, we need to check if the first list starts the second list and then remove it from the start of the second list. We can do this by dropping elements from both lists until the first is empty.

To drop the number of elements in one list from another list, if the first list is empty then return the second list. Otherwise drop the number of elements in the tail of the first from the tail of the second:

```
-   (* drop the number of elements in a first list from a
    second list *)
    fun drop [] 12 = 12 |
        drop (_::t1) (_::t2) = drop t1 t2;
>   val drop = fn : 'a list -> 'b list -> 'b list
```

No operations are performed on the list heads so they may be of arbitrary different types. Note that **drop** is polymorphic. For example:

```
-   drop [1,2,3] [1,2,3,4,5,6];
>   [4,5,6] : int list
```

because:

```
drop [1,2,3] [1,2,3,4,5,6] ==>
drop [2,3] [2,3,4,5,6] ==>
drop [3] [3,4,5,6] ==>
drop [] [4,5,6] ==>
[4,5,6]
```

Note that the lists may be of different types and that the first list need not start the second list. The length of the first list determines how many elements are dropped from the second list. For example:

```
-   drop [true,false,true] ["a","b","c","d","e"];
>   ["d","e"] : string list
```

because:

```
drop [true,false,true] ["a","b","c","d","e"] ==>
drop [false,true] ["b","c","d","e"] ==>
drop [true] ["c","d","e"] ==>
drop [] ["d","e"] ==>
["d","e"]
```

To return to deleting one list from another list. If the second list is empty then deletion fails so return the empty list. If the first list starts the second list then drop the first list from the start of the second list. Otherwise, drop the first list from the tail of the second list and put the head of the second list back onto the result:

```
-   (* delete one list from another *)
    fun delete1 _ [] = [] |
        delete1 l1 (l2 as h2::t2) =
        if starts1 l1 l2
        then drop l1 l2
        else h2::delete1 l1 t2;
>   val delete1 = fn : ''a list -> ''a list -> ''a list
```

We know that **starts1** is of type **''a list -> ''a list -> bool** so **l1** and **h2::t2** must be of type **''a list**. This is another polymorphic function. For example:

```
-   delete1 [3,4,5] [1,2,3,4,5,6];
>   [1,2,6] : int list
```

because:

```
delete1 [3,4,5] [1,2,3,4,5,6] ==>
 starts1 [3,4,5] [1,2,3,4,5,6] ==>
 false
1::delete1 [3,4,5] [2,3,4,5,6] ==>
 starts1 [3,4,5] [2,3,4,5,6] ==>
 false
1::2::delete1 [3,4,5] [3,4,5,6] ==>
 starts1 [3,4,5] [3,4,5,6] ==>
 true
 drop [3,4,5] [3,4,5,6] ==>
 [6]
1::2::[6] ==> [1,2,6]
```

Going back to the original:

```
delete "cat" "the cat sat" ==>
implode (delete1 ["c","a","t"]
                 ["t","h","e"," ","c","a","t",
                  " ","s","a","t"]) ==>
 starts1 ["c","a","t"]
         ["t","h","e"," ","c","a","t"," ","s","a","t"] ==>
 false
implode ("t"::
        delete1 ["c","a","t"]
                ["h","e"," ","c","a","t"," ","s","a","t"]) ==>
 starts1 ["c","a","t"]
         ["h","e"," ","c","a","t"," ","s","a","t"] ==>
 false
implode ("t"::"h"::
        delete1 ["c","a","t"]
                ["e"," ","c","a","t"," ","s","a","t"]) ==>
```

```
    starts1 ["c","a","t"]
           ["e"," ","c","a","t"," ","s","a","t"] ==>
    false
implode ("t"::"h"::"e"::
        delete1 ["c","a","t"]
               [" ","c","a","t"," ","s","a","t"]) ==>
    starts1 ["c","a","t"]
           [" ","c","a","t"," ","s","a","t"] ==>
    false
implode ("t"::"h"::"e"::" "::
        delete1 ["c","a","t"]
               ["c","a","t"," ","s","a","t"]) ==>
    starts1 ["c","a","t"]
           ["c","a","t"," ","s","a","t"] ==>
    true
    drop ["c","a","t"]
         ["c","a","t"," ","s","a","t"])) ==>
  [" ","s","a","t"]
implode ("t"::"h"::"e"::" "::[" ","s","a","t"]) ==>
implode ["t","h","e"," "," ","s","a","t"] ==> "the  sat"
```

Note that we have not made **drop** local to **delete1** because we will need it later on.

### 8.3.4 Insert one string before another in a third string
Consider inserting one string before another string in a third string:

```
-   insertb "kidney " "beans" "eat beans";
>   "eat kidney beans" : string
```

The three strings are **explode**d and passed to an auxiliary function for list insertion. The result is then **implode**d

```
-   local
      fun insertb1 ... = ...
    in
      (* insert one string before another in a third *)
      fun insertb s1 s2 s3 =
            implode
             (insertb1
              (explode s1) (explode s2) (explode s3))
    end;
>   val insertb = fn string -> string -> string -> string
```

To insert one list before another list in a third list, if the third list is empty then the second list cannot be found so return the third list. If the second list starts the third list then put the first list on the front of the third list. Otherwise insert in the tail of the third list and put the head of the third list onto the result:

```
-   (* insert one list before another in a third *)
    fun insertb1 _ _ [] = [] |
        insertb1 l1 l2 (l3 as h3::t3) =
        if starts1 l2 l3
        then l1@l3
```

```
            else h3::insertb1 l1 l2 t3;
>    val insertb1 = fn : "a list -> "a list -> "a list -> "a list
```

**starts1** is of type `''a list -> ''a list -> bool` so **l2** and **h3::t3** must
be of type `''a list`. **l1** is appended to **h3::t3** so it must also be of type `''a
list`. This is another polymorphic function for lists of equality type. For
example:

```
-    insertb1 [3,4] [5,6] [1,2,5,6];
>    [1,2,3,4,5,6] : int list
```

because:

```
insertb1 [3,4] [5,6] [1,2,5,6] ==>
 starts1 [5,6] [1,2,5,6] ==>
 false
1::insertb1 [3,4] [5,6] [2,5,6] ==>
 starts1 [5,6] [2,5,6] ==>
 false
1::2::insertb1 [3,4] [5,6] [5,6] ==>
 starts1 [5,6] [5,6] ==>
 true
1::2::[3,4]@[5,6] ==>
 [1,2,3,4,5,6]
```

Thus:

```
insertb "cat" "fish" "the fish" ==>
implode (insertb1 ["c","a","t"] ["f","i","s","h"]
                  ["t","h","e"," ","f","i","s","h"]) ==>
 starts1 ["f","i","s","h"]
         ["t","h","e"," ","f","i","s","h"] ==>
 false
implode ("t"::insertb1 ["c","a","t"] ["f","i","s","h"]
                       ["h","e"," ","f","i","s","h"]) ==>
 starts1 ["f","i","s","h"]
         ["h","e"," ","f","i","s","h"] ==>
 false
implode ("t"::"h"::insertb1 ["c","a","t"] ["f","i","s","h"]
                            ["e"," ","f","i","s","h"]) ==>
 starts1 ["f","i","s","h"]
         ["e"," ","f","i","s","h"] ==>
 false
implode ("t"::"h"::"e"::insertb1 ["c","a","t"]
                                 ["f","i","s","h"]
                                 [" ","f","i","s","h"]) ==>
 starts1 ["f","i","s","h"]
         [" ","f","i","s","h"] ==>
 false
implode ("t"::"h"::"e"::" "::insertb1 ["c","a","t"]
                                      ["f","i","s","h"]
                                      ["f","i","s","h"]) ==>
```

```
starts1 ["f","i","s","h"]
         ["f","i","s","h"] ==>
true
["c","a","t"]@["f","i","s","h"] ==>
["c","a","t","f","i","s","h"]
implode ("t"::"h"::"e"::" "::["c","a","t","f","i","s","h"]) ==>
implode ["t","h","e"," ","c","a","t","f","i","s","h"] ==>
"the catfish"
```

### 8.3.5 Insert one string after another in a third string

Consider inserting one string after another string in a third string:

```
-   inserta "more " "eat " "eat beans";
>   "eat more beans" : string
```

The three strings are **explode**d and passed to an auxiliary function for list insertion. The result is then **implode**d

```
-   local
      fun inserta1 ... = ...
    in
      (* insert one string after another in a third *)
      fun inserta s1 s2 s3 =
              implode (inserta1
                      (explode s1) (explode s2) (explode s3))
    end;
>   val inserta = fn string -> string -> string -> string
```

To insert one list after another list in a third list, if the third list is empty then the second list cannot be found so return the third list. If the second list starts the third list then drop the second list, put the first list on the front of the remains of the third list and put the second list before the first list. Otherwise insert in the tail of the third list and put the head of the third list onto the result:

```
-   (* insert one list after another in a third *)
    fun inserta1 _ _ [] = [] |
        inserta1 l1 l2 (l3 as h3::t3) =
          if starts1 l2 l3
          then l2@l1@drop l2 l3
          else h3::inserta1 l1 l2 t3;
>   val inserta1 = fn : ''a list -> ''a list -> ''a list -> ''a list
```

**starts1** is of type **''a list -> ''a list -> bool** so **l2** and **h3::t3** must be of type **''a list**. **l1** is appended to the remains of **h3::t3** so it must also be of type **''a list**. This is another polymorphic function on lists of equality type. For example:

```
-   inserta1 [4,5] [2,3] [1,2,3,6];
>   [1,2,3,4,5,6] : int list
```

because:

```
inserta1 [4,5] [2,3] [1,2,3,6] ==>
 starts1 [2,3] [1,2,3,6] ==>
 false
1::inserta1 [4,5] [2,3] [2,3,6] ==>
```

```
starts1 [2,3] [2,3,6] ==>
true
[2,3]@[4,5]@drop [2,3] [2,3,6] ==>
[2,3]@[4,5]@[6] ==>
[2,3,4,5,6]
1::[2,3,4,5,6] ==>
[1,2,3,4,5,6]
```

Thus:

```
-    inserta "more " "eat " "eat beans";
>    "eat more beans" : string
```

because:

```
inserta "more " "eat " "eat beans" ==>
implode (inserta1 ["m","o","r","e"," "]
                  ["e","a","t"," "]
                  ["e","a","t"," ","b","e","a","n","s"]) ==>
  starts1 ["e","a","t"," "]
          ["e","a","t"," ","b","e","a","n","s"] ==>
  true
  ["e","a","t"," "]@["m","o","r","e"," "]@
   drop ["e","a","t"," "]
        ["e","a","t"," ","b","e","a","n","s"] ==>
  ["e","a","t"," "]@
   ["m","o","r","e"," "]@["b","e","a","n","s"] ==>
  ["e","a","t"," ","m","o","r","e"," ","b","e","a","n","s"]
  implode
  ["e","a","t"," ","m","o","r","e"," ","b","e","a","n","s"] ==>
  "eat more beans"
```

In **inserta1** the expression:

```
12@11@drop 12 13
```

is not very efficient. First of all **12** is dropped from **13** which involves going along **13** for the length of **12**. Then **11** is joined to the remains. But then **12** is appended back on which again involves going down the length of **12**.

We could write a new function to combine dropping **12** and putting it back on the front of **11**. Instead of simply dropping each element of **12** we can join them back on to the result of appending **11** once all of **12** is dropped:

```
-    (* drop the number of elements from a second list in a
        third list and append a first list preceded by the
        elements of the second list *)
     fun dropjoin 11 [] 13 = 11@13 |
         dropjoin 11 (h2::t2) (_::t3) = h2::dropjoin 11 t2 t3;
>    val dropjoin = fn : 'a list -> 'a list -> 'a list -> 'a list
```

**append** is of type **'a list -> 'a list -> 'a list** so **11** and **13** must be of type **'a list** as must the final result. **h2** is joined onto the final result so it must be of type **'a**. For example:

```
-    dropjoin [4,5] [2,3] [2,3,6];
>    [2,3,4,5,6] : int list
```

because:

```
dropjoin [4,5] [2,3] [2,3,6] ==>
2::dropjoin [4,5] [3] [3,6] ==>
2::3::dropjoin [4,5] [] [6] ==>
2::3::[4,5]@[6] ==>
[2,3,4,5,6]
```

Now, we can define:

```
-   local
      fun dropjoin ... = ...
    in
      fun inserta1 l1 l2 [] = [] |
          inserta1 l1 l2 (l3 as h3::t3) =
            if starts1 l2 l3
            then dropjoin l1 l2 l3
            else h3::inserta1 l1 l2 t3
    end;
>   val inserta1 = fn : ''a list -> ''a list -> ''a list -> ''a list
```

Note that **dropjoin** is local to **inserta1** which is local to **inserta**.

## 8.3.6 Replace one string with another in a third string

Finally, consider replacing one string with a second string in a third string:

```
-   replace "cat" "dog" "a catfish";
>   "a dogfish" : string
```

The strings are **explode**d and passed to an auxiliary function to replace one list with another in a third list. The result is then **implode**d:

```
-   local
      fun replace1 ... = ...
    in
    (* replace one string with another in a third *)
    fun replace s1 s2 s3 =
          implode
            (replace1 (explode s1) (explode s2) (explode s3))
    end;
>   val replace = fn : string -> string -> string -> string
```

To replace one list with another in a third list, if the third list is empty then the first list cannot be found so return the empty list. If the first list starts the third list then drop it from the start of the third list and append the second list. Otherwise, replace in the tail of the third list and put the head of the third list onto the result:

```
-   (* replace one list with another in a third *)
    fun replace1 _ _ [] = [] |
        replace1 l1 l2 (l3 as h3::t3) =
          if starts1 l1 l3
          then l2@drop l1 l3
          else h3::replace1 l1 l2 t3;
>   val replace1 = fn : ''a list -> ''a list -> ''a list -> ''a list
```

For example:

```
-   replace1 [4,3] [3,4] [1,2,4,3,5,6];
>   [1,2,3,4,5,6] : int list
```

because:

```
replace1 [4,3] [3,4] [1,2,4,3,5,6] ==>
 starts1 [4,3] [1,2,4,3,5,6] ==>
 false
1::replace1 [4,3] [3,4] [2,4,3,5,6] ==>
 starts1 [4,3] [2,4,3,5,6] ==>
 false
1::2::replace1 [4,3] [3,4] [4,3,5,6] ==>
 starts1 [4,3] [4,3,5,6] ==>
 true
 [3,4]@drop [4,3] [4,3,5,6] ==>
 [3,4]@[5,6] ==>
 [3,4,5,6]
1::2::[3,4,5,6] ==>
 [1,2,3,4,5,6]
```

Thus:

```
-    replace "cat" "dog" "a catfish";
>    "a dogfish" : string
```

because:

```
replace "cat" "dog" "a catfish" ==>
implode (replace1 ["c","a","t"] ["d","o","g"]
                  ["a"," ","c","a","t","f","i","s","h"]) ==>
 starts1 ["c","a","t"]
         ["a"," ","c","a","t","f","i","s","h"]  ==>
 false
implode ("a"::replace1 ["c","a","t"] ["d","o","g"]
                       [" ","c","a","t","f","i","s","h"]) ==>
 starts1 ["c","a","t"] [" ","c","a","t","f","i","s","h"] ==>
 false
implode
 ("a"::" "::replace1 ["c","a","t"] ["d","o","g"]
                     ["c","a","t","f","i","s","h"]) ==>
 starts1 ["c","a","t"] ["c","a","t","f","i","s","h"] ==>
 true
 ["d","o","g"]@drop ["c","a","t"]
                    ["c","a","t","f","i","s","h"] ==>
 ["d","o","g"]@["f","i","s","h"] ==>
 ["d","o","g","f","i","s","h"]
implode ("a"::" "::["d","o","g","f","i","s","h"]) ==>
implode ["a"," ","d","o","g","f","i","s","h"] ==>
"a dogfish"
```

## 8.4 Digit string to number value conversion

Suppose we have a string made up of digits and we want to convert it to
the equivalent integer value. First of all, let's look at the form of an integer.

Consider:

4637

We can factor this as multiples of powers of ten:

4*1000 + 6*100 + 3*10 + 7*1 ==>
$4*10^3 + 6*10^2 + 3*10^1 + 7*10^0$

Thus, each digit in an integer represents a multiple of a power of 10. If we number the digits from 0 to N from right to left then the general form is:

*digitN ... digit2 digit1 digit0* ==>
*digitN*$*10^N$ ... *digit2*$*10^2$ + *digit1*$*10^1$ + *digit0*$*10^0$

It is impractical to hold a table of all possible powers of 10 and expensive computationaly to generate them as they are needed. Instead, we can factor the expression for the value of a digit sequence to identify a recursive form. Consider again:

*4637* ==>
$4*10^3 + 6*10^2 + 3*10^1 + 7*10^0$ ==>
$10*(4*10^2 + 6*10^1 + 3*10^0)+ 7*10^0$ ==>
$10*(10*(4*10^1 + 6*10^0)+ 3*10^0)+ 7*10^0$ ==>
$10*(10*(10*(4*10^0) + 6*10^0) + 3*10^0) + 7*10^0$ ==>
$10*(10*(10*4 + 6) + 3) + 7$

The general form is:

*digitN . . . digit2 digit1 digit0* ==>
*digitN*$*10^N$ . . . + *digit2*$*10^2$ + *digit1*$*10^1$ + *digit0*$*10^0$ ==>
$10*($*digitN*$*10^{N-1}$ + . . . + *digit2*$*10^1$ + *digit1*$*10^0$ )+ *digit0*$*10^0$ ==>
$10*(10*($*digitN*$*10^{N-2}$ + . . .)+ *digit2*$*10^0$ )+ *digit1*$*10^0$ )+ *digit0*$*10^0$ ==>
$10*(10*(. . .(10*$*digitN*$*10^0$ )+ . . .)+ *digit2*$*10^0$ )+ *digit1*$*10^0$ )+ *digit0*$*10^0$ ==>
$* 10*(10*(. . .(10*$*digitN*$+ . . .)+ *digit2*$)+ *digit1*$)+ *digit0*

We can evaluate this from the inside out. For example:

```
10*(10*(10*4+6)+3)+7
10*(10*(40+6)+3)+7 ==>
10*(10*46+3)+7 ==>
10*(460+3)+7 ==>
10*463+7
4630+7 ==>
4637
```

This suggests that we keep a running total and work from left to right. Each time we multiply the running total by **10** and then add the next digit value to it. For example:

```
RT == 0 digits == 4637
RT == 10*0+4 == 4 digits == 637
RT == 10*4+6 == 46 digits == 37
RT == 10*46+3 == 463 digits == 7
RT == 10*463+7 == 4637
```

Let us assume that we will be working with a list of single digit strings. We **explode** the initial string and call another function to process it:

```
-   (* convert digit string to integer *)
    fun value intstring = getval 0 (explode intstring);
>   val value = fn : string list -> int
```

The **0** is the initial value for the running total.

If the list is empty, return the running total. Otherwise, find the value of the tail with the running total multiplied by **10** and the value of the head digit added to it:

```
-   (* convert list of digit strings to integer using running
       total *)
    fun getval rt [] = rt |
        getval rt (h::t) = getval (10*rt+ conv h) t;
>   val getval = fn : int -> string list -> int
```

Here, **conv** is a function which will return the integer value corresponding to a string digit.

There are two ways to convert a digit string to the equivalent value. One is to use a lookup function:

```
-   exception CONV;
>   exception CONV
```

```
-   (* convert single digit string to integer by pattern
       matching *)
    fun conv "0" = 0 |
        conv "1" = 1 |
        ...
        conv "9" = 9 |
        conv _ = raise CONV;
>   val conv = fn : string -> int
```

Note the exception which is raised when a non-digit string is the argument.

ASCII, the American Standard Code for Information Interchange, is an international standard for representing characters as integers. We could also convert digit strings to values using the built in function **ord** which returns the ASCII value of a single letter string:

```
-   ord "0";
>   48 : int
-   ord;
>   fn : string -> int
```

Now, the ASCII value of each digit is one more than the previous digit:

```
ord "0" == 48
ord "1" == 49
ord "2" == 50
...
ord "9" == 57
```

so a digit string can be converted to its integer value by taking the ASCII value for **0** away from its ASCII value:

```
ord "0" - ord "0" == 48-48 == 0
ord "1" - ord "0" == 49-48 == 1
ord "2" - ord "0" == 50-48 == 2
...
ord "9" - ord "0" == 57-48 == 9
```

Thus:

```
–     (* convert single digit string to integer by ASCII value
       arithmetic *)
      fun conv d = ord d-ord "0";
>     val conv = fn : string -> int
```

To return to finding the value of a string of digits:

```
–     value "3241";
>     3241 : int
```

because:

```
value "3241" ==>
getval 0 ["3","2","4","1"] ==>
getval (10*0+conv "3") ["2","4","1"] ==>
getval (0+3) ["2","4","1"] ==>
getval 3 ["2","4","1"] ==>
getval (10*3+conv "2") ["4","1"] ==>
getval (30+2) ["4","1"] ==>
getval 32 ["4","1"] ==>
getval (10*32+ conv "4") ["1"] ==>
getval 320+4 ["1"] ==>
getval 324 ["1"] ==>
getval (10*324+ conv "1") [] ==>
getval (3240+1) [] ==>
getval 3241 [] ==>
3241
```

## 8.5 Let expression

Sometimes it is useful to be able to introduce a temporary variable to hold a partial result during evaluation. SML provides let expressions to do this. At simplest one may write:

```
let val name = expression1
in expression2
end
```

This associates the value of *expression1* with *name* for the evaluation of *expression2*. After the **end** the *name* may no longer be used: it is local to *expression2*

The type of a let expression is that of the final expression *expression2*.

Note the **val** before the *name*. A common mistake is to forget the **val**.

Note the **end** at the end. A common mistake is to forget the **end**.

For example, to work out **3*3+4*4** with a local squaring function:

```
–     let val sq = fn (x:int) => x*x
      in sq 3+ sq 4
      end;
>     25 : int
```

Here, **sq** is local to **sq 3+sq 4**.

For a let expression, the **fun** form may be used, for example:

```
–     let fun sq (x:int) = x*x
```

```
    in sq 3+ sq 4
    end;
>    25 : int
```

Instead of a name a pattern of names may be used. Then, the value of the defining expression must have the same structure as the pattern. Names in the pattern are bound to corresponding components of the value of the defining expression.

For example, to multiply the first two elements of a list together:

```
-   let val (h1::h2::_) = [22,33,44,55,66]
    in h1*h2
    end;
>    726 : int
```

Here:

```
h1 == 22
h2 == 33
_  == [44,55,66]
```

in `h1*h2`.

A particularly useful form is to have a tuple pattern to pick up components of a tuple value from a function. Then the tuple components may be manipulated locally.

## 8.6 Unzip revisited

In the last chapter, we looked at turning a list of pair tuples into a tuple of lists:

```
-   local
    fun unzip1 (f,s) [] = (f,s) |
        unzip1 (f,s) ((f1,s1)::t) = unzip1 (f1::f,s1::s) t
    in
     val unzip = unzip1 ([],[])
    end;
>    val unzip1 = fn : ('a * 'b ) list -> 'a list * 'b list
```

and saw that we built the lists in reverse order:

```
-   unzip [(1,1),(2,4),(3,9),(4,16)];
>    ([4,3,2,1],[16,9,4,1]) : (int list) * (int list)
```

because the elements from the $N$th pair always precede those from the $N-1$th pair.

Now we can use a let expression to match the tuple of lists from processing the tail of the original list and then put the elements from the head pair in the right positions. If the tuple list is empty then return a tuple of empty lists. If the tuple list is not empty then process the tail to form a tuple of a list of the first elements from the tail and a list of the second elements from the tail. Then put the first element from the head tuple onto the first elements list and the second element from the head tuple onto the second elements list:

```
-   (* convert list of two element tuples to two singleton
        lists *)
    fun unzip [] = ([],[]) |
        unzip ((f,s)::t) = let val (f1,s1) = unzip t
                           in (f::f1,s::s1)
                           end;
>    val unzip = fn : ('a*'b) list -> ('a list)*('b list)
```

Here `f1` holds the list of first elements from the tail and `s1` holds the list of second elements from the tail. For example:

```
-   unzip [(1,1),(2,4),(3,9),(4,16)];
>   ([1,2,3,4],[1,4,9,16]) : (int list)*(int list)
```

because:

```
unzip [(1,1),(2,4),(3,9),(4,16)] ==>
 f == 1
 s == 1
 t == [(2,4),(3,9),(4,16)]
 let val (fl,sl) = unzip [(2,4),(3,9),(4,16)] ==>
   f == 2
   s == 4
   t == [(3,9),(4,16)]
   let val (fl,sl) = unzip [(3,9),(4,16)] ==>
     f == 3
     s == 9
     t == [(4,16)]
     let val (fl,sl) = unzip [(4,16)] ==>
       f == 4
       s == 16
       t == []
       let val (fl,sl) = unzip [] ==>
         ([],[])
       f == 4
       s == 16
       t == []
       let val (fl,sl) = ([],[])
         fl == []
         sl == []
       in (f::fl,s::sl) ==>
         ([4],[16])
     f == 3
     s == 9
     t == [(4,16)]
     let val (fl,sl) = ([4],[16])
       fl == [4]
       sl == [16]
     in (f::fl,s::sl) ==>
       ([3,4],[9,16])
   f == 2
   s == 4
   t == [(3,9),(4,16)]
   let val (fl,sl) = ([3,4],[9,16])
     fl == [3,4]
     sl == [9,16]
   in (f::fl,s:;sl) ==>
     ([2,3,4],[4,9,16])
 f == 1
 s == 1
 t == [(2,4),(3,9),(4,16)]
 let val (fl,sl) = ([2,3,4],[4,9,16])
```

```
fl == [2,3,4]
sl == [4,9,16]
in (f::fl,s::sl) ==>
([1,2,3,4],[1,4,9,16])
```

Instead of passing an accumulation tuple we now hold the same information in local variables.

## 8.7 Finding words in a string

Suppose we have a string and we want to convert it to a list of words:

```
-  getwords "the cat went to sleep";
>  ["the","cat","went","to","sleep"] : string list
```

As always, we **explode** the string into individual letters:

```
-  local
     fun getwords1 ... = ...
   in
     (* convert string to list of words *)
     fun getwords s = getwords1 (explode s)
   end;
>  val getwords = fn : string -> string list
```

We assume that **getwords1** returns a string list.

The original string list contains letter sequences separated by space sequences.

To get a word, we need to pick up each letter until we find a space and then return a tuple of the word and the rest of the list following the space. For example:

```
-  getword ["t","h","e"," "," ","c","a","t"];
>  ("the",[" ","c","a","t"]) : string * string list
```

If the letters list is empty then return the empty string and the empty list in a tuple. If the letters list starts with a space then return the empty string and the rest of the letters list after the space. Otherwise the list starts with the first letter of the word. Process the rest of the letters list, which starts with the rest of the word, to form a tuple of the rest of the word and the letters after it. Then put the first letter of the word list onto the rest of the word and return it with the rest of the letters:

```
-  (* return, from singleton string list, next word and
      list of singleton strings following it *)
   fun getword [] = ("",[]) |
       getword (" "::t) = ("",t) |
       getword (h::t) =
   let val (rw,rl) = getword t
   in (h^rw,rl)
   end;
>  val getword = fn : string list -> string*string list
```

Note the tuple pattern **(rw,rl)**. **getword** is called recursively to return a tuple of the rest of the word and the rest of the letters. Thus **rw** matches the rest of the word and **rl** matches the rest of the letters. For example:

```
-  getword ["t","h","e"," "," ","c","a","t"]);
>  ("the",[" ","c","a","t"]) : string * string list
```

because:

```
getword ["t","h","e"," "," ","c","a","t"]) ==>
  h == "t"
  t == ["h","e"," "," ","c","a","t"]) ==>
  let val (rw,rl) =
   getword ["h","e"," "," ","c","a","t"]) ==>
    h == "h"
    t == ["e"," "," ","c","a","t"]) ==>
    let val (rw,rl) =
     getword ["e"," "," ","c","a","t"]) ==>
      h == "e"
      t == [" "," ","c","a","t"]) ==>
      let val (rw,rl) =
       getword [" "," ","c","a","t"]) ==>
       ("",[" ","c","a","t"])
      h == "e"
      t == [" "," ","c","a","t"]) ==>
      let val (rw,rl) = ("",[" ","c","a","t"])
       rw == ""
       rl == [" ","c","a","t"]
      in (h^rw rl) ==>
       ("e",[" ","c","a","t"])
    h == "h"
    t == ["e"," "," ","c","a","t"]) ==>
    let val (rw,rl) = ("e",[" ","c","a","t"])
     rw == "e"
     rl == [" ","c","a","t"]
    in (h^rw,rl) ==>
     ("he",[" ","c","a","t"])
  h == "t"
  t == ["h","e"," "," ","c","a","t"]) ==>
  let val (rw,rl) = ("he",[" ","c","a","t"])
   rw == "he"
   rl == [" ","c","a","t"]
  in (h^rw, rl) ==>
  ("the",[" ","c","a","t"])
```

To find all the words, we need to skip spaces until we find a letter. Then we pick up the first word and put it on the front of processing the rest of the list:

```
-    (* get list of words from list of singleton strings *)
     fun getwords1 [] = [] |
         getwords1 (" "::t) = getwords1 t |
         getwords1 l =
           let val (w1,rl) = getword l
           in w1::getwords1 rl
     end;
>    val getwords1 = fn : string list -> string list
```

Remember that **getword** returns a tuple of the next word and the list of letters after it. **w1** will match the word and **rl** will match the rest of the list. For example:

```
-    getwords "the cat sat down";
>    ["the","cat","sat","down"] : string list
```

because:

```
getwords "the cat sat down" ==>
getwords1 ["t","h","e"," ","c","a","t"," ",
           "s","a","t"," ","d","o","w","n"] ==>
  let val (w1,rl) =
       getword ["t","h","e"," ","c","a","t"," ",
                "s","a","t"," ","d","o","w","n"] ==>
       ("the",
        ["c","a","t"," ","s","a","t"," ","d","o","w","n"])
       w1 == "the"
       rl == ["c","a","t"," ","s","a","t"," ","d","o","w","n"]
  in w1::getwords1 rl ==>
"the"::
(getwords1
  ["c","a","t"," ","s","a","t"," ","d","o","w","n"]) ==>
       let val (w1,rl) =
            getword ["c","a","t"," ","s","a","t",
                     " ","d","o","w","n"] ==>
       ("cat",["s","a","t"," ","d","o","w","n"])
       w1 == "cat"
       rl == ["s","a","t"," ","d","o","w","n"]
       in w1::getwords1 rl ==>
"the"::"cat"::
  getwords1 ["s","a","t"," ","d","o","w","n"] ==>
    let val (w1,rl) =
         getword ["s","a","t"," ","d","o","w","n"] ==>
         ("sat",["d","o","w","n"])
         w1 == "sat"
         rl == ["d","o","w","n"]
  in w1::getwords1 rl ==>
"the"::"cat"::"sat"::getwords1 ["d","o","w","n"] ==>
                  let val (w1,rl) =
                       getword ["d","o","w","n"] ==>
                       ("down",[])
                       w1 == "down"
                       rl == []
                  in w1::getwords1 rl ==>
"the"::"cat"::"sat"::"down"::getwords1 [] ==>
"the"::"cat"::"sat"::"down"::[] ==>
["the","cat","sat","down"]
```

## 8.8 Counting words

Consider counting how often each word occurs in a list of words. For each distinct word, a count is held as a tuple of the word and the number found so far. All the count tuples are held in a list which is initially empty.

For each word, the count list is updated. If the count list is empty then the word has not yet been found so a new list is made with a tuple for that word with a count of 1. If the word is that in the first tuple in the count list then the count in the tuple is incremented and the new tuple is put back onto the rest of the count list. Otherwise, the first tuple is put onto the result of updating the tail of the count list for the word:

```
-   (* increment count for given word in count list *)
    fun wupdate w [] = [(w,1)] |
        wupdate w ((w1,c1)::t) = if w=w1
                                 then (w1,c1+ 1)::t
                                 else (w1,c1)::wupdate w t;
>   val wupdate = fn : ''a -> (''a * int) list -> (''a * int) list
```

This function will serve to update the count in a tuple list for any equality type of index element. For example:

```
-   wupdate "beans" [("eat",2),("more",1),("beans",3)];
>   [("eat",2),("more",1),("beans",4)] : (string * int) list
```

because:

```
wupdate "beans" [("eat",2),("more",1),("beans",3)] ==>
("eat",2)::wupdate "beans" [("more",1),("beans",3)] ==>
("eat",2)::("more",1)::wupdate "beans" [("beans",3)] ==>
("eat",2)::("more",1)::("beans",4)::[] ==>
[("eat",2),("more",1),("beans",4)]
```

Now to count the occurrence of each distinct word in a word list, if it is empty an empty count list is returned. Otherwise, use the first word to update the count list from processing the rest of the words. We can use **foldr** to apply **wupdate** to each word in turn with an empty count list as the base case:

```
-   local
      fun wupdate ... = ...
    in
      (* update count list from word list *)
      val count = foldr wupdate []
    end;
>   val count = fn : ''a list -> (''a * int) list
```

For example:

```
-   count ["the","cat","saw","the","saw"];
>   [("saw",2),("the",2),("cat",1)] : (string * int) list
```

because:

```
count ["the","cat","saw","the","saw"] ==>
foldr wupdate [] ["the","cat","saw","the","saw"] ==>
wupdate "the"
 (foldr wupdate [] ["cat","saw","the","saw"]) ==>
wupdate "the"
 (wupdate "cat" (foldr wupdate [] ["saw","the","saw"])) ==>
wupdate "the"
 (wupdate "cat"
  (wupdate "saw" (foldr wupdate [] ["the","saw"]))) ==>
wupdate "the"
 (wupdate "cat"
  (wupdate "saw"
   (wupdate "the" (foldr wupdate [] ["saw"])))) ==>
```

```
wupdate "the"
 (wupdate "cat"
  (wupdate "saw"
   (wupdate "the"
    (wupdate "saw" (foldr wupdate [] []))))) ==>
wupdate "the"
 (wupdate "cat"
  (wupdate "saw"
   (wupdate "the"
    (wupdate "saw" [] )))) ==>
wupdate "the"
 (wupdate "cat"
  (wupdate "saw"
   (wupdate "the" [("saw",1)]))) ==>
wupdate "the"
 (wupdate "cat"
  (wupdate "saw" [("saw",1),("the",1)])) ==>
wupdate "the"
 (wupdate "cat" [("saw",2),("the",1)]) ==>
wupdate "the" [("saw",2),("the",1),("cat",1)] ==>
[("saw",2),("the",2),("cat",1)] ==>
```

## 8.9 Summary

In this chapter we looked at the use of **explode** to turn a string into a list and **implode** to turn a list of strings into a single string. We then wrote functions to find, delete, insert and replace text in text by manipulating lists of single letters. Next we met the let expression for introducing temporary local variables. We then used let expressions to accumulate partial results when processing lists. Typically, we accumulated a tuple of the result so far and what was left over. At the end, we had nothing left over and returned the final result.

In the next chapter we are going to look at a technique for defining our own data types. We will use this to represent the results of more elaborate text processing, including simple lexical analysis.

## 8.10 Exercises

1) Write a function to find the length of a string using **explode** and **length**. Do not use the built in **size**. What is the type of this function?
2) Write a function which counts how often a string occurs in another string:

     – **scount "the" "the pathetic bathe theory with lather";**
     > 5 : int

   What is the type of this function?
3) Write a function which deletes all occurrences of a string in another string:

     – **deleteall "the" "the cat ate the haggis";**
     > " cat ate  haggis" : string

   What is the type of this function?

4) Write a function which replaces all occurrences of a string with another string in a third string:

```
-   replaceall "the" "our" "the cat stole the pie";
>   "our cat stole our pie" : string
```

What is the type of this function?

5) Write a function which inserts a string after all occurrences of another string in a third string:

```
-   insertafterall " big" "the" "the dog saw the cat";
>   "the big dog saw the big cat" : string
```

What is the type of this function?

6) Write a function which inserts a string before all occurrences of another string in a third string:

```
-   insertbeforeall "happy " "happy" "happy happy";
>   "happy happy happy happy" : string
```

What is the type of this function?

7) Write a function to convert an integer into a string of digits:

```
-   iconv 312;
>   "312" : string
```

Use the system function **chr** which turns an ASCII value into the equivalent single letter string:

```
-   chr 48;
>   "0" : string
-   chr;
>   fn : int -> string
```

Can your function deal with an initial value of **0**? What is the type of this function?

8) Octal integers use the digits:

```
0  1  2  3  4  5  6  7
```

Each place indicates a multiple of a power of 8:

```
452 == 4*8*8+5*8+2
```

Write a function to convert an octal number represented as a string of octal digits to a decimal integer:

```
-   oconv "452";
>   298 : int
```

What is the type of this function?

9) A string contains a sequence of octal and decimal integers separated by spaces. An octal integer starts:

```
#O
```

A decimal integer starts:

```
#D
```

Write a function which given such a string returns an equivalent list of tuples of string number type and integer number value:

```
-   numbs "#O32 #D32 #O45";
>   [("octal",26),("decimal",32),("octal",37)] : (string * int) list
```

What is the type of this function?

# CHAPTER 9

# Concrete data types

## 9.1 Introduction

In Chapter 1 we talked about how model making is based on constructing new types for a problem. Programming then involves using the given types in a programming language to represent those new types. We have seen that SML provides base types for integers, reals, booleans and strings and we have used these directly to represent property values. However, sometimes the types we want for a problem can be represented by a subset of one of the base types but we still have to deal with all possible values for that base type. We have used catch all variables to pick up the base type values we are not really interested in but this can distort our functions.

For example, in the traffic light function from Chapter 4:

```
-    fun  change "red" = "red & amber" |
         change "red & amber" = "green" |
         change "green" = "amber" |
         change "amber" = "red" |
         change s = s^" not a light state";
>    val change = fn : string -> string
```

we represented light states as strings. However, there are only four light states and an infinite variety of strings so we had to introduce the final case for **s** to catch any other string and return a plausible value. If this function were part of a larger system then we would need special cases all over the place to deal with an invalid light state.

We also saw that we could use exceptions to stop evaluation when something goes wrong. However, it would be nice to exclude the possibility of a function being called with an inappropriate value right from the start.

SML enables the definition of new types as ranges of discrete values represented as names. These are known as concrete data types. Patterns for a new concrete type may only take those defined values. Thus, there is no need to worry about values outside of those required.

## 9.2 New types

A new type may be introduced by what is called a datatype binding. At its simplest, this may be used to define the constituent values for a new type by listing base values explicitly. The binding is said to introduce new value constructors, that is the names representing the discrete values. These are used to build new values of that type just by mentioning them in expressions.

This simple form of datatype binding takes the form:

```
datatype type_constructor = value_constructor1 |
                            value_constructor2 |
                            value_constructor3 ...
```

which defines the base values of type *type_constructor*, a name, to be the value constructor names *value_constructor1* or *value_constructor2* or *value_constructor3*, etc.

The new type is an equality type, that is = and <> are defined for its values. For example, we could represent traffic light states with the datatype:

```
-   datatype traffic_light = red | red_amber | green | amber;
>   datatype traffic_light = red | red_amber | green | amber
    con red = red : traffic_light
    con red_amber = red_amber : traffic_light
    con green = green : traffic_light
    con amber = amber : traffic_light
```

Here, the system tells us that we have defined the datatype traffic_light with the value constructors **red, red_amber, green** and **amber** with the same constructor names as values. An equality test for **traffic_light** values is also defined so these values may appear in patterns. We can now define a function to change a traffic light from one state to the next:

```
-   (* change traffic light state *)
    fun change red = red_amber |
        change red_amber = green |
        change green = amber |
        change amber = red;
>   val change = fn : traffic_light - > traffic_light
-   change amber;
>   red : traffic_light
```

Note that we no longer need the catch all case. We can only use the values **red, red_amber, green** and **amber**.

As another example, we could define the boolean type **bool** with:

```
-   datatype bool = true | false;
>   datatype bool = true | false
    con true = true : bool
    con false = false : bool
```

This defines the value constructors **true** and **false** for the new type **bool**. An equality test for **bool** is also defined so that the values **true** and **false** may be tested explicitly and used in pattern matching. Thus, we could define negation:

```
-   (* boolean negation *)
    fun not true = false |
        not false = true;
>   val not = fn : bool - > bool
```

```
–    not true;
>    false : bool
```

We can also define other boolean operations, for example conjunction:

```
–    (* conjunction *)
     fun band false false = false |
         band false true = false |
         band true false = false |
         band true true = true;
>    val band = fn: bool –> bool –> bool
```

## 9.3 Example – simple lexical analysis

Suppose we are told about the following word classes:

```
article – the, a
noun – cat, mat, rat
verb – sat on, ate
```

We might represent word classes as a datatype:

```
–    datatype class = article | noun | verb;
>    datatype class = article | noun | verb
     con article = article : class
     con noun = noun : class
     con verb = verb : class
```

Suppose we are given a sentence as a string and we want to turn it into a list of the corresponding word classes:

```
–    lex "the cat sat on the mat";
>    [article,noun,verb,article,noun] : class list
```

This is the problem of lexical analysis: the recognition of individual lexemes or symbols from a character representation of a lexeme sequence. We can use string matching to identify each word:

```
–    (* recognize word classes in singleton string list *)
     fun lex1 [] = [] |
         lex1 ("a"::"t"::"e"::t) = verb::lex1 t |
         lex1 ("a"::t) = article::lex1 t |
         lex1 ("c"::"a"::"t"::t) = noun::lex1 t |
         lex1 ("m"::"a"::"t"::t) = noun::lex1 t |
         lex1 ("r"::"a"::"t"::t) = noun::lex1 t |
         lex1 ("s"::"a"::"t"::" "::"o"::"n"::t) = verb::lex1 t |
         lex1 ("t"::"h"::"e"::t) = article::lex1 t |
         lex1 (_::t) = lex1 t;
>    val lex1 = fn: string list –> class list
```

For each word we list its characters followed by a variable **t** to pick up the tail of the string list. Having recognized a word, we return its class followed by the result of recognizing the words in the rest of the list.

The order of the clauses is alphabetical but with long words before short words starting with the same letters. Pattern matching is top to bottom. If two words start with the same letters then we must check for the longer one first. Otherwise, the shorter one will be matched in instances of the longer one.

The last clause has a wildcard match to ignore any other characters, including spaces, and just check the rest of the list. Instead, we could have defined an error class and returned that. Alternatively, we could have raised an exception. Given a string, we explode it and pass it to **lex1**:

```
-   local
      fun lex1 ... = ...
    in
    (* lexical analyzer *)
    fun lex words = lex1 (explode words)
    end;
>   val lex = fn: string -> class list
```

For example:

```
-   lex "the cat sat on";
>   [article, noun,verb] : class list
```

because:

```
lex "the cat sat on" ==>
lex1 ["t","h","e"," ","c","a","t"," ",
 "s","a","t"," ","o","n"] ==>
article::
 lex1 [" ","c","a","t"," ","s","a","t"," ","o","n"] ==>
article::lex1 ["c","a","t"," ","s","a","t"," ","o","n"] ==>
article::noun::lex1 [" ","s","a","t"," ","o","n"] ==>
article::noun::lex1 ["s","a","t"," ","o","n"] ==>
article::noun::verb::lex1 [] ==>
article::noun::verb::[] ==>
[article,noun,verb]
```

## 9.4 Structured datatype binding

In the above example, we constructed a datatype to represent a discrete range of values. We can also define discrete values which are associated with other values which need not be discrete.

For example, in the above lexical analyzer it would be useful to know not just what classes of words were found but also which words were found. That is we would like each discrete class value to be associated with a string value. For this example, we could do this already with a tuple of a class and a string. However, every tuple would have to consist of a class value and a string.

SML generalizes datatype bindings to associate discrete value constructors with arbitrary values. Within the values of a datatype, different value constructors may be associated with different types. Such associations might be termed structured concrete types.

Here, the datatype binding form is extended to:

**datatype** *type_constructor* =
        *value_constructor1* **of** *type_expression1* |
        *value_constructor2* **of** *type_expression2* | ...

where the extension:

    **of** *type_expression*

is optional. This specifies a new type *type_constructor* with values of the form:

*value_constructor1 value1*
*value_constructor2 value2*

...

where *value1* is a value corresponding to *type_expression1*, *value2* is a value corresponding to *type_expression2*, and so on. Here:

*value_constructor1*
*value_constructor2*

...

are functions which build structured values of type *type_constructor*. They do so by associating the value constructors with the values. Thus, they look like function calls for which evaluation stopped after the argument was evaluated.

Note that the values may be of any types including arbitrary structures of lists, tuples, datatypes and functions.

For example, supposing we want the lexical analyzer to return the word as well as the class. We could add a string field to each class constructor:

```
-   datatype class = article of string |
                      noun of string | verb of string;
>   datatype class = article of string |
                      noun of string | verb of string
con article = fn: string -> class
con noun = fn: string -> class
con verb = fn: string -> class
```

Once again, we have the discrete value constructors **article, noun** and **verb** but now each is a function from a string to a class. Effectively, each value constructor may be associated with any string value. For example:

```
article "the"
noun "cat"
verb "sat on"
```

are all valid **class** values.

Let us now modify the lexical analyzer to return the words as well as the classes:

```
-   lex "the cat ate the rat";
>   [article "the",noun "cat",verb "ate",
    article "the",noun "rat"] : class list
```

For each word, we apply the value constructor to the appropriate string:

```
-   (* find words and their classes from string list *)
    fun lex1 [] = [] |
        lex1 ("a"::"t"::"e"::t) = verb "ate"::lex1 t |
        lex1 ("a"::t) = article "a"::lex1 t |
        lex1 ("c"::"a"::"t"::t) = noun "cat"::lex1 t |
        lex1 ("m"::"a"::"t"::t) = noun "mat"::lex1 t |
        lex1 ("r"::"a"::"t"::t) = noun "rat"::lex1 t |
        lex1 ("s"::"a"::"t"::" "::"o"::"n"::t) =
        verb "sat on"::lex1 t |
        lex1 ("t"::"h"::"e"::t) = article "the"::lex1 t |
        lex1 (_::t) = lex1 t;
>   val lex1 = fn : string list -> class list
```

For example:

```
-   lex1 ["a"," ","r","a","t"," ","a","t","e"];
>   [article "a",noun "rat",verb "ate"] : class list
```

because:

```
lex1 ["a"," ","r",a,t," ","a",t,"e"] ==>
article "a"::lex1 [" ","r",a,t," ","a",t,"e"] ==>
article "a"::lex1 ["r",a,t," ","a",t,"e"] ==>
article "a"::noun "rat"::lex1 [" ","a",t,"e"] ==>
article "a"::noun "rat"::lex1 ["a",t,"e"] ==>
article "a"::noun "rat"::verb "ate"::lex1 [] ==>
article "a"::noun "rat"::verb "ate"::[] ==>
[article "a",noun "rat",verb "ate"]
```

## 9.5 Structured pattern matching

Structured datatype patterns consist of a value constructor followed by a pattern for the associated value.

For example, to extract the string from a **class** we match each discrete value:

```
-   (* select word value from word class *)
    fun word (article a) = a |
        word (verb v) = v |
        word (noun n) = n;
>   val word = fn : class -> string
```

Here, we have a datatype pattern consisting of a constructor name followed by a variable for the associated value.

Note that the whole datatype pattern is in brackets, as if it were a function call argument for another function. For example:

```
-   word (article "an");
>   "an" : string
```

Now we can convert a list of **class** back into a string sentence:

```
-   (* convert word class list to string *)
    fun words [] = "" |
        words [w] = word w |
        words (h::t) = word h^" "^words t;
>   val words = fn: class list -> string
```

Note the case for one word to avoid putting a space at the end of the sentence. For example:

```
-   words [article "the",noun "cat",
            verb "sat on",article "the",noun "rat"];
>   "the cat sat on the rat" : string
```

because:

```
words [article "the",noun "cat",
       verb "sat on",article "the",noun "rat"] ==>
"the"^" "^words [noun "cat",
                 verb "sat on",article "the",noun "rat"] ==>
"the"^" "^"cat"^" "^
 words [verb "sat on",article "the",noun "rat"] ==>
```

```
"the"^" "^"cat"^" "^"sat on"^" "^
 words[ article "the",noun "rat"] ==>
"the"^" "^"cat"^" "^"sat on"^" "^"the"^" "^
 words [noun "rat"] ==>
"the"^" "^"cat"^" "^"sat on"^" "^"the"^" ""rat" ==>
"the cat sat on the rat"
```

This is a simple example of a pretty printer, a program to recreate a textual representation from an internal representation.

We can count how often each word class appears in a list of word classes, using accumulation variables for the different classes:

```
    -   (* count word classes with accumulation tuple *)
        fun count1 (ac,nc,vc) [] = (ac,nc,vc) |
            count1 (ac,nc,vc) (article _::t) =
             count1 (ac+1,nc,vc) t |
            count1 (ac,nc,vc) (noun _::t) = count1 (ac,nc+1,vc) t |
            count1 (ac,nc,vc) (verb _::t) = count1 (ac,nc,vc+1) t;
    >   val count1 = fn: int * int * int -> class list -> int * int * int

    -   local
          fun count1 ... = ...
        in
         (* count word classes *)
         val count = count1 (0,0,0)
        end;
    >   val count = fn : class list -> int*int*int
```

For example:

```
    -   count [article "the",noun "cat",
                verb "sat on",article "the",noun "rat"];
    >   (2,2,1) : int * int * int
```

because:

```
count [article "the",noun "cat",
       verb "sat on",article "the",noun "rat"] ==>
count1 (0,0,0) [article "the",noun "cat",
                   verb "sat on",article "the",noun "rat"] ==>
count1 (1,0,0)
          [noun "cat",
           verb "sat on",article "the",noun "rat"] ==>
count1 (1,1,0) [verb "sat on",article "the",noun "rat"] ==>
count1 (1,1,1) [article "the",noun "rat"] ==>
count1 (2,1,1) [noun "rat"] ==>
count1 (2,2,1) [] ==>
(2,2,1)
```

Note, that in structured datatype patterns, the wildcard pattern may only be substituted for value constructors with no arguments. That is, it is not possible to write a pattern to match arbitrary value constructors. For example, we cannot simplify:

```
    -   fun word (article a) = a |
                (noun n) = n |
                (verb v) = v;
    >   val word = fn : class -> string
```

to:

```
fun word (_ w) = w
```

The system cannot deduce what type is intended.


## 9.6 Union types

Datatypes are particularly useful when we wish to construct functions to handle mixed types. In SML, a function's range and domain must be of single types. To get the effect of mixed type domains and ranges we can unite different types using a datatype.

For example, suppose we want to construct a function which will take either an integer or a real argument and return the equivalent integer. If we write:

```
-   fun makeint (x:int) = x |
        makeint (y:real) = floor y;
```

then a type error occurs because **x** and **y** have different types. We can get round this by defining:

```
-   datatype numb = itype of int | rtype of real;
>   datatype numb = itype of int | rtype of real
    con itype = fn: int -> numb
    con rtype = fn: real -> numb
```

Here, an integer is represented by:

**itype** *integer*

and a real by:

**rtype** *real*

For example:

```
-   itype 4;
>   itype 4 : numb
-   rtype 4.2;
>   rtype 4.2 : numb
```

We can now define the function to convert an integer or a real to an integer as:

```
-   (* convert integer or real to numb *)
    fun makeint (itype i) = i |
        makeint (rtype r) = floor r;
>   val makeint = fn : numb -> int
```

so:

```
-   makeint (itype 3);
>   3 : int
-   makeint (rtype 4.71);
>   4 : int
```

Note that we must disguise the integer and real values with a layer of constructor to make them both **numb** type.

For example, suppose we want to represent various shapes of boxes. We have cubes, where all sides are the same, cubic rectangles where two sides are the same, and rectangles where all sides are different. We can use datatype to represent boxes:

```
–   datatype box = cube of int |
                   cubic of int * int |
                   rectangle of int * int * int;
>   datatype box = cube of int |
                   cubic of int * int |
                   rectangle of int * int * int
    con cube = fn : int –> box
    con cubic = fn : int * int –> box
    con rectangle = fn : int * int * int –> box
```

For example, a cube with 3 metre sides is:

```
cube 3
```

a cubic rectangle with two 3 metre sides and a 4 metre side is:

```
cubic (3,4)
```

and a rectangle with 3 metre, 4 metre and 5 metre sides is:

```
rectangle (3,4,5)
```

Suppose we have a list of boxes and we require a list of volumes. First of all, to find the volume of each box case:

```
–   (* find box volume *)
    fun vol (cube s) = s*s*s |
        vol (cubic (s,d)) = s*s*d |
        vol (rectangle (l,b,h)) = l*b*h;
>   val vol = fn : box –> int
```

Note that there is a separate pattern for each box type, with an appropriate pattern following the value constructor. We can then map this over a list of boxes:

```
–   (* find box volumes from box list *)
    val vols = map vol;
>   val vols = fn : box list –> int list
```

For example:

```
–   vols [cube 3,cubic (3,4),rectangle (3,4,5)];
>   [27,36,60] : int list
```

because:

```
vols [cube 3,cubic (3,4),rectangle (3,4,5)] ==>
map vol [cube 3,cubic (3,4),rectangle (3,4,5)] ==>
vol (cube 3)::
 vol (cubic (3,4))::vol (rectangle (3,4,5))::[] ==>
[27,36,60]
```

## 9.7 Example – converting digit strings to number lists

Suppose we have a sequence of integer and decimal numbers with spaces in between them represented as a string, for example:

```
–   "3 4.2 7 8.91";
>   "3 4.2 7 8.91" : string
```

Suppose we want to convert this to a list of **numb** type as used above:

```
–   findnumbs "3 4.2 7 8.91";
>   [itype 3,rtype 4.2,itype 7,rtype 8.91] : numb list
```

First of all, we could use **getwords** from the last chapter to split the string up:

```
-    getwords "3 4.2 7 8.91";
>    ["3","4.2","7","8.91"] : string list
```

**getwords** does not know about the difference between letters and digits. All it does is split a string up where it finds spaces.

Next we could construct a function which given a string number returns the appropriate **numb**. First of all, we will modify **getval** from the last chapter to return a tuple of an integer and the rest of the list from a list of single character strings. For an integer string, the rest of the list will be empty. For a real string, the rest of the list will start after the decimal point:

```
-    (* find integer at start of singleton string list,
        returning rest of list also *)
     fun findint i [] = (i,[]) |
         findint i ("."::t) = (i,t)|
         findint i (h::t) = findint (10*i+ord h-ord "0") t;
>    val findint = fn : int -> string list -> int * string list
```

For example:

```
-    findint 0 ["1","2","3"];
>    (123,[]) : int*string list
```

and:

```
-    findint 0 ["4","5",".","6","7"];
>    (45,["6","7"]) : int * string list
```

Next we require a function to convert the digit string after the decimal point to a real value. Note that the decimal part of a real number may be factored as a sum of digits divided by decreasing negative powers of ten. For example:

```
0.3124 ==> 3/10+0.0124 ==> 3/10+1/100+0.0024 ==>
3/10+1/100+2/1000+0.0004 ==> 3/10+1/100+2/1000+4/10000+0.0
```

To convert the string representation of the decimal part we need to multiply each digit by the appropriate negative power of **10.0**, and then generate the next negative power of **10.0** for the next digit:

```
-    (* convert singleton digit list to decimal fraction *)
     fun findreal p10 r [] = r |
         findreal p10 r (h::t) =
         findreal (p10/10.0) (r+real (ord h-ord "0")*p10) t;
>    val findreal = fn : real -> real -> string list -> real
```

Here, **r** accumulates the decimal part of the real number and **p10** is the next power of 10. For example:

```
-    findreal 0.1 0.0 ["2","4","1"];
>    0.241 : real
```

because:

```
findreal 0.1 0.0 ["2","4","1"] ==>
findreal 0.01 0.2 ["4","1"] ==>
findreal 0.001 0.24 ["1"] ==>
findreal 0.0001 0.241 [] ==>
0.241 : real
```

To return to our number to **numb** conversion, we call **findint** with the digit sequence to return an initial integer and the rest of the string list. If the rest of string list is empty then we return an **itype** for the integer. Otherwise we call **findreal** to convert the decimal part and then form the final **rtype**:

```
-    (* convert singleton digit list to numb *)
     fun findnumb (i,[]) = itype i |
         findnumb (i,t) = rtype (real i+findreal 0.1 0.0 t);
>    val findnumb = fn : int * string list -> numb

-    (* convert string to numb *)
     fun nconv l = findnumb (findint 0 (explode l));
>    val nconv = fn : string -> numb
```

For example:
```
-    nconv "123";
>    itype 123 : numb
```
because:
```
nconv "123" ==>
findnumb (findint 0 (explode "123")) ==>
findnumb (findint 0 ["1","2","3"]) ==>
findnumb (123,[]) ==>
itype 123
```
Also:
```
-    nconv "12.34";
>    rtype 12.34 : real
```
because:
```
nconv "12.34" ==>
findnumb (findint 0 (explode "12.34")) ==>
findnumb (findint 0 ["1","2",".","3","4"]) ==>
findnumb (12,["3","4"]) ==>
rtype (real 12+findreal 0.1 0.0 ["3","4"]) ==>
rtype (real 12+0.34) ==>
rtype 12.34
```

Finally, given the initial string, we use **getwords** to break it up into a list of separate number strings and then **map nconv** over the list:

```
-    (* convert string of numbers to list of numb *)
     fun findnumbs l = map nconv (getwords l);
>    val findnumbs = fn : string -> numb list
```
For example:
```
-    findnumbs "1 2.3 4";
>    [itype 1,rtypr 2.3,itype 4] : numb list
```
because:
```
findnumbs "1 2.3 4" ==>
map nconv (findwords "1 2.3 4") ==>
map nconv ["1","2.3","4"] ==>
nconv "1"::map nconv ["2.3","4","5.6"] ==>
```

```
nconv "1"::nconv "2.3"::map nconv ["4","5.6"] ==>
nconv "1"::nconv "2.3"::nconv "4"::map nconv [] ==>
[itype 1,rtype 2.3,itype 4]
```

## 9.8  Example – lexical analysis of arithmetic expressions

### 9.8.1.Introduction

Suppose we are processing strings representing arithmetic expressions consisting of:

```
operators – + – * / ( )
identifiers – one or more letters
integers – one or more digits
```

As above, we wish to construct a list of individual symbols from a string.

For an identifier, we will return the string and for an integer we will return the value. For an operator, we will return a constant:

```
( == lbra
) == rbra
+ == add
– == diff
* == mult
/ == divide
```

We will use different value constructors to differentiate the different types:

```
–   datatype symbol = ident of string | numb of int |
                       lbra | rbra | add | diff | mult |
                       divide;
```
```
>   datatype symbol = ident of string | numb of int |
                       lbra | rbra | add | diff | mult | divide
    con ident = fn: string –> symbol
    con numb = fn: int –> symbol
    con lbra = lbra : symbol
    ...
```

so examples of valid **symbol**s include:

```
numb 42
ident "total"
lbra
add
```

### 9.8.2  Analyzer function

We will develop the techniques used in the lexical analyzer discussed above to extract a **symbol list** from a **string**. First of all, we recognize the operators:

```
–   (* recognize arithmetic symbols from singleton string
       list *)
    fun arithlex1 [] = [] |
        arithlex1 ("("::t) = lbra::arithlex1 t |
        arithlex1 (")"::t) = rbra::arithlex1 t |
        arithlex1 ("+"::t) = add::arithlex1 t |
        arithlex1 ("-"::t) = diff::arithlex1 t |
```

```
arithlex1 ("*"::t) = mult::arithlex1 t |
arithlex1 ("/"::t) = divide::arithlex1 t |
...
```

For an identifier, we recognize that the **string list** starts with a letter and for an integer we recognize that it starts with a digit:

```
arithlex1 (l as h::t) =
 if h>="a" andalso h<="z"
 then getident l
 else
  if h>="0" andalso h<="9"
  then getint l
  else arithlex1 t
```

Otherwise, we have an invalid character so we ignore it.

### 9.8.3 Mutual declarations

In **arithlex1** above, two auxiliary functions **getident** and **getint** are called. These will also need to call **arithlex1** to continue processing. If we try and define them independently, say **getint** and **getident** before **arithlex1**, then the system will complain that **arithlex1** has not been defined. Similarly, if we define **arithlex1** first then the system will object that **getint** and **getident** have not been defined.

SML allows such mutual references through the simultaneous declaration:

```
fun name1 ... = ...
and name2 ... = ...
and name3 ... = ...
...
```

Here, the bodies of *name1, name2, name3* and so on may all refer to each other. In the above example we need:

```
fun arithlex1 ... = ... getident ... getint ...
and getident ... = ... arithlex1 ...
and getint ... = ... arithlex1 ...
```

### 9.8.4 Recognizing identifiers

The function **getident** will call another function to split the character sequence into the letter sequence for the name and the rest of the character sequence:

```
(* find identifier starting singleton string list,
   returning rest of list also *)
and get_letters [] = ("",[]) |
    get_letters (l as h::t) =
     if h >= "a" andalso h <= "z"
     then
     let val (rest_of_name,rest_of_chars) = get_letters t
     in (h^rest_of_name,rest_of_chars)
     end
     else ("",l)
>   val get_letters = fn : string list -> string * string list
```

Now, **getident** will convert the letters into a symbol and call the analyzer **arithlex1** recursively:

```
(* find identifier followed by symbols in singleton
   string list *)
and getident c =
    let val (name_letters,rest_of_chars) = get_letters c
    in ident name_letters::arithlex1 rest_of_chars
    end
```
>    val getident = fn : string list – > symbol list

## 9.8.5 Recognizing integers

The function **getint** will call another function to split the character sequence into the digit sequence for the number and the rest of the character sequence:

```
(* find number in singleton string list, returning rest of
   list also *)
and get_digits [] = ([],[]) |
    get_digits (l as h::t) =
    if h >= "0" andalso h <= "9"
    then
      let val (rest_of_number,rest_of_chars) = get_digits t
      in (h::rest_of_number,rest_of_chars)
      end
    else ([],l)
```
>    val get_digits = fn : string list – > string list * string list

It will then use **getval** from Chapter 8 to convert the number digits into the **numb** datatype value and call the analyzer **arithlex1** recursively:

```
(* find number followed by symbols in singleton string
   list *)
and getint c =
    let val (number_digits,rest_of_chars) = get_digits c
    in numb (getval 0 number_digits)::arithlex1
    rest_of_chars
    end;
```
>    val getint = fn : string list – > symbol list

## 9.8.6 Complete analyzer

Finally, we need to define the top-level lexical analysis function:

```
–    local
      fun arithlex1 ... = ...
      and get_letters ... = ...
      and getident ... = ...
      and get_digits ... = ...
      and getint ... = ...
    in
      (* arithmetic lexical analyzer *)
      fun arithlex s = arithlex1 (explode s)
    end;
```
>    val arithlex = fn: string – > symbol list
–    arithlex "(total+57)/(19-sum)";
>    [lbra,ident "total",add,numb 57,rbra,divide,lbra,numb 19,
     diff,ident "sum",rbra] : symbol list

### 9.8.7 Pretty printer

We can convert a sequence of symbols back into the original string:

```
-   symbs_to_string [lbra,ident "total",add,numb 57,rbra,
                     divide,lbra,numb 19,diff,ident
                     "sum",rbra];
>   "(total + 57)/(19-sum)": string
```

As for our simple sentences above, we write a function to convert an individual **symbol** into the equivalent string:

```
-   (* convert symbol to string *)
    fun sconv lbra = "("|
        sconv rbra = ")" |
        sconv add = "+" |
        sconv diff = "-" |
        sconv mult = "*" |
        sconv divide = "/" |
        sconv (ident i) = i |
        sconv (numb n) = iconv n;
>val sconv = fn : symbol -> string
```

Note that we need to convert a number to a string. We can do so with **iconv** from the Chapter 8 Exercise 7 which you will have already solved ...

```
-   fun iconv 0 = "0" |
        iconv n = iconv1 n
>   val iconv = fn : int -> string
    and iconv1 0 = "" |
        iconv1 n =
        (iconv1 (n div 10))^(chr (n mod 10+ord "0"));
>   val iconv1 = fn : int -> string
```

Finally, we apply **sconv** to each element of the **symbol** list:

```
-   (* arithmetic symbol list pretty printer *)
    fun symbs_to_string [] = "" |
        symbs_to_string (h::t) = sconv h^symbs_to_string t;
>   val symbs_to_string = fn : symbol list -> string
```

## 9.9 Pattern matching summary

In general a function may be defined by:

> **fn** *pattern1* **=>** *expression1* |
>      *pattern2* **=>** *expression2* | ...

where a *pattern* may be:

i)   a constant
ii)  a bound variable
iii) a list of *patterns*
iv)  a tuple of *patterns*
v)   a datatype *pattern*
vi)  the wildcard pattern _

When a function is called with an argument, the argument is matched against each *pattern* in turn until a match is found. That is:

i)   constants in the *pattern* must be in the same positions in the argument
ii)  bound variables in the *pattern* will be set to the values in the corresponding

argument positions

iii) tuples in the *pattern* must correspond in position and structure to tuples in the argument

iv) lists in the *pattern* must correspond in position and structure to lists in the argument

v) datatypes in the *pattern* must correspond in position, constructor and structure to datatypes in the argument

vi) wildcard patterns match any values in the corresponding argument positions

Once a match is found, the value of the corresponding *expression* is returned.

## 9.10 Summary

In this chapter we have looked at the use of datatypes to define new types. First of all we saw how to define a type with a fixed number of discrete values, identified as constructor names. We then saw how to parameterize constructor names with associated further values. Finally, we looked at forming discriminated union types where disparate types are combined into a single type. We also met mutual declarations as a way of enabling functions to refer to each other.

In the next chapter we will use datatypes to define recursive structures. In particular, we will see how to define an equivalent to the SML `list` type and how to build tree structures. We will then use tree structures to represent the result of parsing symbol sequences from lexical analyzers, for subsequent manipulation.

## 9.11 Exercises

1) A group of functions is required to produce an index from a book. An index is a list of word records. Each word record is a tuple of a string word followed by a list of integer page numbers. The list is in ascending alphabetical word order, for example:

   - `[("apple",[1,2,3]),("banana",[2]),("cherry",[2,4])];`
   > `[("apple",[1,2,3]),("banana",[2]),("cherry",[2,4])] :`
   `(string * int list) list`

   a) Write a function to add an integer page number to the end of a list of integer page numbers provided that the new page number is not already in the list. What is the type of this function?

   b) Write a function to add a word and page number to an index. It should find the word in the index and add the page number to the page number list if it is not already in the list. If the word is not in the index then a new entry should be made. What is the type of this function?

   A book is preprocessed to produce a list of entries which may be string words or integer page numbers, using the following concrete datatype:

   `datatype entry = word of string | page of int`

For example:

- ```
  [page 1,word "the",word "cat",word "sat",word "by",
   word "the",page 2,word "dog",word "by",word "the",
   page 3,word "mat"];
  ```
- > ```
    [page 1,word "the",word "cat",word "sat",word "by",
     word "the",page 2,word "dog",word "by",word "the",
     page 3,word "mat"] : entry list
    ```

c) Write a function to update an index from an entry list. The function should have bound variables for the entry list, the current page number and the index. If the first entry is a word then it is added to the index at the current page and the rest of the entry list is used to update the new index. If the first entry is a page number then that page number is used as the current page number for updating the index from the rest of the entry list. What is the type of this function?

d) Write a function to create an index from an entry list, for example:

```
index [page 1,word "the",word "cat",word "sat",word "by",
       word "the",page 2,word "dog",word "by",word "the",
       page 3,word "mat"] ==>

[("by",[1,2]),("cat",[1]),("dog",[2]),
 ("mat",[3]),("sat",1),("the",[1,2])]
```

What is the type of this function?

2) Yet another automatic car park records the registration number of every car that enters and leaves in a list. It also adds a time signature to the list every hour. Registration numbers and times are represented by the concrete datatype:

```
datatype park = enter of string | exit of string | time of int
```

An example list is:

- ```
  [time 5,enter "ABC123",enter "DEF456",time 6,exit
   "ABC123", enter "GHI789",time 7,exit "GHI789",exit
   "DEF456"];
  ```
- > ```
    [time 5,enter "ABC123",enter "DEF456",time 6,exit "ABC123",
     enter "GHI789",time 7,exit "GHI789",exit "DEF456"] : park list
    ```

Car park lists are to be processed to produce a list of tuples of car registration numbers and times spent in the car park. In the list, a positive time is the time spent in the car park and a negative time is the entry time.

a) Write a function to add a registration number and an entry time as a tuple to a tuple list in registration number alphabetic order. For example:

- ```
  addrn "DEF456" ~4 [("ABC13",~2),("GHI789",~3)];
  ```
- > `[("ABC13",~2),("DEF456",~4),("GHI789",~3)] : (string * int) list`

What is the type of this function?

b) Write a function which updates a tuple list by finding the tuple for a given registration number and adding a given exit time to the negative entry time in the tuple. For example:

- ```
  updatern "DEF456" 7 [("ABC13",~2),
                       ("DEF456",~4),("GHI789",~3)];
  ```
- > `[("ABC13",~2),("DEF456",3),("GHI789",~3)] : (string * int) list`

What is the type of this function?

c) Write a function which given a car park list, the current time, and a tuple list, processes the car park list to produce a final tuple list as follows. If the car park list is empty then return the tuple list. If the car park list starts with a time then process the rest of the list using that time as the current time. If the car park list starts with a registration number for a vehicle entering the car park then add a new tuple for the registration number and negated current time to the tuple list, and process the rest of the car park list. If the car park list starts with the registration number for a vehicle leaving the car park then add the current time to the negated entry time in the corresponding tuple and process the rest of the car park list. What is the type of this function?

3) A road is used by cars, buses and lorries. A roadside detector records in a list every vehicle that passes by. Every 10 minutes it also records the time. The following datatype is used to represent these events:

```
datatype event = car | bus | lorry | time of int * int
```
An example list is:

```
-   [time(14,10),bus,car,car,lorry,time(14,20),car,car,lorry,
     car];
>   [time(14,10),bus,car,car,lorry,time(14,20),car,car,lorry,car] : event list
```

A summary list is required with a record for each time period giving the start time and numbers of cars, buses and lorries before the next time. For example, for the above list:

```
-   [(time(14,10),2,1,1),(time(14,20),3,0,1)];
>   [(time(14,10),2,1,1),(time(14,20),3,0,1)] : (event*int*int*int) list
```

a) Write a function that converts a vehicle list into a summary list. It has bound variables for the current time, a tuple of counts for cars, buses and lorries, and a vehicle list. If the list starts with a vehicle then the appropriate count is incremented and the rest of the list is processed with the current time. If the list starts with a time then a tuple for the current time and counts is put on the front of the result of processing the rest of the list with the current time set to the time from the list and all counts set to 0. What is the type of this function?

b) Write a function of a summary list which returns a list of all time periods for which there were no buses. What is the type of this function?

c) Write a function of a summary list which returns a list of all summary entries for which the time is a precise hour. What is the type of this function?

d) Write a function that returns the result of applying function **f** to all elements of a list satisfying property **p**. What is the type of this function?

e) Define the functions from b) and c) using the function from d).

4) In a cafe, menu items are represented by the following datatype:

```
datatype item = vgn of string * real |
                vgt of string * real |
                omn of string * real
```

The constructors are:

```
vgn == vegan == no animal produce
vgt == vegetarian == no meat
omn == omnivorous == may contain animal produce
```

The string is the item's name and the real is its price.

A menu is held as a list, for example:

```
-   [vgn("tofu",3.6),vgt("quiche",2.7),omn("haggis",1.9)];
>   [vgn("tofu",3.6),vgt("quiche",2.7),omn("haggis",1.9)] : item list
```

a) Write a function to find all the vegan items on a list. What is the type of this function?

b) Write a function to find the cheapest omnivorous item on the list. What is the type of this function?

An order is a tuple of a food item and a quantity, for example:

```
("tofu",3) == 3 orders of tofu
```

c) Write a function which looks up an item and returns the price. What is the type of this function?

d) Write a function which, given an order tuple and a menu, returns the total cost of the order. What is the type of this function?

e) Write a function which, given a list of order tuples and a menu, returns the total cost of all the orders. What is the type of this function?

f) Write a function which, given a list of lists of order tuples and a menu, returns a list of total order costs, one for each order list. What is the type of this function?

5) Logical expressions are composed of truth values and operators, for example:

```
TRUE
TRUE OR FALSE
NOT TRUE AND FALSE
NOT (TRUE AND FALSE)
NOT (TRUE AND FALSE) OR TRUE
NOT (TRUE AND FALSE) OR TRUE AND FALSE
NOT (TRUE AND FALSE) OR (TRUE AND FALSE)
NOT (TRUE AND FALSE) OR (TRUE AND FALSE) OR FALSE
```

Symbols for logical values and operators may be represented by the datatype:

```
datatype symbol = STRUE | SFALSE | SAND | SOR | SNOT | LBRA |
                  RBRA
```

Write a lexical analysis function to produce a list of symbols from a string representing a logical expression.

6) Polynomials are composed of names, integers and the operators +, * and ^, for example:

```
3*x^3+4*x^2+6*x+8
```

Here, ^ means "to the power of".

a) define a datatype to represent polynomial symbols.

b) write a lexical analysis function to produce a list of symbols from a string representing a polynomial.

7) A simple programming language consists of bracketed prefix integer arithmetic operations, functions introducing bound variables and function calls. For example:

```
((+ 2) 3)
(fn x => ((+ x) 1) 3)
(fn y => ((* y) y) (fn x => ((+ x) 1) 4))
(fn x => (fn y => ((* x) y) 3) 5)
```

a) define a datatype to represent symbols for bound variable names, integers and:

( ) + – * / fn =>

b) write a lexical analysis function to produce a list of symbols from a string representing a program.

# CHAPTER 10

# Defining lists and trees

## 10.1 Linked structures

SML provides **lists** as a universal linked structure. We can now use datatypes to define specialized linked structures and then generalize to universal lists.

Consider a linked list of integers:

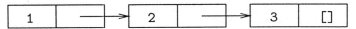

Here, we have a sequence of nodes. Each node holds an integer value and a link to the next node. The end of the sequence is marked by a terminating link.

A datatype for this structure is:

```
-   datatype ilist = icons of int * ilist | INIL;
>   datatype ilist = icons of int * ilist | INIL
    con icons = fn: int * ilist -> ilist
    con INIL = INIL : ilist
```

Here we have a base case for an empty list:

```
INIL
```

and a recursion case:

```
icons of int * ilist
```

for an integer followed by another integer list.

Note the recursive reference to **ilist** in the recursion case. The above example is:

```
-   icons(1,icons(2,icons(3,INIL)));
>   icons(1,icons(2,icons(3,INIL))) : ilist
```

We can now write functions to process linked lists of integers. Once again, the structure of the datatype helps determine the structure of the function with a base case for a terminating link **INIL** and a recursion case for **icons**. For example, to find the sum of the elements of an integer list:

```
-   (* sum ilist *)
    fun isum INIL = 0 |
        isum (icons(v,l)) = v+isum l;
>   val isum = fn: ilist -> int
```

Thus:

```
-   isum (icons(1,icons(2,icons(3,INIL))));
>   6 : int
```

because:

```
isum (icons(1,icons(2,icons(3,INIL)))) ==>
1+isum (icons(2,icons(3,INIL))) ==>
1+2+isum (icons(3,INIL)) ==>
1+2+3+isum INIL ==>
1+2+3+0 ==>
6
```

## 10.2 String linked lists

Suppose we now want to define linked lists of strings, for example:

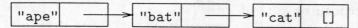

We can use a similar datatype to that for integer lists:

```
-   datatype slist = scons of string * slist | SNIL;
>   datatype slist = scons of string * slist | SNIL
    con scons = fn: string * slist -> slist
    con SNIL = SNIL : slist
```

so the above example is:

```
-   scons("ape",scons("bat",scons("cat",SNIL)));
>   scons("ape",scons("bat",scons("cat",SNIL))) : slist
```

Once again, we can write functions with a base case for the terminating link **SNIL** and a recursion case for **scons**. For example, to join all the elements of a string list together:

```
-   (* implode slist *)
    fun implode SNIL = "" |
        implode (scons(s,l)) = s^implode l;
>   val implode = fn: slist -> string
```

Thus:

```
-   implode (scons("ape",scons("bat",scons("cat",SNIL))));
>   "apebatcat" : string
```

because:

```
implode (scons("ape",scons("bat",scons("cat",SNIL)))) ==>
"ape"^implode (scons("bat",scons("cat",SNIL))) ==>
"ape"^"bat"^implode (scons("cat",SNIL)) ==>
"ape"^"bat"^"cat"^implode SNIL ==>
"ape"^"bat"^"cat"^"" ==>
"apebatcat"
```

## 10.3 Generalized lists

If we compare the datatypes for integer lists:

```
datatype ilist = icons of int * ilist | INIL
```

and string lists:

```
datatype slist = scons of string * slist | SNIL
```
we can see that they are essentially the same apart from the use of the types **int** and **string**. We can generalize to lists of any type by replacing the specific type with a type variable:

```
-   datatype 'a list = cons of 'a * 'a list | NIL;
>   datatype 'a list = cons of 'a * 'a list | NIL
    con cons = fn: 'a * 'a list -> 'a list
    con NIL = NIL : 'a list
```

Now, we can write the above examples as:

```
-   cons(1,cons(2,cons(3,NIL)));
>   cons(1,cons(2,cons(3,NIL))) : int list
-   cons("ape",cons("bat",cons("cat",NIL)));
>   cons("ape",cons("bat",cons("cat",NIL))) : string list
```

Note that, in the first example, the system deduces that the whole structure is of type **int list** because the individual elements are of type **int**. Similarly, in the second example, the system deduces that the whole structure is a **string list** because the individual elements are **string**.

Now, as earlier, we can write polymorphic functions to process lists of arbitrary type. For example, to find the length of a list:

```
-   (* length of list *)
    fun length NIL = 0 |
        length (cons(h,t)) = 1+length t;
>   val length = fn: 'a list -> int
```

or to map a function over a list:

```
-   (* apply function to each in list *)
    fun map f NIL = NIL |
        map f (cons(h,t)) = cons(f h,map f t);
>   val map = fn: ('a -> 'b) -> 'a list -> 'b list
```

In SML systems, lists are based on a similar datatype: the constructor equivalent to **cons** is changed into the infix operator **::** and the constructor **NIL** is changed to **nil**.

## 10.4  List efficiency

A disadvantage of list structures is that they are not very efficient to access. To get to an arbitrary element, it is necessary to go past all the preceding elements. Suppose a list has $N$ elements. Then, at worst $N-1$ elements must be ignored to get to the last one. On average, finding an arbitrary element involves scanning the $N/2$ preceding elements.

For example, with a 5-element list:

```
to get to    skip
element 5    4 elements
element 4    3 elements
element 3    2 elements
element 2    1 element
element 1    0 elements
```

Thus to get to each of these 5 elements in succession involves skipping:

```
4+3+2+1+0 == 10
```

elements in total or:

```
10 div 5 == 2
```

elements on average, which is close to $N/2$.

For long lists, this overhead can becomes prohibitive. For example, with a million elements, half a million must be skipped on average.

## 10.5 Introducing trees

For data with an order between elements, tree structures enable far faster access at the cost of an increase in storage requirements.

In general, a tree consists of a hierarchy of nodes. Each node has a value and branches to sub-nodes. In an ordered tree, the placing of values in sub-nodes is determined by some relationship between those values and the node's value. The top-most node is called the root. Nodes with empty branches are called leaves.

Here, we will consider ordered binary trees where each node has at most two branches, called the left and right branches:

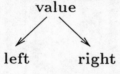

For a given node, all the values on a node's left branch are less than the node value and all the values on a node's right branch are greater than the node's value. For example, let us construct a binary tree from the values:

**7 3 1 5 10 8 12**

We start with a node for **7** as the root:

7

**3** comes before **7** so we add it on a new left branch:

**1** comes before **7** so it goes on **7**'s left branch. **1** comes before **3** so we add it on a new left branch:

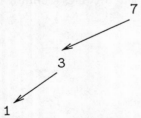

**5** comes before **7** so it goes on **7**'s left branch. **5** comes after **3** so we add it on a new right branch:

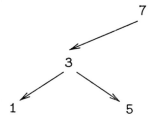

**10** comes after **7** so we add it on a new right branch:

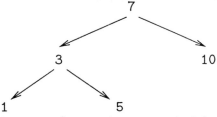

**8** comes after **7** so it goes on **7**'s right branch. **8** comes before **10** so we add it on a new left branch:

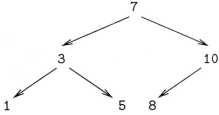

**12** comes after **7** and after **10** so we add it on a new right branch:

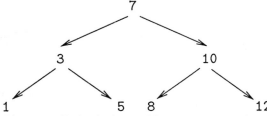

This is called a balanced binary tree: each node has the same number of sub-nodes on the left and right branches. With 1 node in a balanced binary tree there is one layer:

**node1**

With 3 nodes in a balanced binary tree there are two layers:

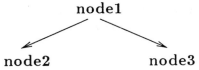

With 7 nodes in a balanced binary tree there are three layers:

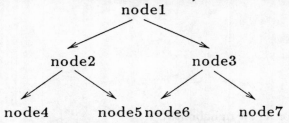

In general, with $N$ nodes in a balanced binary tree, the number of layers is one more than the number of times $N$ can be divided by 2:

$(\log_2 N)+1$

Thus:

```
N           (log2 N)+1  N div 2
1           1           0
3           2           1
7           3           3
15          4           7
31          5           15
63          6           31
...         ..          ...
1023        10          511
```

Hence, searching for a value in a balanced binary tree takes at most $(\log_2 N)+1$ steps because that is the maximum number of layers. For example, the above tree has 7 nodes and so there are $(\log_2 7)+1$ == 3 layers. Consider finding **12** in the above tree:

1) **12 after 7** – right and down
2) **12 after 10** – right and down
3) **12 is 12** == **3** steps

In the equivalent ordered linear list:

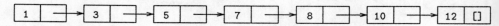

finding **12** takes 7 steps.

## 10.6 Binary tree datatype

Implicit in the above description of binary trees is a recursive definition:

a **binary tree** is **empty**
or
a **binary tree** is a **node** with:
 a **value**
 and
 **left** and **right** branches to **binary trees**

We can represent binary trees of integers with the datatype:

```
-   datatype itree = iempty | inode of int * itree * itree;
>   datatype itree = iempty | inode of int * itree * itree
```

```
con iempty = iempty : itree
con inode = fn: int * itree * itree -> itree
```

**iempty** is the empty node.

Note the recursive references to **itree** in:

```
inode of int * itree * itree
```

For example, the above tree is:

```
inode(7,
      inode(3,
            inode(1,iempty,iempty),
            inode(5,iempty,iempty)),
      inode(10,
              inode(8,iempty,iempty),
              inode(12,iempty,iempty)))
```

To add a value to a binary tree: if the tree is empty then make a new node for that value with empty branches. Otherwise, if the new value comes before the node value then add it to the left branch. Otherwise add it to the right branch:

```
-    (* add integer to ascending order binary tree *)
     fun iadd v iempty = inode(v,iempty,iempty) |
         iadd v (inode(iv,l,r)) =
           if v<=iv
           then inode(iv,iadd v l,r)
           else inode(iv,l,iadd v r);
>    val iadd = fn: int -> itree -> itree
```

Note that this does not build a balanced tree. For example, adding **7** to an empty tree:

```
iadd 7 iempty ==> inode(7,iempty,iempty)
```

Now adding **3**:

```
iadd 3 (inode(7,iempty,iempty)) ==>
inode(7,
      iadd 3 iempty,
      iempty) ==>
inode(7,
      inode(3,iempty,iempty),
      iempty)
```

Next adding: **1**:

```
iadd 1 (inode(7,inode(3,iempty,iempty),iempty)) ==>
inode(7,
      iadd 1 (inode(3,iempty,iempty)),
      iempty) ==>
inode(7,
      inode(3,
            iadd 1 iempty,
            iempty),
      iempty) ==>
inode(7,
      inode(3,
            inode(1,iempty,iempty),
            iempty),
      iempty)
```

Then adding 5:

```
iadd 5 (inode(7,inode(3,inode(1,iempty,iempty),iempty),
iempty)) ==>
inode(7,
      iadd 5 (inode(3,inode(1,iempty,iempty),iempty)),
      iempty) ==>
inode(7,
      inode(3,
            inode(1,iempty,iempty),
            iadd 5 iempty),
      iempty) ==>
inode(7,
      inode(3,
            inode(1,iempty,iempty),
            inode(5,iempty,iempty)),
      iempty)
```

To traverse an ordered binary tree to construct a list of elements in ascending order: if the tree is empty then return the empty list; otherwise append the list from the left branch onto the node value and the list from the right branch:

```
-     (* traverse ascending order binary integer tree *)
      fun itrav iempty = [] |
          itrav (inode(v,l,r)) = (itrav l)@(v::itrav r);
>     val itrav = fn: itree -> int list
```

For example:

```
-     itrav (inode(7,
                    inode(3,
                          inode(1,iempty,iempty),
                          inode(5,iempty,iempty)),
                    iempty));
>     [1,3,5,7] : int list
```

because:

```
itrav (inode(7,
             inode(3,
                   inode(1,iempty,iempty),
                   inode(5,iempty,iempty)),
             iempty)) ==>
itrav (inode(3,
             inode(1,iempty,iempty),
             inode(5,iempty,iempty)))@
 7::itrav iempty ==>
itrav (inode(1,iempty,iempty))@
 3::itrav (inode(5,iempty,iempty))@
  7::itrav iempty ==>
itrav iempty@1::(itrav iempty)@
 3::itrav iempty@5::itrav iempty@
 7::itrav iempty ==>
[]@1::[]@3::[]@5::[]@7::[] ==>
1::3::5::7::[]
```

## 10.7 Polymorphic trees

We can now generalize the above tree datatype to binary trees of arbitrary type. Once again, we replace **int** with a type variable **'a**:

```
-   datatype 'a tree = empty | node of 'a * 'a tree * 'a tree;
>   datatype 'a tree = empty | node of 'a * 'a tree * 'a tree
    con empty = empty : 'a tree
    con node = fn: 'a * 'a tree * 'a tree -> 'a tree
```

Consider the function to add a value to an integer tree:

```
fun iadd v iempty = inode(v,iempty,iempty) |
    iadd v (inode(iv,l,r)) =
    if v<iv
    then inode(iv,iadd v l,r)
    else inode(iv,l,iadd v r);
```

Here, the comparison operator **<** is used on **iv** which is the value from an **inode** and therefore an **int**. Hence **<** denotes integer "less than". To generalize this function we need to abstract from the comparison operator:

```
-   (* add value to polymorphic binary tree *)
    fun add less v empty = node(v,empty,empty) |
        add less v (node(nv,l,r)) =
        if less v nv
        then node(nv,add less v l,r)
        else node(nv,l,add less v r);
>   val add = fn: ('a -> 'a -> bool) -> 'a -> 'a tree -> 'a tree
```

so **less** is a:

```
'a -> 'a -> bool
```

function.

**add** will operate on a tree of arbitrary type provided it is supplied with an appropriate comparison operator for that type. For example, for trees of strings:

```
-   fun sless (s1:string) s2 = s1<=s2;
>   val sless = fn: string -> string -> bool
-   val sadd = add sless;
>   val sadd = fn: string -> string tree -> string tree
```

Similarly, for trees of reals:

```
-   fun rless (r1:real) r2 = r1<=r2;
>   val rless = fun: real -> real -> bool
-   val radd = add rless;
>   val radd = fn: real -> real tree -> real tree
```

The traversal function for polymorphic trees is more or less the same as that for integer trees, as no type specific operations are carried out:

```
-   (* inorder polymorphic binary tree traversal *)
    fun trav empty = [] |
        trav (node(v,l,r)) = trav l@v::trav r;
>   val trav = fn: 'a tree -> 'a list
```

This function is polymorphic.

## 10.8 Grammar and parsing

Consider the English sentences:

```
the mouse saw a big peach
the mouse ate the peach
a big cat saw the mouse
the big cat ate the small mouse
```

We can characterize the structure of these sentences with a set of rules:

A *sentence* is a *noun phrase* followed by a *verb* followed by a *noun phrase*

A *noun phrase* is an article followed by a *noun part*

A *noun part* is an *adjective* followed by a *noun*

A *noun part* is a *noun*

An *article* is one of: `a` `the`

A *noun* is one of: `mouse cat peach`

An *adjective* is one of: `big small`

A *verb* is one of: `saw ate`

These rules or grammar define the syntax of a class of sentences: that is, they specify which sequences of symbols are considered to be well formed.

For computer use, syntax is often defined using a notation called BNF (Backus–Naur form). BNF was originally developed to define the syntax of ALGOL 60, an early and extremely influential language. BNF and variants are now widely used to define programming language syntax.

A BNF rule or production consists of a left hand side and a right hand side separated by the symbol `::=`, which is read as "is". The left hand side is the rule name or non-terminal symbol within angle brackets `<` and `>`. The right hand side is a sequence of options separated by the option symbol `|`, which is read as "or". Each option is a sequence of terminal symbols or lexemes and non-terminal symbols. Thus, the above grammar is:

```
<sentence> ::= <noun phrase> <verb> <noun phrase>
<noun phrase> ::= <article> <noun part>
<noun part> ::= <adjective> <noun> | <noun>
<article> ::= a | the
<noun> ::= cat | mouse | peach
<adjective> ::= big | small
<verb> ::= saw | ate
```

A set of productions may be used to check whether or not a sequence of symbols is well formed, by starting with the first rule and trying to match one of its right hand side options. To match a right hand side option, match each element in the sequence. To match a terminal symbol, look for that symbol. To match a non-terminal symbol, try to match one of its options. If a match fails then back up a stage and try again.

Consider checking:

```
the cat ate the small peach
```

starting with **sentence**:

To find a **<sentence>** find a **<noun phrase>** followed by a **<verb>** followed by a **<noun phrase>**.

To find a <noun phrase> find an <article> followed by a <noun part>.

 To find an <article> find an **a**, which fails.
 To find an <article> find a **the** which succeeds.
 To find a <noun part>, find an <adjective> followed by a <noun>.
  To find an <adjective> find a **big**, which fails.
  To find an <adjective> find a **small**, which fails.
 To find a <noun part>, find a <noun>.
  To find a <noun> find a **cat**, which succeeds.
To find a <verb>, find a **saw**, which fails.
To find a <verb>, find an **ate**, which succeeds.
To find a <noun phrase> find an <article> followed by a <noun part>.

 To find an <article> find an **a**, which fails.
 To find an <article> find a **the** which succeeds.
 To find a <noun part>, find an <adjective> followed by a <noun>.
  To find an <adjective> find a **big**, which fails.
  To find an <adjective> find a **small**, which succeeds.
  To find a <noun> find a **cat**, which fails.
  To find a <noun> find a **mouse**, which fails.
  To find a <noun> find a **peach**, which succeeds.

We can write SML functions to parse sentences directly from the rules. For each rule, a function processes a sequence of symbols and returns a tuple consisting of a boolean to indicate whether or not the function has succeeded and the rest of the symbols.

We assume that we have a datatype:

```
datatype symbol = art of string | adj of string |
                  n of string | v of string | sfail
```

to represent symbols and a lexical analyzer which generates a **symbol list** from a **string**. Note the constructor **sfail** which is used later to indicate a failure to find a symbol. We do not want to use an exception because that would halt the parsing. Instead, we need to note that an option has failed and try another one.

First of all, to find an <article>:

```
-   (* recognize <article> and return rest of symbols *)
    fun article (art a::t) = (true,t) |
        article s = (false,s)
>   val article = fn: symbol list -> bool * symbol list
```

look for an **art** symbol. If one is not found then return **false** and the whole symbol sequence. Otherwise, return **true** and the rest of the symbols following the **art**. For example:

```
-   article [art "the",n "cat",v "ate"];
>   (true,["n "cat",v "ate"]) : bool * symbol list
```

Similarly, to find an <adjective>:

```
     (* recognize <adjective> and return rest of symbols *)
     and adjective (adj a::t) = (true,t) |
         adjective s = (false,s)
>    val adjective = fn : symbol list -> bool * symbol list
```

look for an **adj** symbol. If one is not found then return **false** and the whole symbol sequence. Otherwise, return **true** and the rest of the symbols following the **adj**. For example:

```
-    adjective [n "cat",v "ate"];
>    (false,[n "cat",v "ate"]) : bool * symbol list
```

Once again, to find a **<noun>**:

```
     (* recognize <noun> and return rest of symbols *)
     and noun (n nn::t) = (true,t) |
         noun s = (false,s)
>    val noun = fn: symbol list -> bool * symbol list
```

look for an **n** symbol. If one is not found then return **false** and the whole symbol sequence. Otherwise, return **true** and the rest of the symbols following the **n**.

Finally, to find a **<verb>**:

```
     (* recognize <verb> and return rest of symbols *)
     and verb (v vv::t) = (true,t)
         verb s = (false,s)
>    val verb = fn: symbol list -> bool * symbol list
```

look for a **v** symbol. If one is not found then return **false** and the whole symbol sequence. Otherwise, return **true** and the rest of the symbols following the **v**.

Next, to find a **<noun part>**:

```
     (* recognize <noun part> and return rest of symbols *)
     and nounpart [] = (false,[]) |
         nounpart s =
         let val (a,r1) = adjective s
         in
          if not a
          then
           let val (nn,r2) = noun s
           in
            if not nn
            then (false,s)
            else (true,r2)
          end
          else
           let val (nn,r2) = noun r1
           in
            if not nn
            then (false,s)
            else (true,r2)
           end
         end
>    val nounpart = fn: symbol list -> bool * symbol list
```

look for an **<adjective>**. If one is not found then look for a **<noun>**. If one is not found then return **false** and the whole symbol sequence. Otherwise, return **true** and the rest of the symbol sequence following the **<noun>**. If, however, an **<adjective>** is found then look for a **<noun>** following the **<adjective>**. If one is not found then return **false** and the whole symbol sequence. Otherwise, return **true** and the rest of the symbol sequence following the **<noun>**. For example:

```
-   nounpart [adj "big",n "cat",v "sat"];
>   (true,[v "sat"]) : bool * symbol list
```

because:

```
nounpart [adj "big",n "cat",v "sat"] ==>
  let val (a,r1) = adjective s
   adjective [adj "big",n "cat",v "sat"] ==>
   (true,[n "cat",v "sat"])
 in ...
  let val (n,r2) = noun r1
   noun [n "cat",v "sat"] ==>
   (true,v "sat")
 in ... (true,r2) ==>
  (true,v "sat")
```

Again:

```
-   nounpart [n "cat",v "sat"];
>   (true,[v "sat"]) : bool * symbol list
```

because:

```
nounpart [n "cat",v "sat"] ==>
let val (a,r1) = adjective s
 adjective [adj "big",n "cat",v "sat"] ==>
 (false,[n "cat",v "sat"])
in ...
 let val (n,r2) = noun s
  noun [n "cat",v "sat"] ==>
  (true,v "sat")
in ... (true,r2) ==>
 (true,v "sat")
```

Thus, to find a **<noun phrase>**:

```
      (* recognize <noun phrase> and return rest of symbols *)
      and nounphrase [] = (false,[]) |
          nounphrase s =
            let val (a,r1) = article s
            in
             if not a
             then (false,s)
             else
              let val (np,r2) = nounpart r1
              in
               if not np
               then (false,r1)
               else (true,r2)
              end
            end
>   val nounphrase = fn: symbol list -> bool * symbol list
```

look for an `<article>`. If one is not found then return **false** and the whole symbol sequence. Otherwise, look for a `<noun part>`. If one is not found then return **false** and the whole symbol sequence. Otherwise, return **true** and the rest of the symbols following the `<noun part>`. For example:

```
-   nounphrase [art "the",n "cat",v "ate",art "the"];
>   (true,[art "the"]) : bool * symbol list
```

because:

```
nounphrase [art "the",n "cat",v "ate",art "the"] ==>
 let val (a,r1) = article s
  article [art "the",n "cat",v "ate",art "the"] ==>
  (true, [n "cat",v "ate",art "the"])
 in ...
  let val (np,r2) = nounpart r1
   nounpart [n "cat",v "ate",art "the"] ==>
   (true,[v "ate",art "the"])
  in ... (true,r2) ==>
  (true,[v "ate",art "the"])
```

Finally, to find a `<sentence>`:

```
(* recognize <sentence> and return rest of symbols *)
and sentence [] = (false,[]) |
    sentence s =
      let val (np1,r1) = nounphrase s
      in
       if not np1
       then (false,s)
       else
        let val (vv,r2) = verb r1
         in
          if not vv
          then (false,r1
          else
           let val (np2,r3) = nounphrase r2
           in
            if not np2
            then (false,r2)
            else (true,r3)
          end
        end
      end;
>   val sentence = fn: symbol list -> bool * symbol list
```

look for a `<noun phrase>`. If one is not found then return **false** and the whole symbol sequence. Otherwise look for a `<verb>` following the `<noun phrase>`. If one is not found then return **false** and the whole symbol sequence. Otherwise, look for a `<noun phrase>` following the `<verb>`. If one is not found then return **false** and the whole symbol sequence. Otherwise, return **true** and the rest of the symbols following the `<noun phrase>`. For example, to check:

```
the cat ate the small peach
```

we assume that:

```
lex "the cat ate the small peach" ==>
[art "the",n "cat",v "ate",art "the",adj "small",n "peach"]
```

so:

```
-   sentence [art "the",n "cat",v "ate",
             art "the",adj "small",n "peach"];
>   (true,[]) : bool * symbol list
```

because:

```
sentence [art "the",n "cat",v "ate",
          art "the",adj "small",n "peach"] ==>
 nounphrase [art "the",n "cat",v "ate",
             art "the",adj "small",n "peach"] ==>
  article [art "the",n "cat",v "ate",
           art "the",adj "small",n "peach"] ==>
  (true,[n "cat",v "ate",art "the",adj "small",n "peach"])
  nounpart
  [n "cat",v "ate", art "the",adj "small",n "peach"] ==>
   adjective
   [n "cat",v "ate",art "the",adj "small",n "peach"] ==>
   (false,[n "cat",v "ate",art "the",adj "small",n "peach"])
   noun [n "cat",v "ate",art "the",adj "small",n "peach"] ==>
   (true,[v "ate",art "the",adj "small",n "peach"])
   (true,[v "ate",art "the",adj "small",n "peach"])
  verb [v "ate",art "the",adj "small",n "peach"] ==>
  (true,[art "the",adj "small",n "peach"])
  nounphrase [art "the",adj "small",n "peach"] ==>
   article [art "the",adj "small",n "peach"] ==>
   (true,[adj "small",n "peach"])
   nounpart [adj "small",n "peach"] ==>
    adjective [adj "small",n "peach"] ==>
    (true,[n "peach"])
    noun [n "peach"] ==>
    (true,[])
    (true,[])
   (true,[])
  (true,[])
```

## 10.9 Parse trees

A successful recognition sequence or parse may be represented as a parse tree, where each node is marked with a non-terminal symbol and each leaf is a terminal symbol. For the above example, we could represent the parse sequence as:

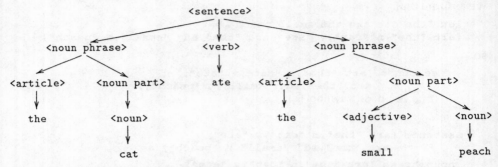

Parse trees are a useful intermediate representation for subsequent processing of structured information defined by syntax rules. In SML, we can use datatypes to represent parse trees. We will start with an option for each production. For example:

```
datatype tree = sentnode of tree * tree * tree |
                 nounphrnode of tree * tree |
                 nounprt1node of tree * tree |
                 nounprt2node of tree |
                 artnode of symbol |
                 vnode of symbol |
                 nnode of symbol |
                 adjnode of symbol |
                 fail
```

Here, the node for a **<sentence>** has three branches for the two **<nounphrase>**s and the **<verb>**.

The node for a **<nounphrase>** has two branches for the **<article>** and the **<nounpart>**.

There are two cases for **<nounpart>**: the first for an **<adjective>** followed by a **<noun>** and the second for a single **<noun>**.

Finally, there are single branch nodes for each of **<article>**, **<verb>**, **<noun>** and **<adjective>**, each with a **symbol** as the leaf.

Note the inclusion of the constructor **fail**. As before, this will be used to indicate failure during parsing.

Thus, the **<verb> ate** would be:

```
vnode (v "ate").
```

The **<noun part> big cat** would be:

```
nounprt1node (adjnode (adj "big"),nnode (n "cat")).
```

The **<noun part> mouse** would be:

```
nounprt2node (nnode (n "mouse")).
```

The **<noun phrase> the big cat** would be:

```
nounphrnode (artnode (art "the"),
             nounprt1node (adjnode (adj "big"),
             nnode (n "cat"))).
```

The above tree would be:

```
sentnode (nounphrnode (artnode (art "the"),
                       nounprt2node (nnode (n "cat"))),
          vnode (v "ate"),
          nounphrnode (artnode (art "the"),
                       nounprt1node (adjnode (adj "small"),
                                     nnode (n "peach"))))
```

Note that there is excess information in this tree. For each terminal symbol we already have a lexical constructor so we do not need a syntactic constructor as well to identify it. Thus, we could simplify the datatype to:

```
datatype tree = sentnode of tree * symbol * tree |
                nounphrnode of symbol * tree |
                nounprt1node of symbol * symbol |
                nounprt2node of symbol |
                fail
```

by dropping the constructors for rules which only recognize terminal symbols. Now the above tree simplifies to:

```
sentnode (nounphrnode (art "the",
                       nounprt2node (n "cat")),
          v "ate",
          nounphrnode (art "the",
                       nounprt1node (adj "small",
                                     n "mouse")))
```

We can now modify the above parser to build the tree during the parse. For an **<article>**:

```
  -   (* recognize <article>
         return symbol leaf and rest of symbols *)
      fun article (art a::t) = (art a,t) |
          article s = (sfail,s)
  >   val article = fn: symbol list -> symbol * symbol list
```

return the **art** and the rest of the symbols or **sfail** and all the symbols. For example:

```
  -   article [art "the",n "cat",v "ate"];
  >   (art "the",[n "cat",v "ate"]) : symbol * symbol list
```

Similarly, for an **<adjective>**:

```
      (* recognize <adjective>,
         return return symbol leaf and rest of symbols *)
      and adjective ((adj a)::t) = (adj a,t) |
          adjective s = (sfail,s)
  >   val adjective = fn: symbol list -> symbol * symbol list
```

return the **adj** and the rest of the symbols or **sfail** and all the symbols. For example:

```
  -   adjective [n "cat",v "ate"];
  >   (sfail,[n "cat",v "ate"]) : symbol*symbol list
```

For a **<noun>**:

```
      (* recognize <noun>,
         return symbol leaf and rest of symbols *)
      and noun ((n nn)::t) = (n nn,t) |
          noun s = (sfail,s)
  >   val noun = fn: symbol list -> symbol * symbol list
```

return the **n** and the rest of the symbols or **sfail** and all the symbols.

For a **<verb>**:

```
(* recognize <verb>,
   return symbol leaf and rest of symbols *)
and verb ((v vv)::t) = (v vv,t) |
    verb s = (sfail,s)
>   val verb = fn: symbol list -> symbol * symbol list
```

return the **v** and the rest of the symbols or **sfail** and all the symbols.

Next, for a **<noun part>**:

```
(* recognize <noun part>,
   return tree node and rest of symbols *)
and nounpart [] = (fail,[]) |
    nounpart s =
     let val (a,r1) = adjective s
     in
      if a=sfail
      then
       let val (nn,r2) = noun s
       in
        if nn=sfail
        then (fail,s)
        else (nounprt2node nn,r2)
       end
      else
       let val (nn,r2) = noun r1
       in
        if nn=sfail
        then (fail,s)
        else (nounprt1node(a,nn),r2)
       end
      end
>   val nounpart = fn: symbol list -> tree * symbol list
```

if there is not an **<adjective>** then return a **nounprt2node** and the rest of the symbols after finding a **<noun>**. If there is an **<adjective>** then return a **nounprt1node** and the rest of the symbols after finding a **<noun>** after the **<adjective>**. Otherwise return **fail** and all the symbols. For example:

```
-   nounpart [n "cat",v "ate"];
>   (nounpart2node (n "cat"),[v "ate"]) : tree*symbol list
-   nounpart [adj "big",n "mouse",v "ate"];
>   (nounpart1node (adj "big",n "mouse"),[v "ate"]) : tree * symbol list
```

For a **<noun phrase>**:

```
(* recognize <noun phrase>,
   return tree node and rest of symbols *)
and nounphrase [] = (fail,[]) |
    nounphrase s =
     let val (a,r1) = article s
     in
      if a=sfail
      then (fail,s)
      else
       let val (np,r2) = nounpart r1
       in
```

```
          if np=fail
          then (fail,s)
          else (nounphrnode(a,np),r2)
         end
       end
>   val nounphrase = fn: symbol list -> tree * symbol list
```

return a **nounphrnode** and the rest of the symbols after finding a **<article>** and a **<noun part>**. Return **fail** and all the symbols if any element fails. For example:

```
–   nounphrase [art "a",adj "small",n "cat",v "ate"];
>   (nounphrnode (art "the",
                        nounpart1node (adj "small",n "cat")),[v "ate"]) :
    tree*symbol list
```

Finally, for a **<sentence>**:

```
(* recognize <sentence>,
     return tree node and rest of symbols *)
and sentence [] = (fail,[]) |
    sentence s =
      let val (np1,r1) = nounphrase s
       in
        if np1=fail
        then (fail,s)
        else
         let val (vv,r2) = verb r1
          in
           if vv=sfail
           then (fail,s)
           else
            let val (np2,r3) = nounphrase r2
             in
              if np2=fail
              then (fail,s)
              else (sentnode(np1,vv,np2),r3)
             end
           end
         end;
>   val sentence = fn: symbol list -> tree * symbol list
```

return a **sentnode** and the rest of the symbols after finding a **<noun phrase>**, **<verb>** and **<noun phrase>**. Return **fail** and all the symbols if any of the elements fail.

Assuming that we have an appropriate lexical analyzer, we can now parse sentences. For example:

```
–   sentence (lex "the cat ate the small peach");
>   (sentnode
      (nounphrnode(art "the",
                        nounprt2node (n "cat")),
       v "ate",
       nounphrnode(art "the",
                        nounprt1node(adj "small",
                                          n "peach"))),[]) : tree * symbol list
```

because:

```
sentence (lex "the cat ate the small peach") ==>
sentence [art "the",n "cat",v "ate",art "the",adj "small",
         n "peach"] ==>
nounphrase [art "the",n "cat",v "ate",art "the",adj "small",
           n "peach"] ==>
 article [art "the",n "cat",v "ate",art "the",adj "small",
          n "peach"] ==>
 (art "the",
  [n "cat",v "ate",art "the",adj "small",n "peach"])
 nounpart
  [n "cat",v "ate",art "the",adj "small",n "peach"] ==>
  adjective
   [n "cat",v "ate",art "the",adj "small",n "peach"] ==>
  (sfail,[n "cat",v "ate",art "the",adj "small",n "peach"])
   noun
    [n "cat",v "ate",art "the",adj "small",n "peach"] ==>
   (n "cat",[v "ate",art "the",adj "small",n "peach"])
  (nounprt2node (n "cat"),
   [v "ate",art "the",adj "small",n "peach"])
 (nounphrnode(art "the", nounprt2node (n "cat")),
  [v "ate",art "the",adj "small",n "peach"])
verb [v "ate",art "the",adj "small",n "peach"] ==>
(v "ate",[art "the",adj "small",n "peach"])
nounphrase [art "the",adj "small",n "peach"] ==>
 article [art "the",adj "small",n "peach"] ==>
 (art "the",[adj "small",n "peach"])
 nounpart [adj "small",n "peach"] ==>
  adjective [adj "small",n "peach"] ==>
  (adj "small",[n "peach"])
  noun [n "peach"] ==>
   (n "peach",[])
 (nounprt1node(adj "small",n "peach"),[])
 (nounphrnode(art "the",nounprt1node(adj "small",
                                      n "peach")),[])
(sentnode
 (nounphrnode(art "the",
              nounprt2node (n "cat")),
 v "ate",
 nounphrnode(art "the",
             nounprt1node(adj "small",
                          n "peach"))),[])
```

## 10.10 Concrete and abstract syntax

It is useful to distinguish between concrete syntax, the structure of representation, and abstract syntax, the meaningful structure. Concrete syntax often contains details which, while fundamental to checking that a symbol sequence is well formed, are not relevant to subsequent processing.

Consider the following grammar of arithmetic expressions:

```
<expression> ::= <term> + <term> |
                 <term> - <term> |
                 <term>
<term> ::= <factor>*<factor> |
           <factor> / <factor> |
           <factor>
<factor> ::= - <base> | <base>
<base> ::= <integer> | ( <expression> )
```

Consider the parse tree for the expression:

```
(6+7)*8
```

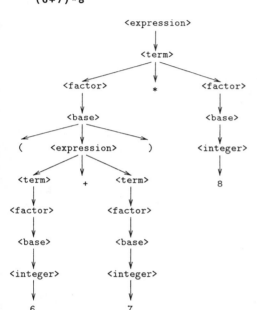

From the point of view of processing arithmetic expression parse trees this contains unnecessary structural information. For example, there are chains of nested subtrees where each level has only one branch. Thus, we see that an **<integer>** is a **<base>** is a **<factor>** is a **<term>** when all we need to know about is the **<integer>**.

For example, the brackets appear explicitly but their presence is already indicated by the nesting of the expression they enclose in the tree. If we miss such details out then we are left with the minimal structural details necessary for further processing.

For example, the above tree might be simplified to:

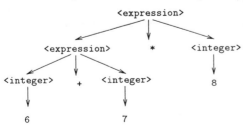

An abstract syntax for arithmetic expressions is:

```
<expression> ::= <expression>+<expression> |
                 <expression>-<expression> |
                 <expression>*<expression> |
                 <expression>/<expression> |
                 -<expression> |
                 <integer>
```

Note that this abstract syntax cannot be used to parse arithmetic expressions because information about operator precedence and brackets is lost. Rather, it defines the structure of resultant parse trees. An equivalent datatype for this abstract syntax is:

```
datatype exp = addexp of exp * exp |
               diffexp of exp * exp |
               multexp of exp * exp |
               divexp of exp * exp |
               negexp of exp |
               integer of int |
               fail
```

Note that operators are not present explicitly but are implied by the corresponding constructors. For example:

```
42 == integer 42
6*7 == multexp (integer 6,integer 7)
6*7+8 == addexp (multexp (integer 6,integer 7),integer 8)
(6+7)*8 == multexp (addexp (integer 6,integer 7),integer 8)
```

## 10.11 Parsing arithmetic expressions

Suppose we wish to construct abstract syntax trees for arithmetic expressions, given the datatype:

```
datatype symbol = lbra | rbra | add | diff | mult | divide |
                  numb of int
```

for symbols.

We will use the exception:

```
-   exception Pfail;
>   exception Pfail
```

to terminate parsing when the first error occurs.

To find an `<expression>`:

```
-   (* recognize <expression>,
       return exp node and rest of symbols *)
    fun exp [] = raise Pfail |
        exp e =
          let val (t1,r1) = term e
            in
             if r1=[] orelse (hd r1<>add andalso hd r1<>diff)
            then (t1,r1)
            else
             let val (t2,r2) = term (t1 r1)
             in
               if hd r1=add
               then (addexp(t1,t2),r2)
               else (diffexp(t1,t2),r2)
             end
```

```
          end
>   val exp = fn: symbol list –> exp * symbol list
```

find a `<term>`. If it is not followed by an `add` or a `diff` then return the datatype
for the `<term>` and the rest of the symbols. Otherwise, find a `<term>` after the
`add` or `diff` and return an `addexp` or `diffexp` and the rest of the symbols.
    To find a `<term>`:

```
    (* recognize <term>,
       return exp node and rest of symbols *)
    and term [] = raise Pfail |
        term t =
         let val (f1,r1) = factor t
         in
          if r1=[] orelse (hd r1<>mult andalso hd r1<>divide)
          then (f1,r1)
          else
           let val (f2,r2) = factor (tl r1)
           in
            if hd r1=mult
            then (multexp(f1,f2),r2)
            else (divexp(f1,f2),r2)
           end
         end
>   val term = fn: symbol list –> exp * symbol list
```

find a `<factor>`. If it is not followed by a `mult` or a `divide` then return the
datatype for the `<factor>` and the rest of the symbols. Otherwise, find a
`<factor>` after the `mult` or `divide` and return a `multexp` or `divexp` and the rest
of the symbols.
    To find a `<factor>`:

```
    (* recognize <factor>,
       return exp node and rest of symbols *)
    and factor [] = raise Pfail |
        factor (diff::t) =
         let val (b1,r1) = base t
          in (negexp b1,r1)
         end |
        factor f = base f
>   val factor = fn: symbol list –> exp * symbol list
```

if there is a `diff` then find a `<base>` after it and return a `negexp` and the rest of
the symbols. Otherwise look for a `<base>`.
    To find a `<base>`:

```
    (* recognize <base>,
       return exp node and rest of symbols *)
    and base (numb ii::t) = (integer ii,t) |
        base (lbra::t) =
         let val (e1,r1) = exp t
         in
          if r1=[] orelse hd r1<>rbra
          then raise Pfail
          else (e1,tl r1)
         end |
        base _ = raise Pfail;
>   val base = fn: symbol list –> exp * symbol list
```

either find a **numb** symbol and return an **integer** and the rest of the symbols or find an **<expression>** between **lbra** and **rbra** and return its datatype and the rest of the symbols.

For example, again assuming a suitable lexical anlyser:

```
-    exp (arithlex "(2+3)*4");
>    (multexp (addexp(integer 2,integer 3),integer 4),[]) :
     exp*symbol list
```

because:

```
exp [lbra,numb 2,add,numb 3,rbra,mult,numb 4] ==>
 term [lbra,numb 2,add,numb 3,rbra,mult,numb 4] ==>
  factor [lbra,numb 2,add,numb 3,rbra,mult,numb 4] ==>
   base [lbra,numb 2,add,numb 3,rbra,mult,numb 4] ==>
    exp [numb 2,add,numb 3,rbra,mult,numb 4] ==>
     term [numb 2,add,numb 3,rbra,mult,numb 4] ==>
      factor [numb 2,add,numb 3,rbra,mult,numb 4] ==>
       base [numb 2,add,numb 3,rbra,mult,numb 4] ==>
       (integer 2,[add,numb 3,rbra,mult,numb 4])
       (integer 2,[add,numb 3,rbra,mult,numb 4])
      (integer 2,[add,numb 3,rbra,mult,numb 4])
      term [numb 3,rbra,mult,numb 4] ==>
       factor [numb 3,rbra,mult,numb 4] ==>
        base [numb 3,rbra,mult,numb 4] ==>
        (integer 3,[rbra,mult,numb 4])
        (integer 3,[rbra,mult,numb 4])
       (integer 3,[rbra,mult,numb 4])
      (integer 3,[mult,numb 4])
     (addexp(integer 2,integer 3),[rbra,mult,numb 4])
    (addexp(integer 2,integer 3),[mult,numb 4])
    term [numb 4] ==>
     factor [numb 4] ==>
      base [numb 4] ==>
      (integer 4,[])
     (integer 4,[])
    (integer 4,[])
   (multexp (addexp(integer 2,integer 3),integer 4),[])
  (multexp (addexp(integer 2,integer 3),integer 4),[])
```

## 10.12 Case expression

In **exp**, **term** and **base** above we used rather clumsy nested conditional expressions to decide what to do after trying to find something at the start of a symbol sequence. For example, in **exp**, after trying to find a **<term>** we have:

```
...
if r1=[] orelse (hd r1<>add andalso hd r1<>diff)
```

```
then ...
else ...
```

to see if there is an appropriate operator after the **term**. Later on we have:

```
if hd r1=add
then ...
else ...
```

to discriminate between finding an addition or a subtraction operator.

SML provides the case expression as a way of using pattern matching to discriminate between cases within expressions. It has the form:

**case** *expression* **of** *match*

where the *match* is a sequence of optional patterns and associated expressions:

*pattern1* => *expression1* |
*pattern2* => *expression2* |
...

as in a function value.

Here, the *expression* is evaluated and matched against each *pattern* in the *match* in turn. When a match succeeds the expression associated with the pattern is evaluated, with the pattern's bound variables set to the corresponding values from the expression's value.

We can use a case expression to simplify **exp** by factoring out the cases for an addition operator, a subtraction operator or nothing appropriate after a **<term>**:

```
fun exp [] = raise Pfail |
    exp e =
     let val (t1,r1) = term e
     in
      case r1 of
        (add::r2) => let val (t2,r3) = term r2
                     in (addexp(t1,t2),r3)
                     end |
        (diff::r2) => let val (t2,r3) = term r2
                      in (diffexp(t1,t2),r3)
                      end |
         _ => (t1,r1)
     end
```

We can also rebuild **term**:

```
and term [] = raise Pfail |
    term t =
     let val (f1,r1) = factor t
     in
      case r1 of
        (mult::r2) => let val (f2,r3) = factor r2
                      in (multexp(f1,f2),r3)
                      end |
        (divide::r2) => let val (f2,r3) = factor r2
                        in (divexp(f1,f2),r3)
                        end |
         _ => (f1,r1)
     end
```

and **base**:

```
and base (numb ii::t) = (integer ii,t) |
    base (lbra::t) =
     let val (e1,r1) = exp t
     in
      case r1 of
       (rbra::r2) => (e1,r2) |
       _ => raise Pfail
     end |
    base _ = raise Pfail;
```

but not **factor**.

## 10.13 Multiple exceptions

We used a single exception to indicate failure during parsing. There are several ways in which parsing can fail and we can define different exceptions to discriminate amongst them. In **exp**, **term**, **factor** and **base** we can encounter an empty list when we are expecting an expression, term, factor or base respectively. In all cases, the problem is that there is no more text to be parsed. In **base** we can fail to find a closing right bracket or we can fail to find any of the symbols that start a base, that is a left bracket or a number. Thus, we can define three exceptions:

```
-   exception No_text; (* text expected *)
>   exception No_text
-   exception Rbra; (* right bracket expected *)
>   exception Rbra
-   exception Numb_or_lbra; (* number or left bracket
                                       expected *)
>   exception Numb_or_lbra
```

and call them at the appropriate points:

```
fun exp [] = raise No_text | ...
and term [] = raise No_text | ...
and factor [] = raise No_text | ...
and base [] = raise No_text |
    base (numb ii::t) = (integer ii,t) |
    base (lbra::t) =
     let val (e1,r1) = exp t
     in
      case r1 of
       (rbra::r2) => (e1,r2) |
       _ => raise Rbra
     end |
    base _ = raise Numb_or_lbra;
```

Now, the raised exception gives slightly more indication as to what has gone wrong:

```
-   exp (arithlex "2*");
uncaught exception No_text

-   exp (arithlex "2*(3+4");
uncaught exception Rbra

-   exp (arithlex "2*+4");
uncaught exception Numb_or_lbra
```

## 10.14 Interpreting arithmetic expressions

We can now write an interpreter to evaluate parse trees for arithmetic expressions. It consists of a function with a case for each sort of **exp** which calls itself recursively for the sub **exp**s and then applies the corresponding arithmetic operator:

```
-   (* interpret arithmetic tree *)
    fun arith (integer i) = i |
        arith (addexp(e1,e2)) = arith e1+arith e2 |
        arith (diffexp(e1,e2)) = arith e1-arith e2 |
        arith (multexp(e1,e2)) = arith e1
        arith e2 |
        arith (divexp(e1,e2)) = arith e1 div arith e2 |
        arith (negexp e) = ~(arith e);
>   val arith = fn: exp -> int
```

For example:

```
-   arith (multexp (addexp (integer 6,integer 7),integer 8));
>   104 : int
```

because:

```
arith (addexp(integer 6,integer 7))*arith (integer 8) ==>
(arith (integer 6)+arith (integer 7))*arith (integer 8) ==>
(6+7)*8 ==>
104
```

We can sew together the lexical analyzer **arithlex** from Chapter 9 with the parser **exp** and the arithmetic interpreter **arith** to form a complete calculator:

```
-   (* interpret arithmetic expression string *)
    fun calc s =
        let val (tree,rest) = exp (arithlex s)
        in
         if rest<>[]
         then raise Pfail
         else arith tree
        end;
>   val calc = fn : string -> int
```

We call **exp** to parse the sequence of symbols from **arithlex**. If there is anything left of the symbols after parsing then **rest** will not be empty and the parsing exception is raised. Otherwise **arith** is called to evaluate the tree. For example:

```
-   calc "(3+4)*6";
>   42 : int

-   calc "(3+4) 6";
uncaught exception Pfail
```

## 10.15 Arithmetic pretty printer

We can also write a pretty printer function which converts an **exp** into an equivalent **string**:

```
    -   (* convert arithmetic tree to string *)
        fun atos (integer i) = iconv i |
            atos (addexp(e1,e2)) = "("^atos e1^"+"^atos e2^")" |
            atos (diffexp(e1,e2)) = "("^atos e1^"-"^atos e2^")" |
            atos (multexp(e1,e2)) = "("^atos e1^"*"^atos e2^")" |
            atos (divexp(e1,e2)) = "("^atos e1^"/"^atos e2^")" |
            atos (negexp e) = "("^"-"^atos e^")";
    >   val atos = fn: exp -> string
```

Note the use of the function **iconv**, which converts an integer into a **string**, and which you wrote for Chapter 8 Exercise 7.

Note that **iconv** cannot convert negative integers. For example:

```
    -   atos (integer 42);
    >   "42" : string
```

Note that all expressions are strictly bracketed, that is brackets are placed round all sub-expressions. For example:

```
    -   atos (addexp (integer 6,integer 7));
    >   "(6 + 7)" : string
```

because:

```
atos (addexp (integer 6,integer 7)) ==>
"("^atos (integer 6)^"+"^atos (integer 7)^")" ==>
"("^"6"^"+"^"7"^")" ==>
"(6+7)"
```

Again:

```
    -   atos (multexp (addexp (integer 6,integer 7),integer 8));
    >   "((6*7) + 8)" : string
```

because:

```
atos (multexp (addexp (integer 6,integer 7),integer 8)) ==>
"("^atos (addexp (integer 6,integer 7))^"*"^
atos (integer 8)^")" ==>
"("^"("^atos (integer 6)^"+"^atos (integer 7)^")"^
"*"^atos (integer 8)^")" ==>
"("^"("^"6"^"+"^"7"^")"^"*"^"8"^")" ==>
"((6+7)*8)"
```

It is possible to pretty print arithmetic expressions without unnecessary brackets by constructing additional cases to consider the precedence of operators in subtrees relative to the operator in the current tree.

## 10.16 Summary

In this chapter we have looked at the use of datatypes in defining our own recursive structures. We saw how to construct type specific and polymorphic lists and binary trees. We then looked at parsing as a way of recognizing structured symbol sequences and constructing parse trees. Finally, we considered parse tree traversal and interpretation. Along the way we met the case expression for pattern matching within expressions.

In the next chapter, we are going to discuss techniques for input and output. This will enable our programs to interact with the screen and keyboard, and with files.

## 10.17 Exercises

For the first three exercises, assume the datatype definition:

```
datatype 'a tree = empty | node of 'a * 'a tree * 'a tree
```

It is worth giving some thought to the generation of suitable test trees from lists for these three exercises.

1) write the following functions. In each case, identify the function's type.
   a) check if a tree appears as a subtree of another tree
   b) generate a list from a tree with reverse in-order traversal, i.e visit the right branch, the node and the left branch
   c) generate a list from a tree with pre-order traversal, i.e visit the node, the left branch and the right branch
   d) generate a list from a tree with post-order traversal, i.e visit the left branch, the right branch and the node

2) Write the following functions. Identify each function's type:
   a) copy a string tree, putting "s" on the end of each node value
   b) copy an integer tree, doubling each node value
   c) copy a tree, applying function f to each node value
   d) define the functions from a) and b) using the function from c)
   e) copy a real tree, squaring each node value provided it is not within 0.001 of 0
   f) copy a string tree, ending each node value with an "s", provided it does not already end with an "s"
   g) copy a tree, applying function f to each node if it satisfies predicate p
   h) define the functions from a), b), e) and f) using the function from g)

3) Write the following functions. Identify the type of each function:
   a) join together all the node values of a string tree in in-order
   b) add together all the node values of an integer tree
   c) flatten a tree by applying function f to the node value and the result of flattening the left and right branches. For an empty branch, return value v
   d) define the functions from a) and b) using the function from c)
   e) define the functions from 1)b), 1)c) and 1)d) using the function from c)

4) Logical expressions have the form:

```
<expression> ::= <term> AND <expression> | <term>
<term> ::= <factor> OR <term> | <factor>
<factor> ::= NOT <base> | <base>
<base> ::= TRUE | FALSE | ( <expression> )
```

For example:

```
TRUE
TRUE OR FALSE
NOT TRUE AND FALSE
NOT (TRUE AND FALSE)
NOT (TRUE AND FALSE) OR TRUE
NOT (TRUE AND FALSE) OR TRUE AND FALSE
NOT (TRUE AND FALSE) OR (TRUE AND FALSE)
NOT (TRUE AND FALSE) OR (TRUE AND FALSE) OR FALSE
```

   a) using the lexical analyzer from Chapter 9 Exercise 5, write a function to check if a string has this form

b) modify the functions from a) to build an **\<expression\>** parse tree from a string using the following datatype:

```
datatype logic =
 TRUE |              - for TRUE
 FALSE |             - for FALSE
 AND of logic*logic | - for <term> AND <expression>
 OR of logic*logic |  - for <factor> OR <term>
 NOT logic           - for NOT <base>
```

Note that brackets are discarded.

c) write a function to pretty print a parse tree from b)

d) write a function to evaluate logical expression parse trees using the following rules:

```
evaluate NOT TRUE == FALSE
evaluate NOT FALSE == TRUE

evaluate FALSE AND FALSE == FALSE
evaluate FALSE AND TRUE == FALSE
evaluate TRUE AND FALSE == FALSE
evaluate TRUE AND TRUE == TRUE

evaluate FALSE OR FALSE == FALSE
evaluate FALSE OR TRUE == TRUE
evaluate TRUE OR FALSE == TRUE
evaluate TRUE OR TRUE == TRUE

evaluate NOT <base> == evaluate NOT (evaluate <base>)

evaluate <base> OR <term> ==
  evaluate (evaluate <base>) OR (evaluate <term>)

evaluate <term> AND <expression> ==
  evaluate (evaluate <term>) AND (evaluate <expression>)
```

5) Polynomials have the form:

```
<polynomial> ::= <term>+<polynomial> | <term>
<term> ::= <integer>*<power> | <power> | <integer>
<power> ::= <name>^<integer> | <name>
<integer> == any sequence of digits
<name> == any sequence of lower case letters
```

For example:

```
3*x^3+4*x^2+6*x+8
```

a) define a datatype to represent **\<polynomial\>** parse trees

b) using the lexical analyzer from Chapter 9 Exercise 6, write a function to parse a **\<polynomial\>** string and return a **\<polynomial\>** parse tree

c) write a function to check that all **\<name\>**s in a **\<polynomial\>** parse tree are the same

d) write a function to evaluate a **\<polynomial\>** parse tree satisfying c) with a given integer value of the **\<name\>**, according to the following rules:

```
evaluate <name> == value for <name>

evaluate <name>^<integer> ==
  value for <name> to the power of <integer>

evaluate <integer>*<power> ==
  <integer>*(evaluate <power>)
```

```
evaluate <term>+<polynomial> ==
(evaluate <term>)+(evaluate <polynomial>)
```

e) write a pretty printer to generate `<polynomial>` strings from `<polynomial>` parse trees

f) write a function to differentiate a polynomial according to the following rules:

```
differentiate <integer> == 0

differentiate <name> == 1

differentiate <name>^<integer> ==
 <integer>*<name>^<integer>-1)

differentiate <integer>*<power> ==
 <integer>*(differentiate <power>)

differentiate <term>+<polynomial> ==
 (differentiate <term>)+(differentiate <polynomial>)
```

It should be applied to a `<polynomial>` parse tree and return a `<polynomial>` parse tree.

6) A simple programming language has the form:

```
<expression> ::= <name> | <integer> | <call>
<call> ::= ( fn <name> => <expression> <expression> ) |
           ((<operator> <expression>) <expression>)
<operator> ::= + | - | * | /
<integer> == any sequence of digits
<name> == any sequence of lower case letters
```

For example:

```
((+ 2) 3)
(fn x => ((+ x) 1) 3)
(fn y => ((* y) y) (fn x => ((+ x) 1) 4))
(fn x => (fn y => ((* x) y) 3) 5)
```

Note that function calls are strictly bracketed. Note that arithmetic operations are prefix and strictly bracketed as if arithmetic operators were functions of type:

```
<integer> -> <integer> -> <integer>
```

a) design a datatype to represent `<expression>` parse trees

b) using the lexical analyzer from Chapter 9 Exercise 7, write functions to parse `<expression>` strings and return `<expression>` parse trees

c) write a pretty printer to generate `<expression>` strings from `<expression>` parse trees

d) write a function that checks that no `<name>`s in expressions are free, i.e. that every `<name>` in an `<expression>` is introduced by an enclosing `<function>`. For example, in:

```
(fn x => ((+ x) y) 3)
```

and:

```
(fn y => ((* y) y) (fn x => ((+ x) y) 11))
```

the `y` in the body of `fn x => ...` is free as it is not introduced anywhere.

e) write a function which given an `<expression>` parse tree checks that every `<function>` introduces a unique `<name>` so, for example:

```
(fn x => ((+ x) 1) (fn x => ((- x) 1) 2))
```

is not allowed as both functions introduce **x**

f) write a function that evaluates **<expression>** parse trees satisfying d) and e) according to the following rules:

```
evaluate ((+ <expression1>) <expression2>) =
  (evaluate <expression1>)+(evaluate <expression2>)
```

```
evaluate ((- <expression1>) <expression2>) ==
  (evaluate <expression1>)-(evaluate <expression2>)
```

```
evaluate ((* <expression1>) <expression2>) ==
  (evaluate <expression1>)*(evaluate <expression2>)
```

```
evaluate ((/ <expression1>) <expression2>) ==
  (evaluate <expression1>)/(evaluate <expression2>)
```

```
evaluate (fn <name> => <expression1> <expression2>) ==
  evaluate replace <name> in <expression1>
          with (evaluate <expression2>)
```

The result should be an integer.

g) change the function from f) so that the final evaluate rule is:

```
evaluate (fn <name> => <expression1> <expression2>) ==
  evaluate replace <name> in <expression1>
          with <expression2>
```

# CHAPTER 11

# Input and output

## 11.1 Introduction

So far we have worked exclusively within SML; that is, our input data have been SML values as have our output results. We are now going to look at how to acquire input data from beyond the SML system from a keyboard or a file. Similarly, we will also look at how to present results on screens or in files without being restricted to SML's value forms.

At its simplest SML input and output (I/O) is based on sequences of characters. System functions are provided for acquiring character sequences as strings from input sources and sending them to output destinations. We will use these as the basis of more elaborate I/O.

There are two complementary approaches to I/O. First of all, for output, a whole string may be assembled, and displayed or sent to a file all at once. Similarly, for input a whole string may be read at once and then the lexical and string processing techniques discussed in previous chapters may be used to extract the represented information. An alternative approach is to output and input values item by item rather than packing or unpacking them all together. Here, nested let expressions are very useful for sequencing I/O. These two approaches may be combined for interactive I/O where a program prompts a user for information and then displays results before prompting for more information.

SML I/O is based on what are called streams as the sources and destinations of data. A stream may either be used for input, in which case its type is:

**instream,**

or for output, in which case its type is:

**outstream,**

but not both at the same time.

In general, a stream is established by opening a file. The system will allocate a new stream. Stream values cannot be displayed but there is never any need to do so. Instead, the stream value is associated with a name and that name is used to pass the stream to the I/O functions.

The built in stream **std_in** may be used for input from the keyboard. Similarly, the built in stream **std_out** may be used for output to the display.

Note that `instream` and `outstream` are not equality types; that is, it is not possible to identify a stream by comparing it with another stream.

## 11.2 Unit type

The **unit** type has one value:

```
()
```

For example:

```
-   ();
>   () : unit
```

The unit type is used to give a neutral result after an activity or to pass a neutral argument to a function.

`()` may be used in pattern matching as a dummy argument. For example:

```
-   fun hello() = "hello";
>   val hello = fn : unit -> string
-   hello();
>   "hello" : string
```

`()` might be thought of as an empty tuple. Many I/O functions return `()` as their result.

## 11.3 Screen output

For basic output, the system function **output** is used:

```
-   output;
>   fn : outstream * string -> unit
```

This takes a tuple argument consisting of an output stream and a string. That string is then displayed on the designated output stream without quotes. **output** returns the unit value `()`.

For example, to display **"banana"** on the screen:

```
-   output (std_out,"banana");
banana> () : unit
```

Note that the string **"banana"** has been displayed on the same line as the SML result. A newline character:

```
\n
```

may be used to make the result of any subsequent **output** use or system output appear on a new line. For example:

```
-   output (std_out,"banana\n");
banana
>   () : unit
```

We can disguise the use of **output** with **std_out** to make a string to screen function:

```
-   (* string write to standard output *)
    fun swrite s = output (std_out,s);
>   val swrite = fn : string -> unit
```

for example:

```
-   swrite "fritters";
fritters> (): unit
```

From this we can write a function to follow the display of a string with a newline:

```
-   (* newline terminated string write to standard output *)
    fun swriteln s = swrite (s^"\n");
>   val swriteln = fn : string -> unit
```

for example:

```
-   swriteln "split";
split
>   () : unit
```

## 11.4 String list output

Suppose we have a list of strings and we want to display it on the screen. We could **implode** the list and then print it directly. For example:

```
-   swrite (implode ["water","for","wetness"]);
waterforwetness> () : unit
```

However, **implode** joins all the list elements together without intervening spaces.

Instead, we could write a recursive function to join the strings together with spaces in between:

```
-   (* space separated implode *)
    fun spimplode [] = "" |
        spimplode [s] = s |
        spimplode (h::t) = h^" "^spimplode t;
>   val spimplode = fn : string list -> string
```

So that:

```
-   spimplode ["water","for","wetness"];
>   "water for wetness" : string
```

We can define:

```
-   (* space separated string list write to standard output *)
    fun slwrite s = swrite (spimplode s);
>   val slwrite = fn : string list -> unit
```

to write a space separated sequence from a list of strings. Thus:

```
-   slwrite ["water","for","wetness"];
water for wetness> () : unit
```

To generate a newline after the string sequence, a newline character may be added to the end of the joined up strings:

```
-   (* newline terminated,
        space separated string list write to standard output *)
    fun slwriteln s = swriteln (spimplode s);
>   val slwriteln = fn : string list -> unit
```

Hence:

```
-   slwriteln ["water","for","wetness"];
water for wetness
>   () : unit
```

A list of strings may be displayed on separate lines by adding a newline character to the end of each:

```
-   (* join newline to each in string list *)
val addnl = map (fn s => s^"\n");
>   val addnl = fn : string list -> string list
```

For example:

```
-   addnl ["able","baker","charlie"];
>   ["able\n","baker\n","charlie\n"] : string list
```

The list can then be **implode**d for display:

```
-   (* separate line string list write to standard output *)
    fun slwritelns s = swrite (implode (addnl s));
>   val slwritelns = fn : string list -> unit
```

Thus:

```
-   slwritelns ["able","baker","charlie"];
able
baker
charlie
>   () : unit
```

## 11.5 Integer list output

In Chapter 8 Exercise 7 you wrote a function to convert an integer to a string:

```
-   (* convert integer to string *)
    fun iconv 0 = "0" |
        iconv n = iconv1 n
>   val iconv = fn : int -> string

    (* convert integer to string ignoring single 0 *)
    and iconv1 0 = "" |
        iconv1 n = iconv1 (n div 10)^chr (n mod 10+ord "0");
>   val iconv1 = fn : int -> string
```

This may be used to output an integer to the screen by converting it to a string:

```
-   (* integer write to standard output *)
    fun iwrite i = swrite (iconv i);
>   val iwrite = fn : int -> unit
```

For example:

```
-   iwrite 777;
777 > () : unit
```

Similarly, to display an integer as the last item on a line, its string is followed by a newline character:

```
-   (* newline terminated integer write to standard output *)
    fun iwriteln i = swriteln (iconv i);
>   iwriteln = fn : int -> unit
```

For example:

```
-   iwriteln 888;
888
>   () : unit
```

A list of integers could be displayed by mapping **iconv** over it to produce a list of strings and then calling **slwrite** to display a space separated sequence:

```
-    (* space separated integerlist write to standard output *)
     fun ilwrite l = slwrite (map iconv l);
>    val ilwrite = fn : int list -> unit
```

For example:

```
>    ilwrite [1,3,5,7];
1 3 5 7> () : unit
```

As for a string list, an integer list display may be followed by a newline by placing a newline character at the end of the space separated joined up strings for the integers:

```
-    (* newline terminated,
         space separated integer list write to standard output *)
     fun ilwriteln s = slwriteln (map iconv s);
>    val ilwriteln = fn : int list -> unit
```

For example:

```
-    ilwriteln [3,6,9,12];
3 6 9 12
>    () : unit
```

## 11.6 Formatted output

It is often desirable to print out items within constant width fields, for example to lay out tables. For a string which is shorter than the width, spaces might be added on the left. This is said to right justify the string within the width:

```
-    (* right justify string in given width field *
     fun rjustify i s = if size s<i
                        then rjustify i (" "^s)
                        else s;
>    val rjustify = fn : int -> string -> string
```

For example:

```
-    rjustify 8 "banana" ;
>    "  banana" : string
```

To display a list of integers right justified within 6 character fields on separate lines:

```
-    slwritelns (map ((rjustify 6) o iconv)
                     [1,22,333,4444,55555,666666]);
         1
        22
       333
      4444
     55555
    666666
>() : unit
```

Recall that:

```
(f o g) x == f (g x)
```

so:

```
map ((rjustify 6) o iconv)
```

applies **rjustify 6** to the result of applying **iconv** to each element of an integer list.

Similarly, to left justify a string, spaces are added to the right:

```
-   (* left justify string in given width field *)
    fun ljustify i s = if size s<i
                       then ljustify i (s^" ")
                       else s;
>   val ljustify = fn : int -> string -> string
```

Formatted output is particularly useful for displaying tables from tuple lists. Each tuple may be assembled into the equivalent table row as a string for display.

For example, suppose we have a list of tuples of names and ages:

```
-   [("Agnes",35),("Bill",3),("Clare",21)];
>   [("Agnes",35),("Bill",3),("Clare",21)] : (string*int) list
```

We want to produce a table with the name left justified in a 10 width column and the age right justified in a 3 width column, with a space in between the name and age. First of all, for one tuple:

```
-   (* layout name/age entry *)
    fun layout (n,a) =
        ljustify 10 n^" "^ rjustify 3 (iconv a)^"\n";
>   val layout = fn : string*int -> string
```

For example:

```
-   layout ("Agnes",35);
>   "Agnes     35\n" : string
```

Then for a list of tuples **layout** may be **map**ed over it:

```
-   map layout [("Agnes",35),("Bill",3),("Clare",21)];
>   ["Agnes     35\n","Bill       3\n","Clare     21\n"] : string list
```

Finally, the list may be **implode**d for display:

```
-   (* tabulate name/age table *)
    fun tabulate t = swrite (implode (map layout t));
>   val tabulate = fn : string -> unit
```

For example:

```
-   tabulate [("Agnes",35),("Bill",3),("Clare",21)];
Agnes     35
Bill       3
Clare     21
>   () : unit
```

We may precede the table with headings by displaying an appropriate string:

```
-   (* tabulate name/age table with heading *)
    fun table t =
        swrite ("Name      Age\n"^ (implode (map layout t)));
>   val table = fn : string -> unit
```

For example:

```
-    table [("Agnes",35),("Bill",3),("Clare",21)];
Name    Age
Agnes    35
Bill      3
Clare    21
>   () : unit
```

The above example is a trifle dense. We could be slightly more long winded by carrying out each stage of the display explicitly:

```
-    fun table t =
        let val heading = swriteln "Name       Age"
        in tabulate t
        end
>    val table = fn : (string*int) list -> unit

     and tabulate [] = () |
         tabulate (h::t) =
         let val line = swrite (layout h)
         in tabulate t
         end;
>    val tabulate = fn : (string * int) list -> unit
```

First **table** writes the heading. It then calls **tabulate** to repeatedly layout and display each tuple on a separate line.

Note the use of let expressions to sequence the display.


## 11.7 Keyboard input

For input, the system function **input** is used:

```
-    input;
>    fn : instream*int -> string
```

This takes a tuple argument consisting of an input stream and the number of characters to be read from that input stream, and returns that number of characters as a single string.

For example, to read a single letter from the keyboard:

```
-    input (std_in,1);
#
>    "#" : string
```

On most systems, the "Enter" or "Return" key must be pressed before **input** will start taking in characters. Both will insert a newline character into the stream which the system will input as **"\n"**.

For example, suppose we want to read a line terminated by a newline from the standard input, and return that line as a list of single characters. The next character is read. If it is a newline character then the empty list is returned. Otherwise that character is placed on the front of reading the rest of the line:

```
-    (* read newline terminate input from standard input *)
     fun sreadln() = let val ch = input (std_in,1)
                     in
                      if ch="\n"
                      then []
                      else ch::sreadln ()
                     end;
>    val sreadln = fn: unit -> string list
```

Note the use of the **unit** argument **()**. For example:

```
-   sreadln();
time for tea
>   ["t","i","m","e"," ","f","o","r"," ","t","e","a"] : string list
```

We can use this to read a single integer from the keyboard:

```
-   (* read newline terminated integer from standard input *)
    fun ireadln() = getval 0 (sreadln());
>   val ireadln = fn : unit -> int
```

Here, **sreadln** is used to get a whole line which is assumed to be a single integer. **getval** is then used to convert the corresponding string to an integer. For example:

```
-   ireadln();
2331
>   2331 : int
```

## 11.8 Interactive I/O

A simple way to interact with a program is for it to prompt for input to the screen, read input up to some end character from the keyboard, process the input, display the output to the screen and prompt for input again.

For example, suppose we have a sequence of pairs of integers and we want to find the first as a percentage of the second. We could:

a)  prompt for the first number
b)  read the first number
c)  prompt for the second number
d)  read the second number
e)  calculate the first as a percentage of the second
f)  display the result
g)  initiate the whole process again:

```
-   (* interactive percent calculator *)
    fun percents () =
          let val prompt1 = swrite "1st number: "
          in
           let val n1 = ireadln()
           in
            let val prompt2 = swrite "2nd number: "
             in
              let val n2 = ireadln()
              in
              let val result = iwriteln (n1*100 div n2)
              in percents ()
              end
             end
            end
          end
        end;
>   val percents = fn : unit -> 'a
```

For example:

```
–    percents();
```
1st number: **45**
2nd number: **90**
50
1st number: **70**
2nd number: **80**
87
1st number: **...**

Note this function never stops! The SML system gives it the arbitrary type **'a** as result.

We could end the function by prompting for a character to decide whether or not to continue:

```
–    (* user terminatable interactive percent calculator *)
     fun percents () =
          let val prompt1 = swrite "1st number: "
          in
           let val n1 = ireadln()
           in
            let val prompt2 = swrite "2nd number: "
            in
             let val n2 = ireadln()
             in
              let val result = iwriteln (n1*100 div n2)
              in
               let val q = swrite "more? enter y or n: "
               in
                let val a = sreadln()
                in
                 if a=["n"]
                 then ()
                 else percents ()
                end
               end
              end
             end
            end
           end
          end;
>    val percents = fn : unit –> unit
```

Now, the function will continue unless an "n" on a line by itself is entered. For example:

```
–    percents();
```
1st number: **24**
2nd number: **40**
60
more? enter y or n: **y**
1st number: **24**
2nd number: **30**
80
more? enter y or n: **n**
>    () : unit

We can now make an interactive calculator by using the lexical analyzer **arithlex1** from Chapter 9 with the parser **exp** and evaluator **arith** from

Chapter 10:

```
    (* interactive arithmetic calculator *)
    fun intcalc () =
        let val prompt = swrite "enter an expression: "
        in
         let val e = sreadln()
         in
          let val (tree,rest) = exp (arithlex1 e)
          in
           if rest<>[]
           then raise Pfail
           else
            let val result = iwriteln (arith tree)
            in intcalc()
            end
          end
         end
        end;
>   val intcalc = fn : unit -> 'a
```

We prompt for input, read a line and parse the result of lexically analysing the input string. If the tree is a failure node or there are symbols left after parsing we halt. Otherwise we output the result of evaluating the tree. In either case we repeat the whole process again. For example:

```
-   intcalc();
enter an expression: 3*4+5
17
enter an expression: ...
```

## 11.9 Handling exceptions

In the above calculator, processing terminates if a parse error is encountered and an exception is raised. It would be more satisfactory if we could intercept the exception, provide an appropriate error message and input another expression.

SML enables the construction of exception handlers which can catch a raised exception before it is detected by the system. An exception handling expression has the form:

*expression* **handle** *match*

where a *match* is a sequence of alternative patterns and associated expressions:

```
pattern1 => expression1 |
pattern2 => expression2 |
...
```

as in a function definition. At its simplest, each *pattern* is the constructor for an exception.

The *match* is known as the handler for the *expression*.

When the *expression* is evaluated, the system remembers that it has an associated handler. Sub-expressions may also have handlers and they are remembered in sequence. If an exception is raised during evaluation then control is returned to the most recent handler. The exception's constructor is matched in turn against each of the handler's *patterns*. If a match is found then the value of the corresponding *expression* is returned. If no match is found then control is returned to the next most recent handler and so on. If none of the remembered handlers has a pattern for the exception then ultimately the system will display an uncaught exception message.

The type of each *expression* in the handler must be the same as the type of the original *expression* .

To apply this to the calculator, first of all we will separate out the input/ output from the actual interpretation:

```
-   fun interpret e = ...
    and intcalc () =
        let val prompt = swrite "enter an expression: "
        in
         let val e = sreadln()
         in
          let val result = writeln (interpret e)
          in intcalc()
          end
         end
        end;
>   val intcalc = fn : unit -> 'a
```

As before, the interpreter calls the parser followed by the calculator. In addition, there is a handler with a case for each possible parsing error:

```
-   fun interpret e =
        let val (tree,rest) = exp (arithlex1 e)
        in
         if rest<>[]
         then "extra text at end of expression"
         else iconv (arith tree)
        end
        handle No_text => "end of text encountered" |
                Rbra => ") expected" |
                Numb_or_lbra => "number or ( expected"
>   val interpret = fn : string list -> string
```

Note that the handler returns strings. The interpreter must also return strings if no exceptions are raised, that is a string error message if the expression text is not empty after parsing or a string for the result of the calculation. For example:

```
-   intcalc();
enter an expression: 3*
end of text encountered
enter an expression: 3*+5
number or ( expected
enter an expression: 3*(4+5
) expected
enter an expression: 3*(4+5) 6
extra text at end of expression
enter an expression: ...
```

Exceptions may also be used to pass back values. They are then declared with associated types, like a datatype:

**exception** *name* **of** *type*

Such an exception is raised with a specific value. For example, we could declare a single parser error exception which returns a string:

```
-   exception Error of string;
>   exception Error of string
```

and call it with different strings to reflect the different errors:

```
fun exp [] = raise Error "end of text encountered" | ...
and term [] = raise Error "end of text encountered" | ...
and factor [] = raise Error "end of text encountered" | ...
and base [] = raise Error "end of text encountered" |
    base (numb ii::t) = (integer ii,t) |
    base (lbra::t) =
    let val (e1,r1) = exp t
    in
      case r1 of
        (rbra::r2) => (e1,r2) |
        _ => raise Error ") expected"
    end |
    base _ = raise Error "number or ( expected";
```

An exception handler pattern may now include appropriate constants, constructors and bound variables. For example:

```
-   fun interpret e =
        let val (tree,rest) = exp (arithlex1 e)
        in
          if rest<>[]
          then "extra text at end of expression"
          else iconv (arith tree)
        end
        handle Error s => s;
>   val interpret = fn : string list -> string
```

Here, **s** matches the string value passed back with **Error**.

The advantage of this approach is that the error message is identified at the point where the error is detected.


## 11.10 File output

For output to a file, the file must be opened for output. The system function **open_out**:

```
-   open_out;
>   fn : string -> outstream
```

takes a file name string as argument, creates a new file with that name, having thrown away any existing file with the same name, and returns an output stream which may then be used in **output**.

After output the file on the stream should be closed by the system function **close_out**:

```
-   close_out;
>   fn : outstream -> unit
```

which takes an output stream argument and returns **()**.

Thus, to send a string to a file:

```
-   (* write string to file *)
    fun fswrite f s
     let val outs = open_out f
    in
     let val ss = output (outs,s)
     in close_out outs
     end
    end;
>   val fswrite = fn : string -> string -> unit
```

First of all, the file with string name associated with **f** is opened, returning a stream value to **outs**. Next, the string **s** is sent to the file on stream **outs**. Finally, the file on stream **outs** is closed.

For example, to send the string **"time for tea"** to the file: **myfile.txt**:

```
-   fswrite "myfile.txt" "time for tea";
>   () : unit
```

Note that we never need to see or know how the stream is represented. We just mention the name associated with the stream value.

We can use this function to send an arbitrary string to an arbitrary file. For example, to send the tuple of names and ages in list **s** to a file **f,** we **map layout** over it and implode the result as before:

```
-   (* write name/age table to file *)
    fun out_age_name f s = fswrite f (implode (map layout s));
>   val out_age_name = fn : string -> string -> unit
```

Note that attempting to output to a closed file raises an exception.

## 11.11 Sequenced file output

Sometimes, it may be more convenient to write to a file item by item rather than assembling all the items into a string and sending them at once. For example, many interactive systems update a file in response to user input from a keyboard. The danger is that if anything goes wrong and the process stops abnormally then the output file will be left open. The underlying computer system should notice this when you leave the SML system and close the file: however, it is bad practice to rely on the underlying system to do so.

We can adapt our screen display functions to write to an explicit output stream by abstracting for the stream. Thus, to write a string we effectively rename **output**:

```
-   (* write string to output stream *)
    fun fswrite stream s = output (stream,s);
>   val fswrite = fn : outstream -> string -> unit
```

Similarly, to put a string at the end of a line:

```
-   (* write newline terminated string to output stream *)
    fun fswriteln stream s = fswrite stream (s^"\n");
>   val fswriteln = fn : outstream -> string -> unit
```

To send a list of strings separated by spaces to a file:

```
-   (* write space separated string list to output stream *)
    fun fslwrite stream s = fswrite stream (spimplode s);
>   val fslwrite = fn : outstream -> string list -> unit
```

and to end the space separated sequence with a new line:

```
-    (* write newline terminated,
        space separated string list to output stream *)
     fun fslwriteln stream s = fswriteln stream (spimplode s);
>    val fslwriteln = fn : outstream -> string list -> unit
```

Finally, to display a list of strings on separate lines:

```
-    (* write string list on separate lines to output stream *)
     fun fslwritelns stream s =
        fswrite stream (implode (addnl s));
>    val fslwritelns = fn : outstream -> string list -> unit
```

We may also generalize the integer display functions. Thus, to send an integer to an output stream:

```
-    (* write integer to output stream *)
     fun fiwrite stream i = fswrite stream (iconv i);
>    val fiwrite = fn : outstream -> int -> unit
```

and to send a integer followed by a newline character:

```
-    (* write newline terminated integer to output stream *)
     fun fiwriteln stream i = fswriteln stream (iconv i);
>    val fiwriteln = fn : outstream -> int -> unit
```

For a list of integers, we map **iconv** over it to produce a list of strings and then call **fslwrite** to write a space separated sequence:

```
-    (* write space separated integer list to output stream *)
     fun filwrite stream l = fslwrite stream (map iconv l);
>    val filwrite stream = fn : outstream -> int list -> unit
```

Finally, an integer list may be followed by a newline:

```
-    (* write newline terminated,
        space separated integer list to output stream *)
     fun filwriteln stream l = fslwriteln stream (map iconv l);
>    val filwriteln = fn : outstream -> int list -> unit
```

For example, consider reading a sequence of lines from the keyboard and writing them to a file. The last line has a "!" on its own at the start:

```
-    (* copy from keyboard to named file *)
     fun keytofile () =
        let val prompt = swrite "file name: "
        in copylines (open_out (implode (sreadln())))
        end
>    val keytofile = fn : unit -> unit

     (* copy from keyboard to output stream *)
     and copylines stream =
        let val prompt = swrite "next line: "
        in
        let val l = implode (sreadln())
        in
         if l = "!"
         then close_out stream
         else
          let val fw = fswriteln stream l
          in copylines stream
          end
        end
```

```
        end;
>    val copylines = fn : outstream -> unit
```

**keytofile** prompts for and reads the file name. It opens the file and passes the associated stream to another function **copylines**. This prompts for and reads a line. If the line is the last one then the file is closed. Otherwise the line is written to the stream for the file and the process continues. For example:

```
-    keytofile();
file name: tempfile.txt
next line: Once upon a time there were three little
next line: computers called Freyr, Aurora and Anubis.
next line: !
>    () : unit
```

will write two lines of text to the file **tempfile.txt**.


## 11.12 File input

To input from a file, the file must be opened for input with the system function **open_in**:

```
-    open_in;
>    fn : string -> instream
```

This takes a file name string argument and returns the corresponding input stream.

Note that attempting to open a nonexistent file causes an exception to be raised.

At the end of input, the file should be closed with the system function **close_in**:

```
-    close_in;
>    fn : instream -> unit
```

which also returns the unit value.

The system function **end_of_stream**:

```
-    end_of_stream;
>    fn : instream -> bool
```

checks whether an input stream has no more characters, that is whether the associated file is empty. It returns **true** at the end of a stream and **false** if there are more characters to come.

For example, to read an entire file and return it as a list of single characters:

```
-    (* read file as string *)
fun fread f = let val ins = open_in f
                 in
                  let val ff = fread1 ins
                  in
                   let val ci = close_in ins
                   in ff
                   end
                  end
                 end
>    val fread = fn : string -> string
```

```
            (* read input stream as string *)
        and fread1 ins = if end_of_stream ins
                            then []
                            else
                            let val ch = input (ins,1)
                            in ch::fread1 ins
                            end;
>   val fread1 = fn: instream -> string list
```

In **fread**, the file named by the string associated with **f** is opened for input returning a stream to **ins**. **fread1** is called to read each character in turn from stream **ins** and assemble them into a list of strings, until the end of the stream is detected. Finally, the file attached to the input stream is closed.

## 11.13 Sequenced file input

It may also be useful to read a file bit by bit rather than all at once, for example in a system where a file is displayed on the screen under the control of the user. Care must be taken to ensure that the file is always closed at the end. As for output, we may abstract over the keyboard functions.

For example, suppose we want to read a line terminated by a newline from a stream, and return that line as a list of single characters:

```
-   (* read singleton string list from input stream *)
    fun fsreadln stream = let val ch = input (stream,1)
                          in
                          if ch="\n"
                          then []
                          else ch::fsreadln stream
                          end;
>   val fsreadln = fn: instream -> string list
```

Suppose we want to read up to a certain character from a stream:

```
-   (* read singleton string list up to given char from input
       stream *)
    fun fread stop stream = let val ch = input (stream,1)
                            in
                            if ch=stop
                            then []
                            else ch::fread stop stream
                            end;
>   val fsreadln = fn: instream -> string -> string list
```

so **fsreadln** is:

```
-   val fsreadln = fread "\n";
>   val fsreadln = fn: instream -> string list
```

Alternatively, we could read until some condition is met:

```
-   (* read singleton string list until condition from input
       stream *)
    fun fread p stream = let val ch = input (stream,1)
                         in
                         if p ch
                         then []
                         else ch::fread p stream
```

```
                                    end;
>   val fread = fn : (string -> bool) -> instream -> string list
```

Thus, **fsreadln** is:

```
-   val fsreadln = fread (fn ch => ch="\n");
>   val fsreadln = fn : instream -> string list
```

For example, to display all the lines in a file containing a specified string:

```
-   (* display lines from file containing string *)
    fun findlines() =
            let val prompt1 = swrite "file name: "
            in
             let val file = implode (sreadln())
             in
              let val prompt2 = swrite "search text: "
              in
               let val s = sreadln()
               in search (open_in file) s
               end
              end
             end
            end
>   val findlines = fn : unit -> unit

    and search stream s =
            if end_of_stream stream
            then close_in stream
            else
             let val next = fsreadln stream
             in
              if contains1 s next
              then
              let val l = swriteln (implode next)
              in search stream s
              end
              else search stream s
            end;
>   val search = fn : instream -> string list -> unit
```

**findlines** prompts for and reads a file name and search text. It then opens the file and passes the associated stream and exploded search text to **search**. **search** checks to see if the end of stream has been reached. If it has then the stream is closed. Otherwise, the next line from the stream is read and **contains1** from Chapter 8 is used to see if the line contains the text. If it does then the line is displayed. In either case, processing continues.

## 11.14 Summary

In this final practical chapter we have seen how to connect our programs to the outside world through input and output. We looked at simple output to the screen and input from the keyboard, and how to interleave them for interaction. We also saw how to extend these techniques to simple file handling.

The next chapter is the last in this book. It provides a brief survey of more advanced aspects of SML and makes suggestions for further reading.

## 11.15 Exercises

1) Write a function to display a real number **r** on the screen with **d** places after the decimal point.

2) Write functions to display a list of real numbers on the screen:
   i)  all on one line, with spaces in between each number
   ii) with each number on a separate line

3) Write a function to print the **n** times table for integer **n**. For example,

```
-  timestable 4;
 1 * 4 =  4
 2 * 4 =  8
...
12 * 4 = 48
>() : unit
```

The columns of numbers should be right justified.

4) Write a function that prompts for and reads a sequence of integers ending with 0 from the keyboard, one on each line, and displays a count of the integers, and their total and average.

5) Write a function which prompts for and reads an integer and then displays a table of all values from 0 to that integer with their squares and cubes, in right justified columns, with a suitable heading. For example:

```
-  powers ();
enter  integer < 100: 3
   n       n*n     n*n*n
   1        1         1
   2        4         8
   3        9        27
>() : unit
```

You may assume that the initial integer is no bigger than 100.

6) Write a function that repeatedly prompts for and reads a line of text from the keyboard, and prints a message to say whether or not it is a palindrome, i.e. reads the same from left to right and right to left, after all spaces have been removed:

```
-  palin();
text: madam im adam
madam im adam is a palindrome
text: ...
```

7) Write a function that, using the functions from Chapter 10 Exercise 4, prompts for and reads a logical expression, and displays the result of evaluating the expression.

8) Write a function that, using the functions from Chapter 10 Exercise 5, prompts for and reads a polynomial, and displays the result of differentiating the polynomial.

9) Write a function that, using the functions from Chapter 10 Exercise 6, prompts for and reads a program in the simple language, and displays the result of evaluating it.

10) Write a function to copy all of one file to another file. Both file names should be string arguments.

11) Write a function to display a file on a screen after prompting for the file

name. On displaying a screen full of text, it should pause and prompt for a
key to be pressed before displaying the next screen.

12) Write a function to edit files of lines of text. It should prompt for and read
a file name, and read the file into a list of string lists, one for each line. It
should then repeatedly prompt for a single letter command followed by
optional arguments and carry them out. The commands are:

```
T                    ==  display list as a sequence of lines
F/<text>         ==  find and display all lines containing the text
                         <text> in the list
D/<text>         ==  delete all occurences of the text <text> in the list
I/<text1>/<text2>   ==  insert text <text1> before all occurrences of
                             text <text2> in the list
R/<text1>/<text2>   ==  replace all occurrences of text <text1>
                             with text <text2> in the list
Q                    ==  write the list back to the file as a sequence of lines
                         and halt
```

13) Stock control records consisting of item names, stock levels and reorder
levels may be held in a text file, for example:

```
socks 200  250
hats   15   10
coats  75   80
pants  30   35
vests  45   40
```

Write a function that prompts for and reads a file name, and reads the file
into a suitable tuple list. It then repeatedly prompts for and reads a single
letter command followed by optional arguments and carries out the
command. The commands are:

```
D                    ==  display the list as a table with a suitable heading
F <name>         ==  find and display the entry for item <name> in the list
D <name>         ==  delete the entry for item <name> from the list
A <name> <stock> <reorder>   ==  add a new entry to the list
                                     for item <item> with stock level
                                     <stock> and reorder level
                                     <reorder>
O                    ==  display all entries in the list whose order level is below
                         the stock level, showing the difference between the
                         reorder level and the stock level
O <file>         ==  write the name and difference between the reorder level
                         and stock level for all entries in the list whose order level
                         is below the stock level to file <file>
C <name> <amount>   ==  add <amount> to the stock level for the list
                             entry for <name>
Q                    ==  write the tuple list back to the original file and halt
```

# CHAPTER 12
# Further SML

## 12.1 Introduction

This book is intended as an introduction to Standard ML and has concentrated on basic language aspects and programming techniques. SML has a number of more advanced features, in particular for imperative programming and encapsulation, which we will now consider. Suggestions for further reading are then given.

## 12.2 Functional and imperative languages

We have treated SML as if it were a pure functional language. Functional languages are a subgroup of the declarative languages: the other subgroup is logic programming languages of which the best known example is the impure Prolog.

Pure declarative languages have the common feature that once a name has been associated with a value, that association cannot be changed. Program parts communicate with each other by passing each other values as arguments or by referring to shared names to access their associated values. However, program parts cannot change the values associated with shared names and so they cannot affect indirectly each other's behaviour. Thus, the order in which different program parts are carried out cannot affect the final result. It may affect whether or not the program ever stops but we will not worry about that here.

This evaluation order independence gives pure declarative languages a number of useful theoretical and practical properties. Primarily, it is relatively easier to construct formal definitions of pure declarative languages as they do not necessarily have to make explicit any concept of evaluation order. Such formal definitions can form the basis for proving programs correct relative to specifications, which is particularly important for safety critical systems. They also enable the development of transformation rules for changing programs without affecting what they do, for example to make them more efficient. Finally, formal definitions may be used to prove the correctness of language implementations, that is that implementations are consistent with the formal definition. On the practical side, pure declarative languages are good candidates for parallel implementations. If the evaluation order cannot affect the final result then, in principle, arbitrary program parts may be evaluated concurrently on separate processors.

In contrast, imperative languages, like C, Pascal and COBOL, are based on changeable associations between names and values, and provide commands for assigning new values to names. Thus, program parts can interact with other by changing the values associated with shared names and so the evaluation order can affect the final result. This makes it much harder to construct formal theories about imperative languages as they must either make the evaluation order explicit, leading to more complex theories, or leave areas of ambiguity where it is not possible to identify one unique result for a program. Programming is also more complex as programmers have to be far more concerned with the precise order in which things happen.

The main advantage of imperative languages is that they correspond more closely to digital computer hardware. Almost all contemporary computers are based on what is known as the von Neumann architecture, after John von Neumann, the mathematician who first characterized it. At the heart of a von Neumann computer is a memory whose contents can be accessed and changed by specifying an associated address. This is the hardware basis for assignment; indeed assignment in imperative languages originated as an abstraction from such hardware.

Declarative languages correspond less well to the von Neumann architecture. When they were first developed their implementations were significantly slower and more demanding of memory than imperative language implementations. There are now excellent pure declarative language implementations which come close to the efficiency of imperative language implementations. Nonetheless, there are circumstances where imperative approaches are advantageous. For example, we have seen that in SML lists and trees are "changed" by making entire new copies with appropriate differences. For large applications, this copying can be very consuming of time and space. In contrast, in an imperative language lists and trees really can be changed by overwriting their elements with new values.

SML seeks the best of both worlds. It has a pure functional subset which we have looked at in the rest of this book. It also has imperative constructs which we will consider briefly now.

## 12.2.1 Imperative aspects of SML

In imperative languages a variable is a changeable association between a name and a value. In declarative languages, a variable is a fixed association between a name and a value. The imperative aspects of SML reflect this and are based upon a fixed association between a name and a changeable value. The implications of this difference will be explored below.

In SML, the polymorphic operator **ref** returns a changeable reference to a value:

```
-   ref;
>   fn : 'a -> 'a ref
```

For example, after:

```
-   val x = ref 1;
>   val x = ref 1 : int ref
```

**x** is associated with a changeable reference to an integer with initial value **1**.

The assignment operator := is used to change **ref** values and returns the **unit** value ():

```
-   op :=;
>   fn : 'a ref * 'a -> unit
```

For example:

```
-   x := 2;
>   () : unit
-   x;
>   ref 2 : int ref
```

sets the value of the **ref** value associated with **x** to **2**.

Note that the value of **x** has not changed, it is still the same **ref** value. However, the value of the **ref** value has changed. Now consider:

```
-   val y = x;
>   val y = ref 2 : int ref
```

**y** and **x** have the same value which is a **ref** value. Thus, assignment to the **ref** value associated with **y**:

```
-   y := 3;
>   () : unit
-   y;
>   ref 3 : int ref
```

appears to change **x**:

```
-   x;
>   ref 3 : int
```

In fact **x** has not changed. Rather the value of the **ref** value associated with both **y** and **x** has changed.

Here lies the difference between SML and other imperative languages. The SML **ref** value is akin to pointers in C or Pascal. In SML, setting one **ref** variable to the value of another results in both sharing the same **ref** value, much like setting two pointer variables in Pascal to the same pointer. However, SML has no concept of a changeable name/value association and thus is fully in the spirit of functional languages.

The polymorphic operator ! is used to get the value from a **ref** value:

```
-   !;
>   fn : 'a ref -> 'a
```

Note the difference between:

```
-   x;
>   ref 3 : int ref
```

which returns the **ref** value associated with **x** and:

```
-   !x;
>   3 : int
```

which returns the value of the **ref** value associated with **x**.

For example, to increment the **ref** value associated with **x**:

```
-   x := !x+1;
>   () : unit
-   x;
>   ref 4 : int ref
```

Now ; may be used a sequence operator. A bracketed sequence of expressions:

( *expression1* ; *expression 2* ; ... *expressionN* )

returns the value of the last expression *expressionN*. For example:

```
-   (x := !x+1;!x);
>   5 : int
```

increments the **ref** value associated with **x** and returns its value.

## 12.2.2 Replacing recursion with iteration

SML provides the iterative construct:

**while** *expression1* **do** *expression2*

which repeatedly evaluates *expression2* so long as *expression1* is **true**. We can use this construct to convert linear recursion to iteration.

Consider the factorial function:

```
fun fac n =
 if n=0
 then 1
 else n*fac (n-1);
```

An iterative equivalent is:

```
fun fac n =
 let val i = ref n;
     val f = ref 1;
 in
  while !i<>0 do
  ( f := !i*!f;
    i := !i-1
  );
  !f
 end;
```

Here, instead of repeatedly creating new instances of **n** through recursion we repeatedly reuse a **ref** value associated with **i** which is set initially to the value of **n**. Similarly, instead of repeatedly accumulating the value of;

```
fac (n-1)
```

we repeatedly reuse a **ref** value associated with **f** which is set initially to the base value of the recursion.

In general, consider:

```
fun name variable =
        if condition variable
        then base variable
        else recursion variable ( name ( decrement variable ))
```

Here, the condition *condition*, base expression *base*, recursion expression *recursion* and decrement expression *decrement* are treated as functions of the defined function's bound variable. The recursion expression is also treated as a function of the recursion call.

This is equivalent to:

```
fun name variable =
      let val count = ref variable ;
          val accumulate = ref ( base variable )
      in
       while not ( condition !count ) do
       ( accumulate := recursion !count !accumulate ;
         count := decrement !count
       );
       !accumulate
       end
```

Now, a count variable *count* is initialized to the starting value of the bound variable *variable* and an accumulation variable *accumulate* is initialized to the base expression. Then, so long as the condition is not true, the recursion expression is applied to the count and accumulation variables to update the accumulation variable, and the decrement expression is applied to the count variable. Finally, the value of the accumulate variable is returned. For example, consider:

```
fun sumlist l =
 if l=[]
 then 0
 else hd l+sumlist (tl l);
condition l == l=[]
base l == 0
recursion l v == (hd l)+v
decrement l == tl l

fun sumlist l =
 let val ll = ref l;
     val s = ref 0
 in
  while !ll<>[] do
  ( s := hd (!ll) + !s;
    ll := tl (!ll)
  );
  !s
 end;
```

This extends to functions of several variables. For example, consider:

```
fun power (x,n) =
 if n=0
 then 1
 else x*power (x,n-1);
condition (x,n) == n=0
base (x,n) == 1
recursion (x,n) v == x*v
decrement (x,n) == n-1

fun power (x,n) =
 let val i = ref n;
     val p = ref 1
```

```
 in
  while !i<>0 do
  ( p := x*!p;
    i := !i-1
  );
  !p
 end;
```

It also extends to nested functions. For example, consider:

```
fun funsum f n =
 if n=0
 then 0
 else f n+funsum f (n-1);
```

*condition* f n == n=0
*base* f n = 0
*recursion* f n v = (f n)+v
*decrement* f n = n-1

```
fun funsum f n =
 let val i = ref n;
     val s = ref 0
 in
  while !i<>0 do
  ( s := f (!i) + !s;
    i := !i-1
  );
  !s
 end;
```

This does not apply universally. Consider:

```
fun map f l =
 if l=[]
 then []
 else f (hd l)::map f (tl l);
```

*condition* f l == l=[]
*base* f l == []
*recursion* f l v = f (hd l)::v
*decrement* f l = tl l

```
fun map f l =
 let val ll = ref l;
     val m = ref []
 in
  while !ll<>[] do
  ( m := f (hd (!ll))::!m;
    ll := tl (!ll)
  );
  !m
 end;
```

Here, the result from the second version is a list in reverse order! This arises because :: is not commutative. In the recursive function we build the list from the last element. In the iterative version we build the list from the first element. In the above examples where the recursive action involved + or * the order did not matter.

Note that we have only considered a simple form of recursion. Transformation of all forms of recursion to iteration is possible. However, more complex forms often involve the introduction of explicit data structures to hold partial accumulated values. Recursion is then converted to an initial iteration down to the base case accumulating partial values in the structures and then iterating back up again, processing the partial accumulated values, to find the final value. For more details consult a book on compiler construction.

Note that while we save on recursion, we have the new, smaller overhead of dereferencing explicitly the **ref** values.

## 12.2.3 Replacing copying with assignment
Suppose we have a list of integers, and that we wish to construct a list of doubles of those integers:

```
fun double [] = [] |
    double (h::t) = 2*h::double t
```

Here we recurse down the list and then return constructing a copy of the list. Suppose that we no longer need the first list thereafter. We could start with a list of **int ref** instead of **int**:

```
-   val l = [ref 1,ref 2,ref 3,ref 4,ref 5];
>   val l = [ref 1,ref 2,ref 3,ref 4,ref 5] : (int ref) list
```

and change the **ref** elements rather than copying:

```
-   fun double [] = () |
        double (h::t) = (h := 2*!h; double t);
>   val double = fn : (int ref) list -> unit
-   double l;
>   () : unit
-   l;
>   [ref 2,ref 4,ref 6,ref 8,ref 10] : (int ref) list
```

Here, we change the head of the list and discard the unit result. We then recursively change the rest of the list. In the above example, **l** is still associated with the same list of **int ref**s. The values of those **int ref**s has changed.

For example, consider counting how often each unique letter appears in a string. First of all we build a list of tuples to hold a count of 0 for each alphabetic letter:

```
-   fun initcounts l counts =
        if l<"a"
        then counts
        else initcounts (chr (ord l-1)) ((l,ref 0)::counts);
>   val initcounts = fn : string -> (string * int ref) list ->
                                    (string * int ref) list
-   val counts = initcounts "z" [];
>   val counts = [("a",ref 0), ... ("z",ref 0)] : (string*int ref) list
```

Next we increment the count for one letter. If we cannot find that letter then we ignore it:

```
-   fun count _ [] = () |
        count l ((l1,c1)::t) =
        if l1=l
        then c1 := !c1+1
        else count l t;
>   val count = fn : string -> (string * int ref) list -> unit
```

For a list of letters, we increment the count for each letter in turn:

```
-   fun countall [] counts = () |
        countall (h::t) counts =
        (count h counts; countall t counts);
>   val countall = fn : string list -> (string * int ref) list -> unit
```

For example:

```
-   countall (explode "ace cab") counts;
>   () : unit
-   counts;
>   [("a",ref 2),("b",ref 1),("c",ref 2),("d",ref 0),("e",ref 1),...] :
    (string * int ref) list
```

Note as above that while we have avoided copying we have the new, smaller overhead of dereferencing explicitly **ref** variables.


## 12.3  Encapsulation with abstract types and modules

In Chapter 6 we introduced the idea of encapsulation. We used local declarations to group a function with the auxiliary functions that only it needs to access and to hide those auxiliary functions from other uses. SML provides two more advanced constructs for encapsulation, abstypes and structures, which we will now survey briefly.


### 12.3.1  Abstract types

In Chapter 1 we said that a type consists of a range of values along with methods to construct, inspect and change such values. In Chapter 2 we then met the **bool**, **int**, **real** and **string** basic types and their associated operations. Note that we have no need to know just how these types are actually implemented in a computer provided they behave consistently when we use them in programs. In Chapter 1 we also suggested that programming could be viewed as the crafting of new types to fit particular needs. That is, we use existing types to define representations for new ranges of values and we build functions to be the methods that manipulate those new value ranges.

Here, we have made our new representations from lists, tuples and datatypes. Such representations are said to be concrete because their low level SML details are explicit and visible. However, someone using a new type has no need to know specific representation details provided the type behaves consistently when manipulated through the methods.

The SML abstype is a way of forming a new type by encapsulating a datatype with method functions so that only appropriate functions are visible. There is no access to the low level datatype details. Values of an abstype can only be constructed and manipulated through the visible method functions. Such a type is said to be abstract rather than concrete as both the representation and method details are hidden.

For example, suppose we wish to make a new type to represent word counts for texts:

```
-      abstype wordcount= words of (string * int) list
       with
        local
         fun inccount w [] = [(w,1)] |
             inccount w ((w1,c1)::t) = if w=w1
                                       then (w1,c1+1)::t
                                       else (w1,c1)::inccount w t
         and findcount _ [] = 0 |
             findcount w ((w1,c1)::t) = if w=w1
                                        then c1
                                        else findcount w t
        in
         (* create new count *)
         fun new() = words []
         (* increment counts for words *)
         and incwords ws (words wl) = words (foldr inccount wl ws)
         (* find count for word *)
         and find w (words wl) = findcount w wl
         (* find all words *)
         and allwords (words wl) = map (fn (w,_) => w) wl
        end
       end;
>      type wordcount
       val new = fn : unit -> wordcount
       val incwords = fn : string list -> wordcount -> wordcount
       val find = fn : string -> wordcount -> int
       val allwords = fn : wordcount -> string list
```

Our new type is called **wordcount**. It has datatype values with constructor **words** for lists of pairs of string words and integer counts. It also has functions to create an empty **wordcount**, to increment the counts for a list of words in a **wordcount**, to find the count for a word in a **wordcount** and to return all the words in a wordcount. Note that these visible functions strip away the outer **words** and then call hidden auxiliary functions.

The user of this new type cannot see how a **wordcount** is actually represented. They can only construct and manipulate **wordcount**s by using the visible functions.

For example, we could create a new **wordcount**:

```
-    val c = new();
>    val c = - : wordcount
```

Note that the system does not show us a concrete value for the new **wordcount**. Instead it displays a -.

We can now increment the counts for a sentence:

```
-    val c1 = incwords ["the","cat","ate","the","haggis"] c;
>    val c1 = - : wordcount
```

view all the unique words:

```
-    allwords c1;
>    ["ate","cat","haggis","the"] : string list
```

and then check the count for a word:

```
-    find "the" c1;
>    2 : int
```

Note that abstypes are not equality types so comparison methods must be defined explicitly.

We might use abstypes as building blocks when developing large systems as a way of controlling system complexity. Once a new type has been tested thoroughly it can be treated as pre-given in constructing other system components. Furthermore, if we supply other people with an abstype then they need not be aware if we decide to change the representation or method details later on, for example to make them more efficient or extend their functionalities. Provided the methods still behave in the same way then users will not notice the difference and need not change their programs.

For example, we might decide to change the representation of the sequence of pairings of words and counts above from a list to a tree:

```
-   abstype wordcount =
     words of string*int*wordcount*wordcount | wcempty
    with
     local
      fun inccount w wcempty = words (w,1,wcempty,wcempty)
          inccount w (words (w1,c1,l,r)) =
           if w=w1
           then words (w,c1+1,l,r
           else
            if w<w1
            then words (w1,c1,inccount w l,r)
            else words (w1,c1,l,inccount w r)
     in
      (* create new count *)
      fun new() = wcempty
      (* increment counts for words *)
      and incwords ws w1 = foldr inccount w1 ws
      (* find count for word *)
      and find _ wcempty = 0 |
          find w (words(w1,c1,l,r)) = if w=w1
                                      then c1
                                      else
                                       if w<w1
                                       then find w l
                                       else find w r
      (* find all words *)
      and allwords wcempty = [] |
          allwords (words(w,_,l,r)) = allwords l@w::allwords r
     end
    end;
>   type wordcount
    val new = fn : unit -> wordcount
    val incwords = fn : string list -> wordcount -> wordcount
    val find = fn : string -> wordcount -> int
    val allwords = fn : wordcount -> string list
```

Here, the representation and methods have changed but the methods still have the same names, types and observable behaviours.

## 12.3.2 Structures

We have been working with what is called the SML Core language. The SML Modules language extends the Core with constructs which support large scale system development from separate components. We will look very briefly now at these constructs.

In general, a module is an independent, self-contained chunk of program, usually consisting of a group of related definitions. For a module to be used elsewhere, what it contains must be made public. Similarly, for something declared in a module to be used elsewhere, it must be known how to invoke it, what arguments if any it requires and what results if any it returns.

In SML, a module is called a structure and consists of a named sequence of declarations. Corresponding to a structure is a signature which is a sequence of the names of the declared values in the structure along with their types. That signature is all that someone else needs to know to access things from the structure.

An abstype must be incorporated in the program that uses it and so its definition can be seen by the user even though only its visible methods may be used. In contrast, the SML Module language enables the completely independent development of program components with only their signatures known to users.

For example, suppose we wish to develop a module for ordered integer lists, starting with functions to insert an integer into an ascending order list and to sort an integer list into ascending order:

```
-   structure ISORTLIST =
    struct
    fun iinsert i [] = [i] |
        iinsert (i:int) (h::t) = if i<h
                                 then i::h::t
                                 else h::iinsert i t
    and isort [] = [] |
        isort (h::t) = iinsert h (isort t)
    end;
>   structure ISORTLIST :
    sig
    val iinsert : int -> int list -> int list
    val isort : int list -> int list
    end
```

The system shows us the structure's signature, indicating that the structure contains two functions called **iinsert** and **isort**.

Someone else can use the functions in a module provided they know the signature and a description of the functions' behaviours. A function in a module is invoked through what is called a long identifier, that is the structure name followed by a "." followed by the function name.

For example, **iinsert** can be invoked from **ISORTLIST**:

```
-   ISORTLIST.iinsert 3 [1,2,4,5];
>   [1,2,3,4,5] : int list
```

A structure may provide a wide variety of general purpose functions which are not all relevant to a particular problem. It may then be constrained by an explicit signature that only refers to some of the functions, thereby restricting those that may be used.

For example, we might want to only make the sorting function from **ISORTLIST** available. The signature:

```
-   signature ONLYISORTSIG =
    sig
     val isort : int list -> int list
    end;
>   signature ONLYISORTSIG =
    sig val isort : int list - > int list end
```

only specifies the sort function. We can now define a new structure which will only allow access to that sort function:

```
-   structure ONLYISORTLIST : ONLYISORTSIG = ISORTLIST;
>   structure ONLYISORTLIST : ONLYISORTSIG
```

Attempts to access **iinsert** from **ONLYISORTLIST** will result in an error message to say that **iinsert** is not declared.

Structures may be generalized as functors through parameterization. Such parameters may abstract over types as well as values. Functors are then specialized by being called with specific types and values to form new structures.

For example, we might want to provide a more general sorted list module, so we could abstract at the comparison **i<h**:

```
-   functor SORTLIST (type ANY
                      val order : ANY -> ANY -> bool) :
    sig type ANY
        val sort : ANY list -> ANY list
        val insert : ANY -> ANY list -> ANY list
        sharing type ANY = ANY
    end =
    struct
     type ANY = ANY
     fun insert v [] = [v] |
         insert v (h::t) = if order v h
                           then v::h::t
                           else h::insert v t
     and sort [] = [] |
         sort (h::t) = insert h (sort t)
    end;
>   functor SORTLIST : < sig >
```

We have indicated that in **SORTLIST**, for some type **ANY** the function **order** returns a boolean after doing something to two values of that type.

Note that we have specified **SORTLIST**'s type explicitly. The **type** and **sharing type** definitions are necessary to ensure type consistency: for explanation see one of the books below.

This functor can be used elsewhere to build new structures to deal with a specific types of list. For example, we can construct a structure specifically for integer lists by calling **SORTLIST** with **ANY** set to **int** and **order** set to an appropriate **int -> int -> bool** function:

```
-   fun iless (i1:int) i2 = i1<i2;
>   val iless = fn : int -> int -> bool
```

```
- structure ISORTLIST = SORTLIST(type ANY = int;
                                 val order = iless);
> structure ISORTLIST :
  sig
    eqtype ANY
    val sort : ANY list -> ANY list
    val insert : ANY -> ANY list -> ANY list
  end
```

Now **ISORTLIST** is like **SORTLIST** with **ANY** set to **int** and **order** set to **iless**. When we invoke **insert** or **sort** from **ISORTLIST** they will only work with integer lists:

```
-   ISORTLIST.insert 3 [1,2,4,5];
>   val it = [1,2,3,4,5] : ISORTLIST.ANY list
```

For more information about structures, see the further reading below.

## 12.4 Other features

SML has two other significant features which we will now summarize.

As well as tuples, lists and datatypes, SML also provides records for defining groups of associated values. A record is like a tuple in that it is a fixed sized sequence of elements of different types. However, in a record each element has an explicit name which may be used to access it.

SML enables the definition of new infix operators. A variant of function declarations is used to define their behaviour. Their associativity and precedence may also be specified.

For more details see the further reading below.

## 12.5 Further reading

A wide range of books on Standard ML is available. The essential references for people who want to implement SML or manipulate formally SML programs are:

R. Milner, M. Tofte, R. Harper, *The definition of Standard ML* (Cambridge, Mass.: MIT Press, 1990)

R. Milner & M. Tofte, *Commentary on Standard ML* (Cambridge, Mass.: MIT Press, 1991)

which provide a succinct formal definition of SML.

C. Myers, C. Clack, E. Poon, *Programming with Standard ML* (Englewood Cliffs, New Jersey: Prentice-Hall, 1993)

is a thorough introduction which includes coverage of abstypes and structures. It also contains a good annotated bibliography on both SML and functional programming.

Å. Wikström, *Functional programming using Standard ML* (Englewood Cliffs, New Jersey: Prentice-Hall, 1987)

is another thorough introductory text. It has material on abstypes but not on structures, and covers an older version of exceptions.

R. Bosworth, *A practical course in functional programming using Standard ML* (New York: McGraw-Hill, 1995)

is another introduction. It provides two medium sized case studies but has no material on abstypes or structures.

R. Harrison, *Abstract data types in Standard ML* (New York: John Wiley, 1993)

is a second level text. It assumes some knowledge of functional programming and contains detailed coverage of the use of abstypes and structures in developing generic abstract data types.

J. D. Ullman, *Elements of ML Programming* (Englewood Cliffs, New Jersey: Prentice-Hall, 1994)

and

R. Stansifer, *ML primer* (Englewood Cliffs, New Jersey: Prentice-Hall, 1992)

are better suited for second language learning of SML. Both cover all of SML. The latter is relatively brief but contains useful examples.

L. C. Paulson, *ML for the working programmer* (Cambridge: Cambridge University Press, 1991)

is a more advanced text. As well as full coverage of SML it also includes material on program proof, and the implementation in SML of an interpreter for $\lambda$ calculus and of a tactical theorem prover.

S. Sokolowski, *Applicative high order programming: the Standard ML perspective* (London: Chapman and Hall, 1991)

focuses on the use of higher order functions. It includes material on program proof, polymorphism and functional language implementation through compilation to code for an abstract stack machine.

C. Reade, *Elements of functional programming* (Reading, Mass.: Addison-Wesley, 1989)

covers a wide range of practical and theoretical functional programming topics. An introduction to SML is followed by material on lazy evaluation, semantics, polymorphic type checking, $\lambda$ calculus and combinators, and functional language implementation through the SECD machine.

## 12.6 SML implementations

The Usenet news group `comp.lang.ml` provides a lively forum for discussion of SML. The "Standard ML Frequently Asked Questions" posting appears monthly and contains details of how to obtain SML implementations, including those summarized below. It may also be found through anonymous ftp from :

`pop.cs.cmu.edu:/usr/rowan/sml-archive/faq.txt`

In particular, Standard ML of New Jersey (NJSML), developed jointly by AT&T Bell Laboratories and Princeton University, runs on many UNIX based systems. MicroML, developed at the University of Umea, and Moscow ML, developed at the Keldysh Institute of Applied Mathematics, Moscow, and the Royal Veterinary and Agricultural University, Denmark, run on IBM PC compatible systems. All are free and may be obtained by anonymous ftp:

NJSML: `ftp.research.att.com:/dist/ml`
MicroML: `ftp.cs.umu.se:/pub/umlexe01.uue`
Moscow ML: `ftp.dina.kvl.dk:/pub/mosml`

# Using an SML system

## A.1 Introduction

Active use of an SML system is fundamental to this book. It is assumed that
you have access to a computer and that you know or can find out how to:

  a)  type text into a text file using an editor
  b)  run the SML system

The following discussion is pertinent to UNIX and DOS systems. It is
assumed for illustrative purposes only that the UNIX prompt is:

```
$
```

the DOS prompt is:

```
C>
```

and the SML system command on both UNIX and DOS is:

```
sml
```

Note that the system you are using may well have a different SML command
and prompts.

On windows based systems you should be able to run SML from within a
UNIX shell window or a DOS window.

## A.2 Getting started

SML systems are interactive, that is you type things at them for immediate
processing. Suppose the system is started by:

```
$ sml
```

or:

```
C> sml
```

After printing various inscrutable start up details, the system will prompt for
input from the keyboard with:

```
-
```

After the prompt you can enter any expression followed by a semi-colon:

```
-   expression ;
```

If the expression goes over several lines then push "Enter" after each line and
the system will prompt for the next line with a:

```
=
```
Don't forget the "**;**" at the very end of the expression.

The system will carry out the expression and display the result. How this is done depends on the system. Here, we assume that it will print out a right angle bracket followed by the expression's final value and type:

>   *value* : *type*

Other SML systems will print out:

**val it =** *value* **:** *type*

The SML system name **it** is always set to the last value to be found when an expression is carried out. We will use the first simpler form here.

## A.3 Leaving the system
You can usually get out of an SML system by using the underlying system's exit interrupt code, often control Z or control D. Check for the system you are using. For example, assuming control Z:

```
-    ^Z
$
```
or
```
-    ^Z
C >
```

## A.4 Panic button
If you need to stop an SML program running and return to the SML input prompt then use control C:

```
....
^C
Execution terminated
-
```

## A.5 Program development
Unfortunately, many SML systems will not let you change things once you have typed them in. Thus, it is best to first of all type everything you want to try out into a text file.

Don't forget the "**;**" after each expression.

It is a useful convention to give files containing SML the suffix **.sml** so that you can see that they are SML files from their names. However, this is not a requirement of SML systems.

Suppose the file is called:

   *file*

Next, start up the SML system and type in:

-   **use "***file***";**

to read in everything from the file.

Note the double quotes round the file name: it is a string. For example, if the file was called:

`test.sml`

then you would enter:

`–    use "test.sml";`

Once the file has been read in, the system will go back to prompting for more input from the keyboard.

If there are errors then leave the SML system, edit the file, re-enter the SML system and read the file back in again.

On a UNIX system, you can suspend a process, in this case the SML system, and return to the system input prompt without terminating the process. You will need to find out what the suspension control sequence is. Often it is control X or control Z. For example:

```
–    ^X
Stopped
$
```

You can then edit the file and restart the SML system, usually by typing `fg` to move a suspended process into the foreground. For example:

```
$ fg
(sml)
```

Note that the system informs you that you have returned to SML but the SML input prompt may not be printed. You can now read the file in again.

On a windows based system you could have one window for the SML system and another for editing the file. First of all, type your SML into the file and then read it into the SML system, having saved but not closed the file. If errors are detected in the file you could move to the edit window, change and save the file, move to the SML window and read in the file again, without stopping the SML system in between.


## A.6 Saving system output

If you want to save the results of an SML session in a file then you can use file redirection under DOS or UNIX. You could run everything in:

*input file*

and save the output in:

*output file*

by entering:

C> `sml` < *input file* > *output file*

or

$ `sml` < *input file* > *output file*

For example, if the input file is called:

`test.sml`

and you want the results in:

`results`

then you would enter:

```
C> sml < test.sml > results
```

or

```
$ sml < test.sml > results
```

# APPENDIX B
# SML syntax

These syntax diagrams are for the SML subset covered in Chapters 1 to 11. They are loosely adapted from the syntax in Milner (1990) referenced in Chapter 12. The main changes are the conflation of various independent syntax constructs into unified diagrams and the treatment of different sorts of constructor simply as *name*.

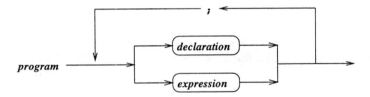

A *program* is one or more *declarations* and *expressions* separated by ;s.

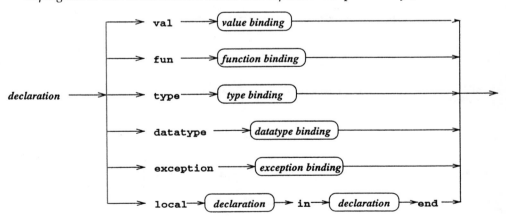

A *declaration* may be for a name/value association, *value binding*, a function, *function binding*, a type synonym, *type binding*, a datatype, *datatype binding*, an exception, *exception binding* or a local declaration.

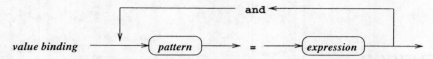

*value binding*

A *value binding* is one or more associations between *pattern*s and *expression*s, separated by **and**s.

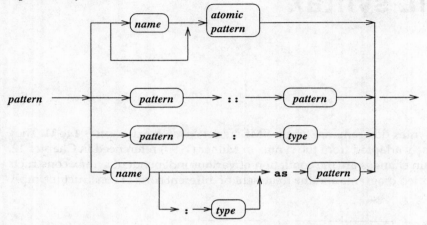

*pattern*

A *pattern* is an *atomic pattern*, a constructor pattern consisting of a structured value constructor *name* followed by an argument *atomic pattern*, a list pattern consisting of two *pattern*s separated by the list constructor **: :**, a *typed pattern* or a layered pattern associating a possibly *type*d bound variable *name* and a *pattern*.

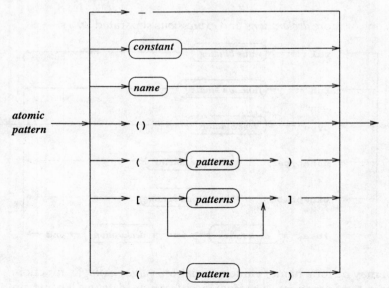

*atomic pattern*

An *atomic pattern* is a wildcard, a *constant* (i.e. an integer, real, boolean or string value), a bound variable or simple value constructor *name*, the unit value, a tuple of *patterns*, an empty list or a list of *patterns*, or a bracketed *pattern*.

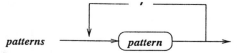

patterns

A *patterns* is one or more *patterns* separated by , s.

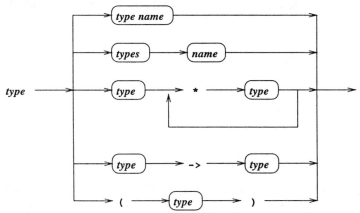

type

A *type* is a *type name* (i.e. a ' followed by a *name*), a type constructor *name* (i.e. **int**, **real**, **bool**, **string** or a type constructor) or a type constructor *name* preceded by a *types* (i.e. for a **list** or a parameterized type constructor), a tuple type, a function type or a bracketed *type*.

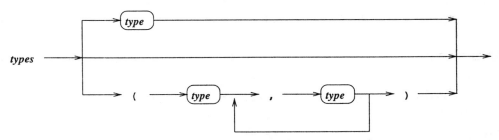

types

A *types* is one *type*, empty or a bracketed sequence of one or more , separated *types*.

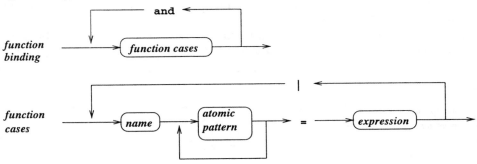

function
binding

function
cases

A *function binding* is one or more *function cases* separated by **and**s.

A *function cases* is a *name* followed by one or more bound variable *atomic patterns* and associated with a body *expression*, or several of this sequence separated by |s.

A *type binding* is an association between a type constructor *name* and a *type*. It may be parameterized by *type names*. A sequence of such associations is separated by **and**s.

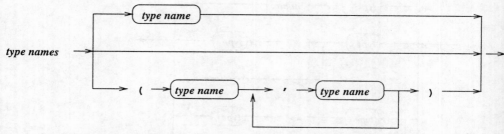

A *type names* is a single *type name*, empty or a bracketed sequence of one or more *type names* separated by **,**s.

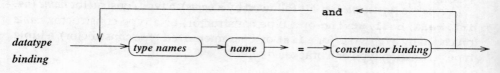

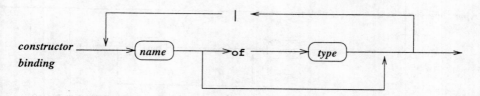

A *datatype binding* associates a type constructor *name* with a *constructor binding*. It may be parameterized by a *type names*. A sequence of such associations is separated by **and**s.

A *constructor binding* is a value constructor *name* which may have an associated *type*. A sequence of these is separated by |s.

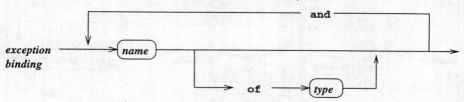

An *exception binding* is a constructor *name* which may have an associated *type*. A sequence of these is separated by **and**s.

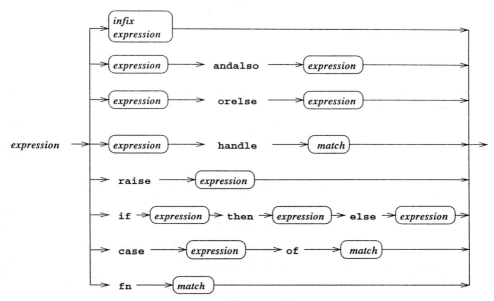

An *expression* is an *infix expression,* two *expressions* separated by an infix boolean operator, an *expression* with a handler *match,* a raised exception *expression,* a conditional expression, a case expression matching an *expression* to a *match,* or a function value defined by a *match.*

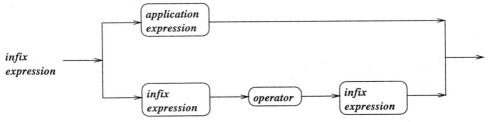

An *infix expression* is a function call *application expression* or two *infix expressions* separated by an infix operator.

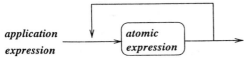

An *application expression* is a single *atomic expression* or a function *atomic expression* followed by argument *atomic expressions.*

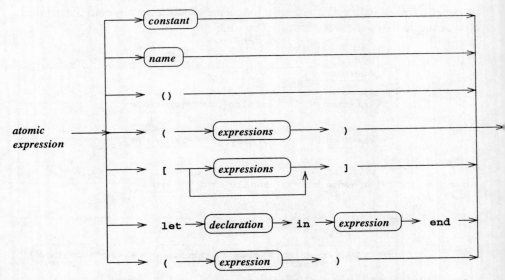

An *atomic expression* is a *constant*, a bound variable or constructor *name*, the unit value, a tuple, an empty list or a non-empty bracketed list, a let expression, or a bracketed *expression*.

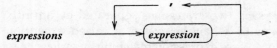

An *expressions* is one or more *expressions* separated by **,**s.

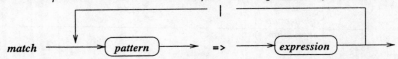

A *match* is an association between a *pattern* and an *expression*. A sequence of such associations is separated by |s.

# SML standard functions and operators

In the type of an overloaded numeric function or operator, all occurrences of the type *num* may be replaced by either **int** or **real**.

## C.1  Standard functions
The following standard functions are introduced in the text:

```
abs : num -> num
~ : num -> num
floor : real -> int
real: int -> real
not: bool -> bool
size : string -> int
ord : string -> int
chr : int -> string
explode : string -> string list
implode : string list -> string
map : ('a -> 'b) -> 'a list -> 'b list
rev : 'a list -> 'a list
```

SML also provides the following arithmetic and trigonometric functions:

```
sqrt : real -> real        – square root
sin : real -> real         – sine of radians
cos : real -> real         – cosine of radians
arctan : real -> real      – arctangent; returns radians
exp : real -> real         – e^x for argument x
ln : real -> real          – natural logarithm
```

## C.2  I/O streams and functions
The following streams and functions are discussed in Chapter 11:

```
open_in : string -> instream
input : instream * int -> string
end_of_stream : instream -> bool
close_in : instream -> unit

std_in : instream
```

```
open_out : string -> outstream
output : outstream*string -> unit
close_out : outstream -> unit
std_out : outstream
```

SML also provides the function:

```
lookahead : instream -> string
```

which returns the next character in the specified input stream as a string without removing it from the stream.

## C.3 Standard operators

The number preceding each operator is its precedence.

```
7   div : int * int -> int
7   mod : int * int -> int
7   / : real * real -> real
7   * : num * num -> num

6   + : num * num -> num
6   - : num * num -> num

6   ^: string*string -> string

5   :: : 'a * 'a list -> 'a list
5   @ : 'a list * 'a list -> 'a list

4   = : ''a * ''a -> bool
4   <> : ''a * ''a -> bool

4   < : num * num -> bool
4   <= : num * num -> bool
4   >= : num * num -> bool
4   > : num * num -> bool

3   o : ('b -> 'c)*('a -> 'b) -> 'a -> 'c
```

# Word index

## 300  WORD INDEX

  list   109
binary tree   224, 226
binding, datatype   202
BNF   230
body, of function   56, 73
**bool**   32
boolean   4
  comparison   47
  operators   5, 37
  pattern matching   87
  precedence   38
  type   32
    user defined   202
  and conditional expression   96
bound variable   36, 55–6, 73
  explicit type   60
branch   224
call *see* see function call

**case**   245
case expression   244
case sensitivity   32
catching exceptions   50, 86
cell, list   105
checking   21
**chr**   ASCII to list   200
**close_in** close in stream   267
**close_out** close out stream   264
collection   3, 7, 16, 105, 155
comments   59
comparison   5
  boolean   47
  equality   45
  function   45
  greater than   46
  greater than or equal   46
  inequality   45
  less than   46
  less than or equal   46
  real   47
composition
  of functions   49
  function for   71
concrete data type   201
concrete syntax   240
conditional expression   13, 95
  and boolean value   96
conjunction   5, 37, 203
cons   105
constructor
  list   105
  type   31, 167, 202, 204–5
  value   202, 204, 205
conversion
  ASCII to string   200
  string to integer   189
  list to string   179
  integer to real   44
  real to integer   44

string to ASCII   191
string to list   179
string to number   209
**cos** cosine function   297
curried function   169

**datatype**   202
datatype   202
  binding   202, 204
  pattern   202, 206
  pattern matching   206
decimal number   32
declaration
  global   54
  local   130
  mutual   213
declarative language   273
delete
  indexed list   122
  list by predicate   161
  substring   182
  value from list   116
dereference operator   275
disjunction   5, 38
display accuracy, real   47
**div** integer division   40, 42
division   40, 42
  with negative operand   48
**do**   276
domain   36, 56

**E** floating point exponent   33
efficiency
  list   223
  tree   226
element
  list   105, 109
  list selection   119
  tuple   35
  tuple selection   155
**else**   13, 95
empty list   105, 107
empty string   34
encapsulation   130, 280
**end**   130, 192
end of input   267
end of line character   34
**end_of_stream** function   267
equality   45
equality type   111
  datatype   202
  not abstypes   282
  not function   45
  not streams   254
  variable   112
evaluation order   37–41, 43, 45–6, 56–7, 73, 273
**exception**   86
exception   50, 86, 262
  multiple   246